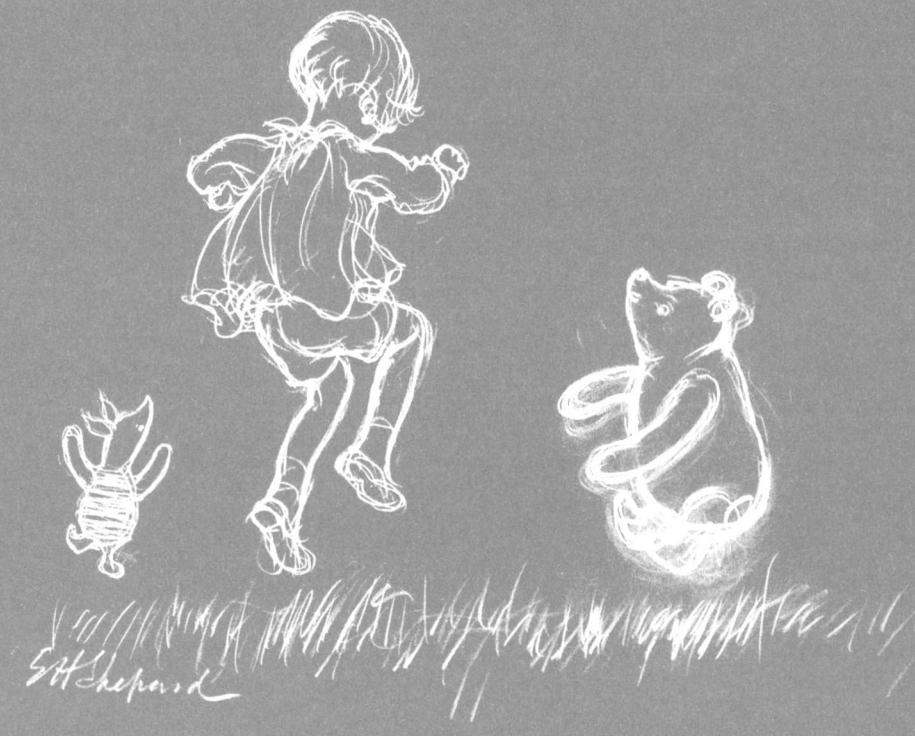

THE MAKING of
WINNIE-THE-POOH

THE MAKING of
WINNIE-THE-POOH

Pooh, Piglet, Eeyore, and Other Beloved Characters

JAMES CAMPBELL

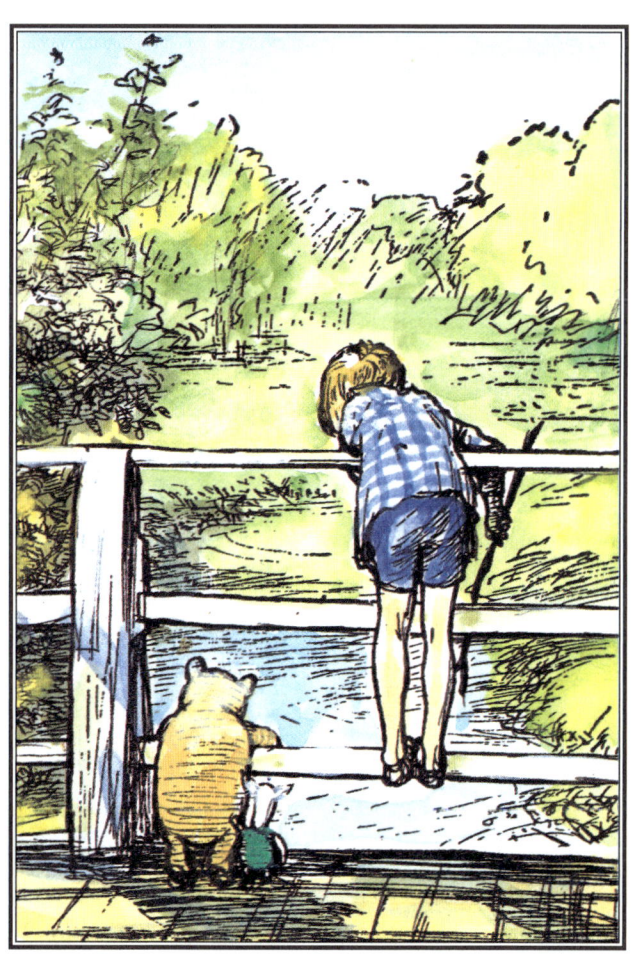

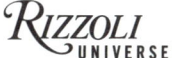

RIZZOLI
UNIVERSE

For Minette Hunt and Diana Campbell
who made it all possible

First published in the United States of America in 2025 by
Rizzoli Universe, a Division of
Rizzoli International Publications, Inc.
49 West 27th Street
New York, NY 10001
rizzoliusa.com

Originally published in Great Britain in 2025 by
LOM ART, an imprint of
Michael O'Mara Books Limited
9 Lion Yard
Tremadoc Road
London SW4 7NQ
mombooks.com

For Rizzoli
Publisher: Charles Miers
Editor: Klaus Kirschbaum
Assistant Editor: Emily Ligniti
Managing Editor: Lynn Scrabis

ISBN: 978-0-7893-4425-0
Library of Congress Control Number: 2025933339
2025 2026 2027 2028 / 10 9 8 7 6 5 4 3 2 1

Designed by Ana Bjezancevic
Printed and bound in China

The authorized representative in the EU for product safety and compliance is
Mondadori Libri S.p.A., via Gian Battista Vico 42, Milan, Italy, 20123
mondadori.it

Visit us online
Instagram.com/RizzoliBooks
Facebook.com/RizzoliNewYork
Youtube.com/user/RizzoliNY

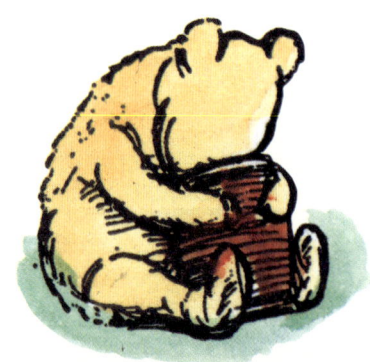

Contents

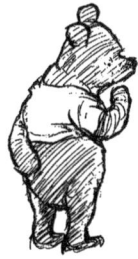

Introduction

The names of the writer A. A. Milne and the illustrator E. H. Shepard are forever united in their joint creation of Winnie-the-Pooh and the characters and stories of the Hundred Acre Wood, yet a hundred years after the first publication of these iconic stories relatively little is now remembered about these two remarkable men and the extent and scope of their literary and artistic output across the twentieth century.

In English-speaking countries, Eeyore, Tigger and Poohsticks, to name but three, have entered the language (and dictionaries) as universal describers. To call someone 'a bit of an Eeyore' is entirely commonplace when referring to a person of a melancholy disposition, while Tigger is synonymous with a bouncy, over-enthusiastic person – even King Charles named his Jack Russell after Tigger, and Queen Camilla is apparently a fan. And the wonderful game of Poohsticks has an enormous global following – there is even a World Poohsticks Championship.

The extraordinary global reach of Winnie-the-Pooh is a phenomenon far beyond the wildest imaginings of A. A. Milne and E. H. Shepard. Since I became involved in the world of Pooh nearly twenty years ago, I have been amazed and overwhelmed by the extent of the reach of these four small books of children's verse and stories, and I have seen at first hand the impact which these characters still have on children of all ages.

The aim of this book is to tell the story of two men, on the face of it very similar, but in fact remarkably different, and how their backgrounds, lives and experiences led them to the creation of one of the most remarkable partnerships in children's literature, and how they worked together, enhancing and complementing each other's creative narrative. Perhaps by looking further into their characters, relationships and working lives, more light might be shone into this unique professional partnership, the fruits of which still resonate over a hundred years later.

They separately and together also produced a substantial body of work, literary and artistic, which documented the rapidly changing society of the twentieth century, now largely forgotten, but which shines a fascinating light on this period of our recent history.

I have been privileged to have been able to access materials unseen, long forgotten or unappreciated and to bring together the worlds of Alan Milne and Ernest Shepard in appreciation of their unique contribution to the lives of all the world's children. I hope you enjoy this book.

James Campbell

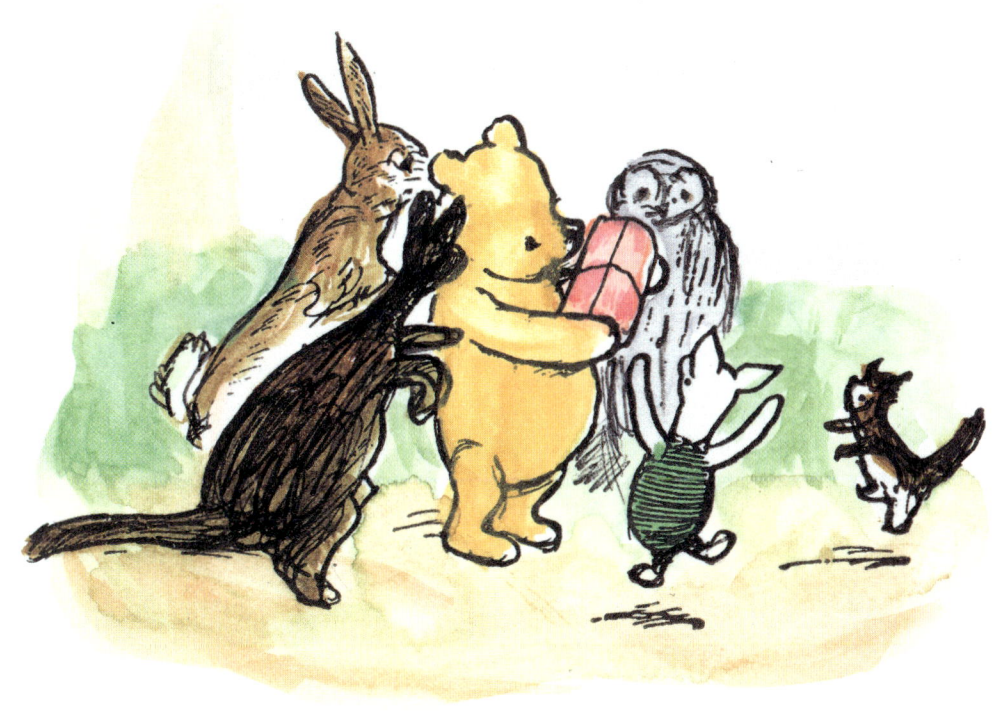

CHAPTER ONE

When They Were Very Young

Alan Alexander Milne was not born on 18 January in 1882 in London's St John's Wood. Alexander Sydney Milne was, however, and his birth was registered under those names. His parents must have had second thoughts, for a return trip to the Registrar produced an amended birth certificate for the baby, now Alan Alexander Milne. His indecisive parents were John Vine Milne and Sarah Maria Heginbotham, both of whom appear to have emerged from confused and impoverished backgrounds determined to better themselves through education, and did so. Both became teachers and met when working at schools in Shropshire. They married late for that time, J. V. (as he was known) being thirty-three and Maria thirty-eight, and it was therefore no surprise that their three sons, Barry, Ken and Alan were all born within four years of their marriage in 1878. J. V. was a natural schoolmaster, gifted at bringing the best out of his pupils. With a relaxed sense of humour, he created a warm and fulfilling educational environment. Maria gave up teaching on marriage and motherhood, and remained in the background, where it seems she was content to stay. She was organized and efficient, managed the domestic environment effectively, and saw to it that her husband and boys were appropriately prepared for whatever might come their way. But she was not demonstrative or particularly loving to her family.

On their marriage the Milnes had bought a failing private school, Henley House in St John's

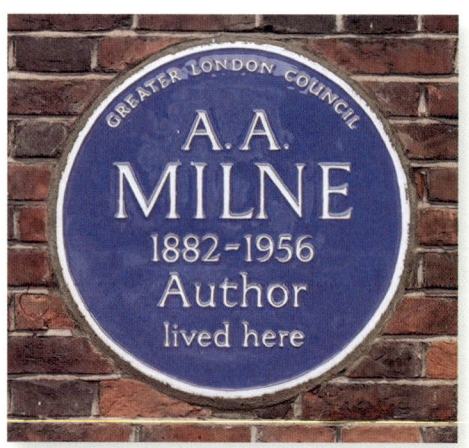

The blue plaque on the site of the now demolished Henley House.

Wood, north London, taking over the premises and the school for a modest premium as the school was effectively worthless. At this time, before the state-funded provision of secondary education had been introduced, most children left school and went to work at the age of twelve. There were the grand and expensive public schools patronized by the aristocracy, the gentry and the wealthy upper middle classes, but these were out of reach for the ordinary middle classes who wanted further education for their children. So there was a proliferation of small, modest schools, generally in large houses where pupils, teachers and staff all lived under the same roof. Henley House, when the Milnes arrived, was barely functioning and had only a handful of pupils, but Maria was methodical, J. V. was competent, gregarious and engaging, with an easy manner, and so quite soon Henley House had a resurgence of new pupils, both boarders and day boys. St John's Wood was an upwardly mobile neighbourhood, within easy reach of Maida Vale, Regent's Park, Kilburn and the fringes of Hampstead and Highgate, all areas with rapidly expanding middle-class populations.

Growing up in a school had its advantages and disadvantages. During the school term there was little family time and the Milne boys were treated largely as the other pupils, but it gave them exposure to learning and books from the earliest age. Alan Milne was precocious from the start, giving both his brothers a run for their money in starting his formal education almost at the same time as they did. This added, not always harmoniously, to the competitiveness which inevitably existed between them.

Well before his fifth birthday, Alan was despatched to the kindergarten of Wykeham House, a school just up the road run by the Misses Budd. J. V. Milne had a great deal of time for these ladies, believing that they delivered a sound grounding in all the necessary subjects, and was very complimentary about their abilities. Alan went there daily with Ken, Barry having already progressed to Henley House, and he adapted immediately to more structured learning. The teaching was formal, precise and strict, and Alan was introduced to reading and writing and, almost inevitably, took to both like a duck to water.

Once back at Henley House for learning as well as living, Alan continued to shine, and to nip at the heels of Ken. A fast bond was developing between the younger two boys, unsurprisingly isolating Barry, a pattern which was to continue for the rest of their lives.

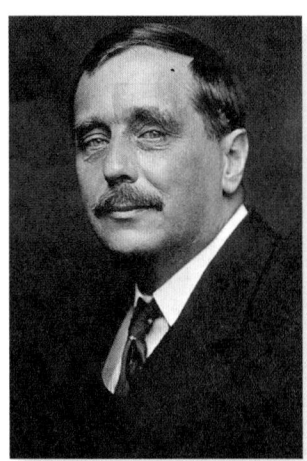

H. G. Wells as a young man.

A young teacher who then joined the school, and was to be a significant influence on Alan, as well as a friend, was H. G. Wells, who was employed to teach science, including mathematics, the subject Alan would eventually read at Cambridge. Although only twenty-two, Wells had remarkable educational qualifications already, was studying at night for his full university degree and teaching for a living by day. He was very much aligned with J. V.'s philosophy of education: he was principled (he refused to teach scripture, as he did not believe in it), approachable and kind. Wells introduced the young Alan to mathematics, including algebra and geometry, as well as to wider science, taking the boys regularly on field trips to apply their new knowledge in the field, or to the new museums in London's South Kensington.

Under the benign and caring oversight of J. V. and the efficient domestic management of Maria, the school flourished, allowing the Milnes to build up their financial resources. They became more ambitious for themselves and their sons. There were more outings to the theatre and concerts, as well as holidays. The whole family would generally go away to the country for an extended summer stay where the boys were allowed a good deal of freedom. They roamed across Kent, Surrey and Berkshire, free to ramble where they pleased, and where they applied practical experience of geography, geology, biology and mathematics to what they saw. These holidays also reinforced the bond between Ken and Alan, and further contributed to the marginalization of Barry, who always seemed rather different from his younger brothers.

J. V. was anxious for his sons to have the best possible education as their start in life. Barry, not particularly academic, was sent to a boarding school in Derbyshire, from where he was articled to a solicitor's practice. Ken and Alan, both clearly bright and intellectually capable, were destined for higher things. With his experience of running Henley House and sending boys onwards to their next schools, J. V. had a good understanding of the various options for his own sons and identified Westminster School in London as being the most appropriate for them.

On the face of it, Westminster was an understandable choice. It had an excellent reputation for learning and an outstanding track record for successful

Oxford and Cambridge entrants. Academically it marched at a level with Eton and Winchester, but was not so connected to upper class society, was much more middle class and accessible, and was relatively more down to earth. On the other hand, unlike Henley House, it was riven with archaic ritual, which made little sense other than for tradition's sake. It had a strong emphasis on the classics and humanities, and less on science, mathematics and more contemporary subjects, and there was little pastoral care. Few Henley House boys had gone on to Westminster, and so in many ways Alan benefitted from the fact that Ken went first and blazed a trail for him to follow. Alan won a Queen's Scholarship before his twelfth birthday and started at Westminster in the autumn term of 1893, going into a class of boys mostly two years older than him.

As predicted, Alan found the initial settling-in period to be challenging and confusing, even with Ken's prior knowledge of the obscure school traditions. He was also frustrated at the over-emphasis on the classics. After Henley House much was arbitrary, unfair and pointless, and Alan pushed back against this. On one occasion he received a poor school report saying that he had done little work, even in mathematics, which greatly distressed Alan's father. In fact, in mathematics he had come not only top in his form, but his marks had been spectacularly good by any standards. It transpired that the report had been written in advance of the examination results in an ill-informed and cursory way, quite typical at the time, but this was never acknowledged nor corrected. It continued to haunt both J. V. and Alan.

After only two terms, Alan was put up into Ken's class so that for the next four years, until Ken left school, they were together, reinforcing the close bond between the brothers. Considering Alan's subsequent career, it was fascinating that English literature did not appear on the curriculum at all and there was no formal English teaching, so that the pupils' knowledge of their own language and literature was woefully inadequate. Even for that period, it was a startling educational omission. However, Alan had at least had a grounding in English, including Shakespeare and classic English literature, at Henley House, and he read voraciously from the school library,

The food was terrible and never improved and, like the damp and unsuitable medieval buildings in which the school was housed, was simply accepted for what it was. Every term, Alan received an allowance from J. V. and had to provide his father with detailed accounts of his expenditure. These were, inevitably, a work of fiction, but certainly much of his relatively modest allowance was spent on extra food. Games were usually on the school playing fields, then as now at Vincent Square. Though by no means a proficient sportsman, here Alan learned and practised the game which was to give him so much pleasure for the remainder of his life, cricket.

One major downside of Westminster was corporal punishment in the form of beatings with a cane, delivered not by the masters, but by senior boys. As bad as the punishment itself, which was painful and humiliating, was the fear of it hanging over the pupils, since the beatings were all too often totally random, having little or no connection to anything which had actually been done. Instead, they were often simply carried out for amusement by bored seniors. There had been no corporal punishment at Henley House for, while it existed as a possibility, J. V. had never been known to raise the cane, which gathered dust in the headmaster's study. Not so at Westminster, where being thrashed was simply an occupational hazard.

During his period at Westminster, Alan became increasingly private and thoughtful and developed a strong sense of personal morality. He disliked bad language and found ribald conversations, off-colour anecdotes and dirty stories embarrassing and uncomfortable. While his fellow pupils were apparently tolerant of this high-minded position, it was further evidence that he was not perhaps cut from quite the same cloth as many of his contemporaries.

Holidays were an escape from the rigours of school life, as the Milnes were now renting a house in the country, Strete Court near Westgate-on-Sea in Thanet, on the north coast of Kent. The change of scene was entirely welcome, with all the family embracing the country air, the proximity of the sea, and, with seven acres of grounds around them, the opportunity to explore and roam to their hearts' content. They continued to be interested in the natural world about them, originally fostered by H. G. Wells back in St John's Wood, but by now the boys had bicycles, which allowed them to go further and further afield. Barry, who had become articled to a solicitor in Dorset, does not seem to have been a regular part of these outings and activities, even in his holidays.

However, Alan's relationship with Ken remained very close. They wrote letters to one another secretly in classes and wrote verse together. Nonetheless, Alan did make other friends. One of these showed him copies of *The Granta*

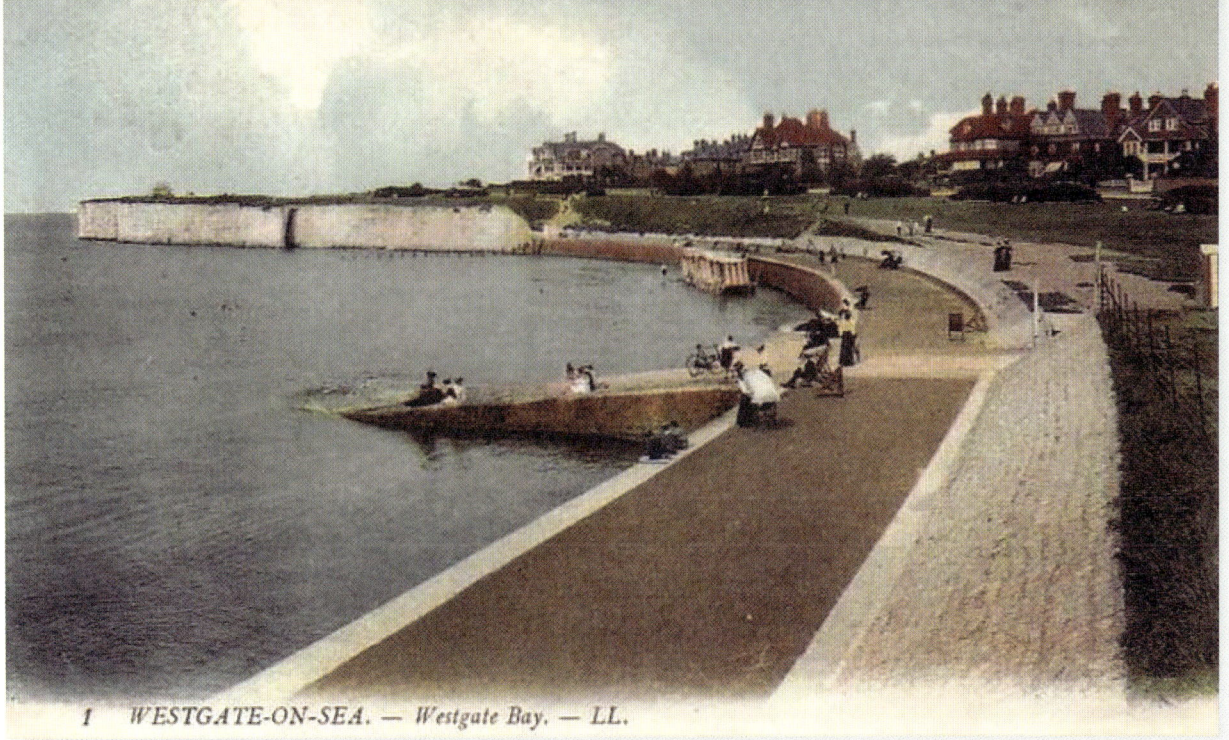

1 WESTGATE-ON-SEA. — Westgate Bay. — LL.

The sandy beaches of Westgate-on-Sea in Thanet, Kent, were a welcome change from the demands of school for the young Milne.

(now just *Granta*), the Cambridge University student magazine, and suggested that Alan's ambition should be to edit this, a suggestion with which he agreed with alacrity, suddenly creating an objective and focus for the future.

That Alan would apply to go to university was a formality so there was little surprise when he won two minor scholarships to Trinity College, Cambridge. By the end of the summer term of 1900 he was more than ready to move on from school. He left Westminster with mixed feelings, with gratitude for where it had allowed him to go, but frustration at the pointlessness of so many of the day-to-day regulations of the school. As time went on his attitude mellowed and he was pleased and enthusiastic when his nephews, Ken's boys, followed in their footsteps to Westminster, although he pointedly sent his own son, Christopher, to Stowe School. The passage of time, nostalgia for the close, shared years with Ken, the sense that his own success had been grounded there, all brought about a gradual change in his feelings about Westminster. Ultimately he made the grand gesture of a legacy in his will which would bring unexpected but most welcome largesse to the school.

Milne was extremely fortunate that a contemporary Westminster Queen's Scholar, Saxon Sydney-Turner, had gone up to Trinity the previous year and had become friends with a dazzling number of the future luminaries of the Bloomsbury Group, including Lytton Strachey, Thoby Stephen, Leonard Woolf and Clive Bell. Milne was introduced to and incorporated into this extraordinary undergraduate society. And, emboldened by this company, as well as by his and others' expectations, he immediately began to submit verse contributions, still written jointly with Ken, to *The Granta*. While nominally a Cambridge University magazine, *The Granta* was an institution like no other in Cambridge. It was managed and run by a small coterie of friends who were linked socially and academically and who shared a certain self-declared intellectual bravura. It was deliberately difficult to break in. Nonetheless Alan persevered, accepted the rejection slips with resignation, and continued to submit. By his second term he was in print, the author initials A. K. M. standing for Alan Ken Milne. Ken, however, now toiling at his solicitor's articles in Weymouth, soon decided to stop participating in their writing projects on the basis that Alan could do quite well enough on his own. Alan also pursued sporting interests, as the College photograph albums show him in football teams in the 1900–01 and 1902–03 seasons.

Alan was nominally studying mathematics, but his real interests lay in other areas of student life, and after the deficit of English literature at Westminster, he embraced the opportunities to engage with this at Cambridge. By his second term he was a 'visiting reader' at meetings of the Shakespeare Society, which met regularly to read through Shakespeare's works, and he was open to any opportunities to broaden his exposure to literature and the arts. Not surprisingly, his mathematics suffered.

He maintained outwardly a light-hearted approach to life, but this concealed an inner reticence, and a seeming inability to release his innermost emotions and feelings. He reserved that little he wished to share about himself for Ken, and for Ken alone. Over and above that which he had built around himself at Westminster, Alan developed at Cambridge a further layer of that buttoned-up-ness that both his son and his future collaborator, Ernest Shepard, would refer to so many years later. He was not known to have had any significant personal relationships while at Cambridge; he was never discovered the worse for drink, nor did he let his own standards of personal behaviour ever lapse.

What he did focus on was writing, editing and making the most of being editor of *The Granta* from 1902. This had been his ambition since Westminster, but it was by no means an easy thing to achieve. Having managed it through hard work and perseverance, he was determined to make a success of it. This was not an ambition shared by his College. He was summoned by his tutor and reprimanded for not having asked permission to take up the editorship of *The*

Granta, as it was felt that this would have a significant and detrimental impact on his degree. He had already been taking a relaxed attitude towards his studies in mathematics, which no longer inspired or even really interested him, and now he was firmly told to pull his socks up and get working for a degree which would represent his abilities. He focused instead on *The Granta* and his own literary work, making this the centre of his time at Cambridge. Unsurprisingly, he only scraped a third-class honours degree in mathematics, which did not seem to concern him that much. He was, however, affected by the distress and shame which it brought to his father. J. V. was overwhelmed by this disastrous close to Alan's university career – he was beside himself with grief as his lofty expectations for his brilliant youngest son came crashing down about his ears. Certainly, for his family, it was an ignominious end to what had been, up until then, a stellar academic career.

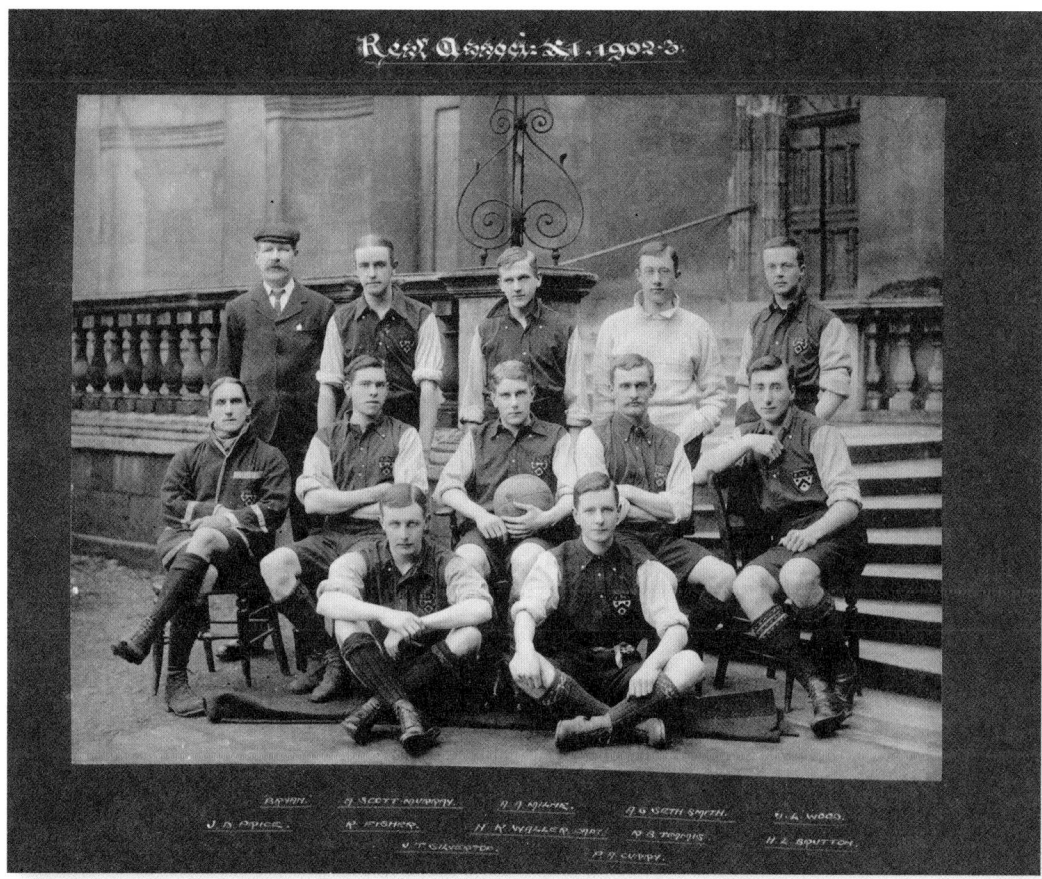

Alan Milne – top row centre – in the Trinity College Cambridge football team, 1902–3.

Ernest Howard Shepard was born on 10 December 1879 in London. His father, Henry Shepard, was an architect by profession and an artist by disposition. Henry came from a respectable, well-off Victorian middle-class family, his father being a highly successful property developer and builder, and Henry was brought up in a large corner house in Bloomsbury's Gordon Square. His mother, Jessie, was the daughter of William Lee, a successful watercolourist, and was a granddaughter of one of the founders of *Punch* magazine.

Ernest was the youngest of Henry and Jessie's three children, following Ethel and Cyril. They were brought up in a substantial white stucco house in Kent Terrace on the western side of London's Regent's Park. It was an unusual childhood in that the family spent much more time together than in most traditional middle-class Victorian families, without the usual rigid demarcation between upstairs and downstairs, between the nursery and the drawing room, and between respect and affection. Henry and Jessie seem to have enjoyed their children, including them in much of their own lives and entertainments. As Ernest was the youngest, he was still at home when Ethel and Cyril were at school, and so he developed a special bond with his mother, to whom he was devoted. It was she, having herself been brought up in an artist's household, who encouraged his earliest efforts at drawing. She often took him with her when she went out to pay calls or to go shopping, and Ernest developed an easy confidence and friendly manner with new people and places. Jessie and Henry would also take the children out to see and experience life in London, with expeditions to the Christmas lights, to the theatre, to enjoy contemporary events and activities, or just to experience life from the top of a bus.

A pencil portrait of Ernest aged two, probably by Minnie Dicksee.

It was a happy, contented and fulfilling family life at Kent Terrace for them all, and for Ernest, it set a benchmark for what a happy home should be like. In his book *Drawn from Memory*, published in 1957, Shepard recounted many warm and evocative stories that took place in a single year of his childhood.

Ernest's parents enjoyed most forms of culture, so reading, drawing, music

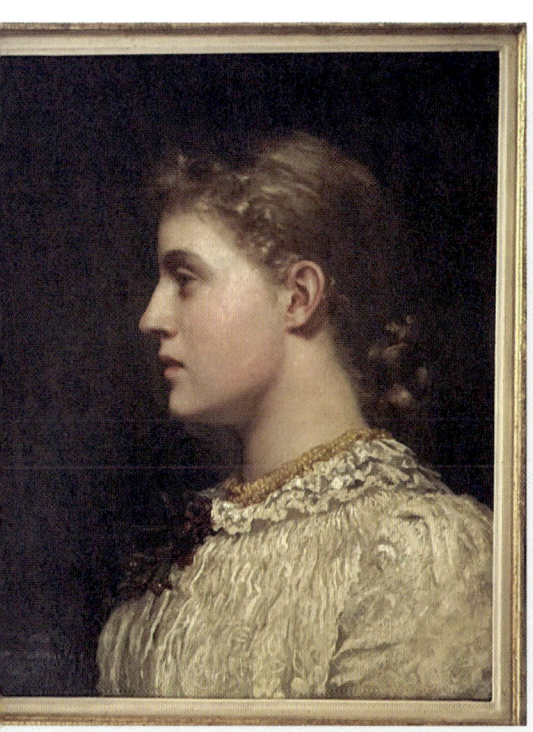

An oil portrait of Shepard's mother, Jessie Lee, by Frank Dicksee.

and conversation were an integral part of family life. There were many evenings at Kent Terrace when Ernest's parents would entertain friends, the doors in the double drawing room on the first floor thrown open for music-making and for amateur theatricals. Ethel was very musical as well as keen on dressing up and writing short plays with a cast of three, which were put on for an indulgent audience of family and close friends. There were also magic lantern shows and conjurors, often in December, when Ernest's birthday and Christmas were good opportunities for celebration. Henry was also a talented amateur artist and early photographer, and so the atmosphere at home was one of relaxed creativity. The children were encouraged to experiment and to be comfortable about performing in front of other people, giving them self-confidence, particularly in front of adults, which was to be of great benefit to them all.

Ethel devoted her life to missionary work in what is now Pakistan and had great empathy for others. When, much later, Ernest's first wife was to die suddenly and unexpectedly, it was Ethel who picked up the pieces, helping to arrange the funeral and supporting her grieving brother, nephew and niece. Cyril, too, was outgoing and amusing, and while later he had a steady job as a Lloyd's underwriter, he spent much of his spare time engaged in amateur theatricals. The connection with *Punch* was also important, as the family link meant that the influence of the magazine percolated through the household, many of its contributors being among those who visited the Kent Terrace drawing room. Jessie was the beating heart of this household, and her wit, gaiety and enthusiasm for life were an inspiration to them all.

Sadly, Jessie became ill and died when Ernest was only ten, and this obviously had an immediate impact on his life. She left a great impression on him, and his reminiscences of her and of her influence on his childhood come across clearly and sharply in *Drawn from Memory*, even though it was written more than sixty years later. Shepard described her death movingly in his second book of memoirs, *Drawn from Life*, which covered the period from then until his marriage in 1904.

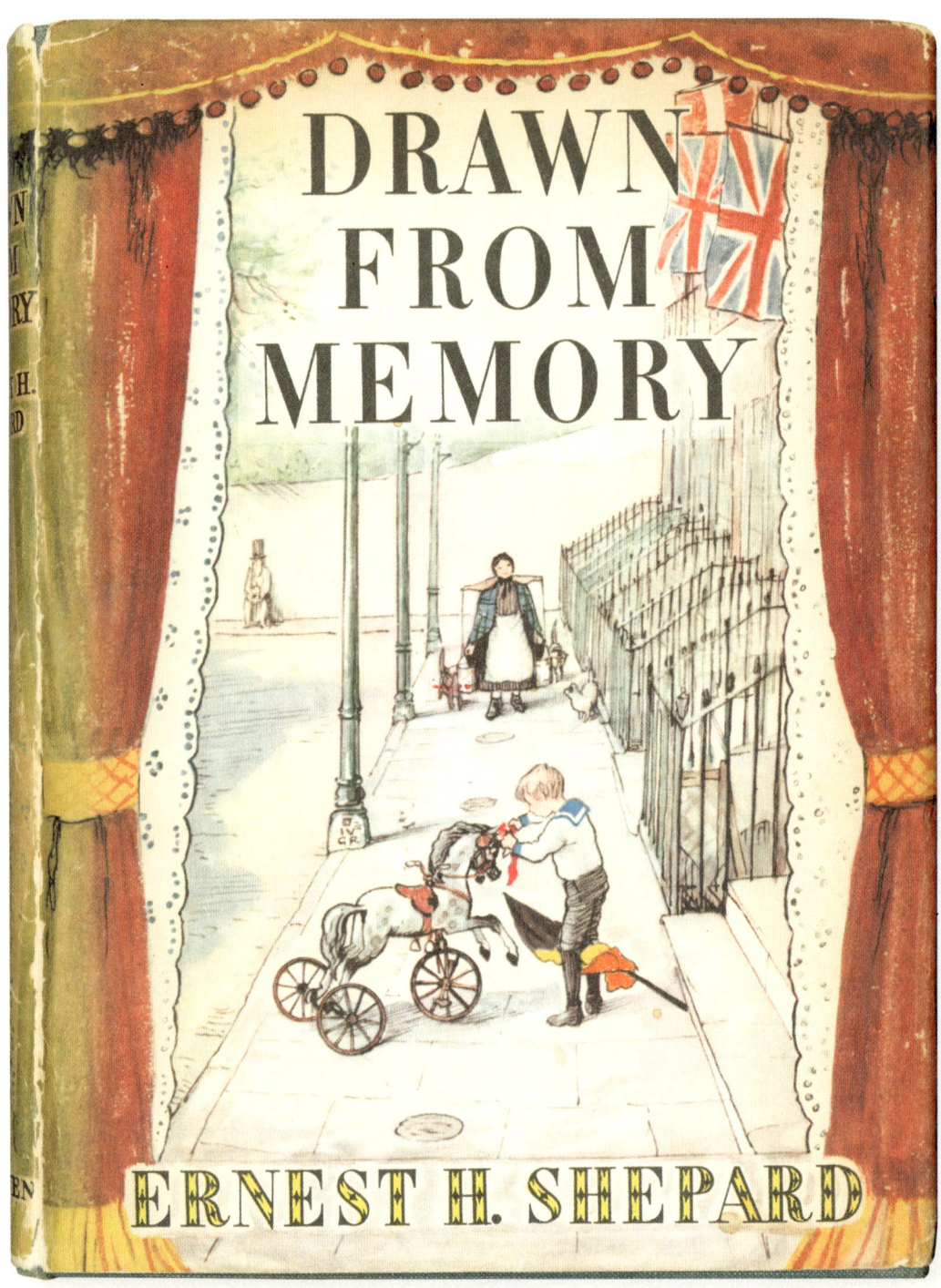

The original dust jacket for the first edition of *Drawn from Memory*, Shepard's memoir of his childhood.

Following Jessie's death the children were sent to stay with their aunts, their father's sisters, in the big house in Gordon Square, and there they lived, with regular visits from their father, for nearly a year. Their lives were never to be the same again, not just because of the loss of their beloved mother, but also because the warm, stable and happy family environment was gone forever. Henry Shepard seems to have lost his way after his wife's death. His health, seemingly both physical and mental, deteriorated and as a result his business and his income suffered. The family moved from Regent's Park to cheaper accommodation in Hammersmith. The two boys, Cyril and Ernest, left their private school in St John's Wood and were enrolled at Colet Court, the preparatory school for St Paul's School, then in Hammersmith, west London. Money remained tight in the Shepard household and in due course Ernest was only able to remain at St Paul's School through the support of his uncle, who was a master there and able to subsidize the fees.

Shepard's early promise as an artist was soon identified at St Paul's, and he was put into an advanced art class. He later complained that by concentrating to such an extent on his art, the school had compromised his wider education. In a similar way to Alan Milne, although for different reasons, he felt ill-educated in English literature and that his knowledge of the classics was not what it ought to have been. When he was sixteen, he was further enrolled for additional life drawing classes on Saturdays at the Heatherley School of Fine Art in west London. There was some initial concern about the young Shepard drawing from the nude at such a tender age, as it was felt that this might affect his moral development. However, Shepard showed a great interest in life drawing, especially drawing nude models, throughout his working life.

He enjoyed his schooldays, possibly because the ordered and consistent life was in contrast to the rather more uncertain times at home. Life there was often confused: the lively but structured household of Kent Terrace was long gone; his father was often distracted or unwell, and for much of the time the children had to shift for themselves. However, it was useful training for the future, when at times Shepard was obliged, by his financial situation or unexpected circumstances, to look after himself, not something most middle-class men would have been able to do.

In the summer holidays, his aunts would take a holiday house in the country and invite the Shepard children to join them. As the aunts were nervous about travelling by train, which was still a relatively new invention, these houses tended to be no further away from London than the home counties. Nonetheless they opened Shepard's eyes to the countryside, and he spent many hours drawing what he saw. He was one of those fortunate people who are quite comfortable both in London and in the countryside, and he spent significant periods of his life in each, enjoying both equally.

His father was interested in military matters and had himself as a younger man joined an informal militia, an early version of the later Territorial Army reserve force, and Shepard also became interested, particularly in the guns and weaponry that were then in use. When the aunts took a house near Aldershot, the home of the British Army, he followed groups of soldiers on exercises on his bicycle and recorded their uniforms and weaponry with increasing accuracy. Back at school, this was an interest shared with other boys, and Ernest became fascinated in particular by artillery, the large field guns and associated ordnance which were transforming the British Army in those years leading up to the Boer War. Later on, this abiding interest in artillery would lead to him to enlist in a field artillery siege battery when he joined up to fight in the First World War.

In a pattern which he was to follow for the remainder of his long life, Ernest began to record the everyday events he saw around him, taking a pencil and small pocket sketchbook everywhere he went and sketching a building, a person or a scene. Often these would go no further, but sometimes he would take these quick sketches and use them as inspiration for more detailed drawings and, later on, for cartoons. Some of his earliest surviving drawings are from this period and include pencil drawings of royal events. In 1893, at the age of thirteen, he drew from life the scenes following the carriage procession for the marriage of the Duke and Duchess of York. This drawing is extraordinarily detailed and accurate, judging by other contemporary illustrations of the same scene, with the crowds, the surrounding buildings and the carriage procession itself drawn with great confidence.

Ernest left St Paul's School in 1896 and moved full-time to the Heatherley School of Fine Art for a year to prepare for the scholarship to the Royal Academy Schools. Throughout his time as a student, Ernest continued to develop a wide network of friends, which often included their families as well. He was also a

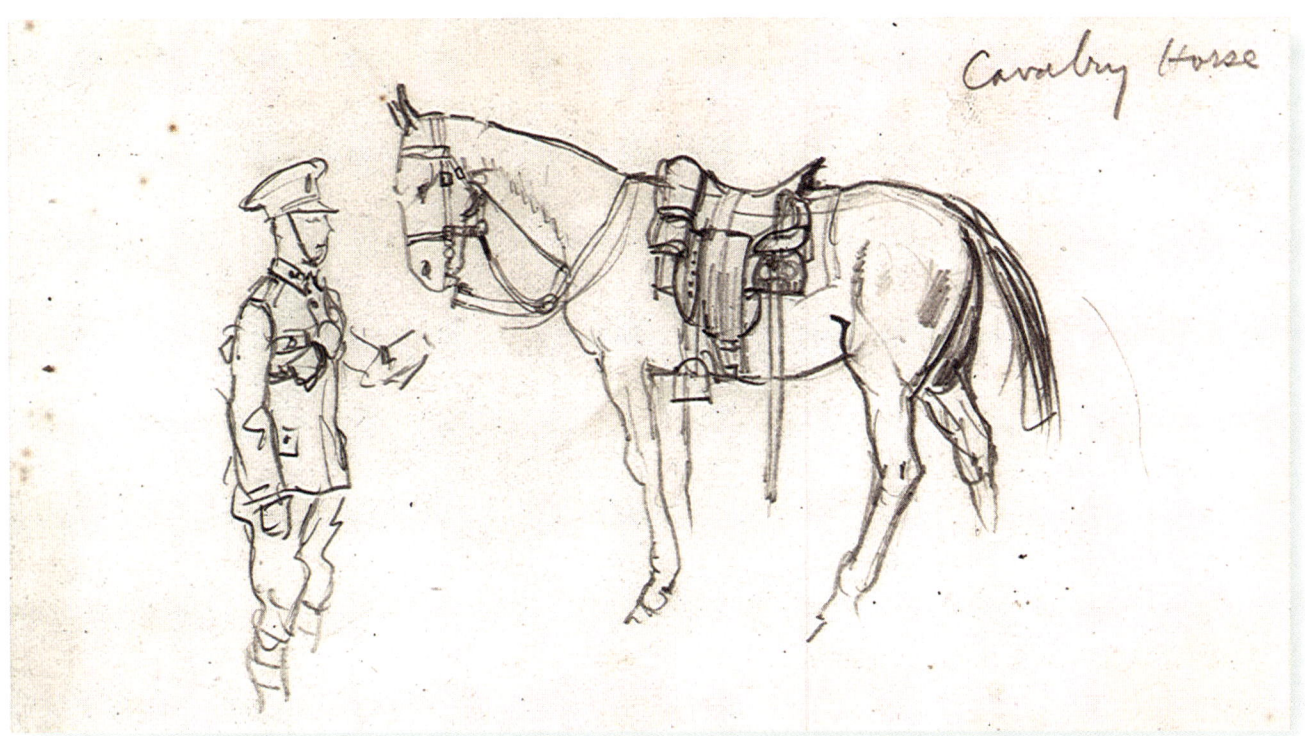

Shepard's extraordinary eye for the minutiae is seen even in small, rough sketches such as this of a cavalry horse and soldier – undated.

keen cyclist and sometimes combined the two pleasures, cycling extraordinary distances to see family or friends for weekends or in the holidays.

He was outgoing and gregarious, enjoyed company and going out, albeit on a very limited budget. He had always enjoyed the theatre and now he started to frequent the music halls, then such a feature of entertainment in London. His high spirits and cheerful demeanour soon led to his lifelong nickname, 'Kipper' or 'Kip', as a fashionable music hall expression of the time for a person who was the life and soul of the party was a 'giddy kipper'.

He was successful in his scholarship application, and with this achieved, the summer before he started at the Royal Academy Schools brought a great and unexpected treat. The aunts were unable to take their usual house in the country and, knowing how disappointed the Shepard children would be, they gave their father the money for him to take the whole family to France. The children had never before been abroad, and the weeks they spent in Normandy were a revelation to Ethel, Cyril and Ernest, not least the delicious food. Henry spent much of his time painting while the children went sightseeing and experienced the culture, language and way of life of another country. It fostered a lifelong appreciation of travel and of France in Ernest.

On his return to London he started his three-year course in the autumn of 1897. He spent the first year in the Lower School, with a thorough grounding in drawing and draughtsmanship, following which he progressed to the Upper School, where there would be life drawing in the evenings for male students only – the Royal Academy thought it was inappropriate for female students to look upon the nude human body. Even at that time, this viewpoint was thought to be rather old-fashioned, certainly by the students.

Ernest made good progress and won further scholarships, both securing his financial position and building a reputation as one of the leading students in the Schools. As his confidence and his skills grew, he tentatively began to submit work speculatively to magazines and made the occasional sale, giving him the feeling that he could make a living as a professional artist. He struggled with oil painting and gradually concluded that it was not his medium. He nonetheless persevered, however, and indeed had an oil painting of Ethel exhibited at the Royal Academy Summer Exhibition. It was 'hung on the line', which was a great compliment as this was at eye level for visitors, and sold immediately, but he realized that his principal area of expertise was as a draughtsman and illustrator. He understood, not least for financial reasons, that his future professional life would need to be based on a commercial practice, working for publications and in the media and print world.

As his time as a student at the Royal Academy Schools drew to a close, he decided to share a studio with a fellow student and friend, George Swaish, and they found a studio house with basic living accommodation in Glebe Place in Chelsea, for which they paid fifty guineas a year. There was a part-time housekeeper who kept an eye on the two young men, but they had to take care of their own domestic responsibilities. In his memoir *Drawn from Life* Ernest explained how for their first meal in their new home they bought a steak and to tenderize it he beat it with an artist's T square. He continued: 'It came out quite thin, like a small blanket, and had to be folded several times to get it into the pan. The steak was as tough as hide.' To begin with, he would live and work in Glebe Place during the week, and then go out to Blackheath to lend a hand with his father's care at the weekends.

Henry Shepard's health had continued to decline, as rheumatoid arthritis gave way to multiple sclerosis, and his children had to rally round to manage the remainder of his life. Ernest had to give up the studio in Glebe Place and all three siblings were together in Blackheath taking turns with his father's care until he died at the age of only fifty-six in May 1902. Alas, years of over-optimism and financial mismanagement along with the costs of his illness meant that the Shepard children were left with virtually no money. The house in Blackheath had to be sold, and the three of them moved into rented accommodation nearby. It was a difficult time for them all.

Ernest's personal life took a turn for the better a couple of years later. While at the Royal Academy Schools, Shepard had met a fellow student, Florence Chaplin, always known as Pie, whose family also had a link with *Punch*. Her grandfather, Ebenezer Landells, was a co-founder of the magazine and had also been closely connected to the *Illustrated London News*, both publications which would turn out to be key to Ernest's future career. Pie was three years older than him, was also an excellent artist and seemed to him as more sophisticated and mature than he was. He fell in love with her but was reticent about expressing his feelings, in part because he felt she was unlikely to be attracted to him due to his age, inexperience, relative immaturity and lack of both prospects and money. Unhappy, he sought refuge in a holiday in Devon with old friends, who realized that he was not his usual jovial self. Eventually he admitted his quandary. To his surprise, they did not laugh at him or tell him that she was out of his league, they simply advised that he should quietly tell her how he felt and take it from there.

So, in due course he plucked up his courage to tell her how he felt and was amazed when he discovered that his feelings were reciprocated. In fact, the two families had much in common, not least the shared connection with *Punch*, and when Pie's widowed mother and Shepard's father had met, each approved of the other. The financial barrier to their marriage seemed at first overwhelming, but Ernest then received payment for two oil paintings, that medium in which he was never comfortable, which were sold for meaningful sums, while Florence received a prestigious and well-paid commission for a mural at Guy's Hospital in London. On the basis of this, and on Ernest taking out life insurance, Pie's mother gave her consent to the marriage. They were married quietly in September 1904 and started life together in Arden Cottage, a two-up, two-down cottage in Shamley Green, near Guildford in Surrey. The couple had two children: Graham, born in 1907, and Mary, born in 1909.

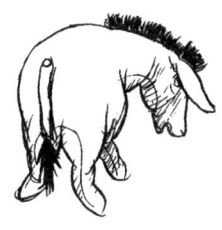

CHAPTER TWO

Punch

It is difficult to overestimate the importance of *Punch* magazine in the century between 1860 and 1960. From modest beginnings it soon became a national institution, indeed, as an English-language publication, it became an international phenomenon. In its heyday it ranked with the monarchy or the BBC as a peculiarly British yet authoritative voice which resonated globally. In today's multi-media world of fast-moving data, the idea that a single weekly publication should have had such a hold on an influential international audience seems extraordinary. But *Punch* somehow managed to be all things to all men – its balance of news, commentary, articles, reviews, cartoons, illustrations and jokes appealed across the board. It played a vital part in the story of A. A. Milne and E. H. Shepard, both of whom aspired from their teens to contribute to it, had personal connections with the magazine, and achieved their ambitions to be part of it.

Milne started writing for *Punch* soon after leaving Cambridge University; Shepard's first cartoons in the magazine were published shortly afterwards. Milne became assistant editor at the precocious age of twenty-four, and both men continued to contribute up until, and even during, their army service in the First World War. Some of Milne's poems for *When We Were Very Young* were first published there and Shepard was asked to illustrate them. Milne continued to be published in *Punch* until the last decade of his life, and Shepard provided cartoons for the magazine well into his seventies. *Punch* was a constant which ran through both their lives like the writing through a stick of rock.

Punch was founded by Henry Mayhew and Ebenezer Landells (the future grandfather-in-law of E. H. Shepard) in 1841 as a weekly humorous magazine. To indicate the ding-dong of robust humour it was named *Punch* after the Punch and Judy puppet show, although the name also indicated that it was intending to land a blow on the reading public. It was to some extent modelled on a Parisian journal called *Le Charivari*, and so *Punch* was subtitled *The London Charivari*. *Punch* set out to be a satirical as well as a humorous magazine, but unlike many of its competitors at that time, it was not gratuitously offensive or rude, and instead used satire, irony and humour to convey its point on issues of the day. As a result, it soon developed a niche market, appealing to readers who were interested in seeing current affairs presented in an amusing but challenging light, although in such a way as to be acceptable in polite society. After a predictably rocky start, partly as the initial capital was only £25 (not much even at that time), and partly as the founders did not have much experience, the magazine was soon sold on to publishers Bradbury and Evans in 1842. It had an unexpected boost after its *Almanack* sold over 90,000 copies, far exceeding expectations.

Originally preliminary drawings to show how a finished piece of artwork might look, *Punch* appropriated the term 'cartoon' for a satirical or humorous drawing with particular emphasis on political issues of the day. From then on, the magazine became as linked to political cartoons as fish was to chips, and it gave the opportunity for an impartial medium to challenge political orthodoxy, or to draw attention to matters which were essentially being swept under the carpet.

From the start, the magazine was a composite of articles about contemporary issues of politics, business, foreign affairs and the arts, some of which were serious, some with a jocular tone, some challenging and some ironic. In the same vein, there were drawings and cartoons, many of which illustrated and complemented the articles, as well as some stand-alone drawings. There was an active correspondence with readers, particularly as the magazine's circulation grew. *Punch* was dominant at a time of great economic and social change, which saw the rise of a literate and increasingly articulate middle class, as well as active demands from the working classes for radical reform to political, economic and social structures across the whole of Europe.

Punch managed to capture an increasing readership through consistently delivering content which attracted a wide spectrum of readers. By the 1850s, members of the royal family and of every other class of society were reading the magazine, each of them attracted by its relevance, willingness to challenge, breadth of interest and humour – quite simply, it made people laugh. The magazine's circulation continued to rise steadily to 100,000 copies per week just before the First World War and approached 200,000 at its peak after the Second

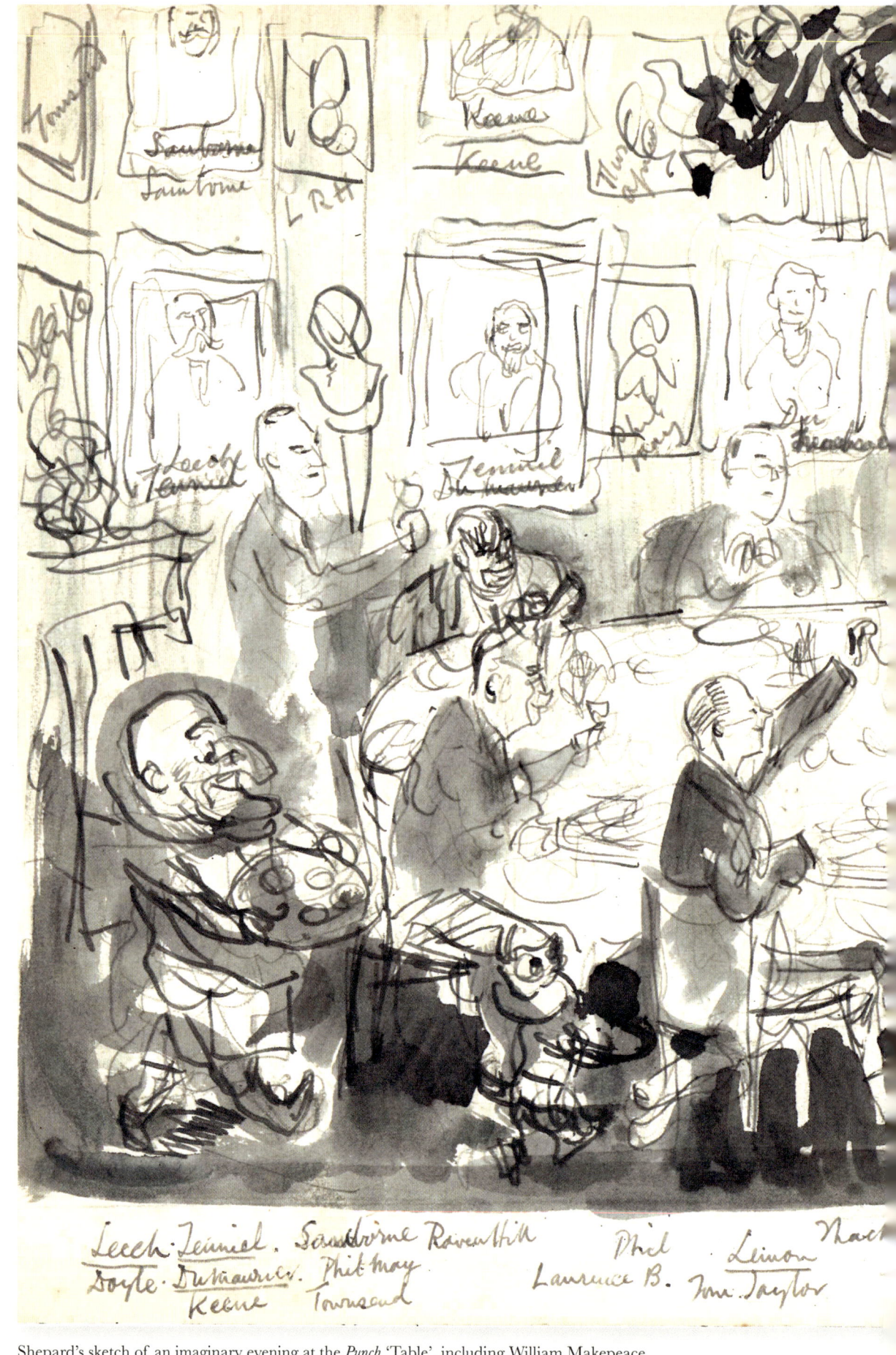

Shepard's sketch of an imaginary evening at the *Punch* 'Table', including William Makepeace Thackeray, John Tenniel and Linley Sambourne, both around the table and in portraits on the wall, presided over by 'Mr Punch' on the left.

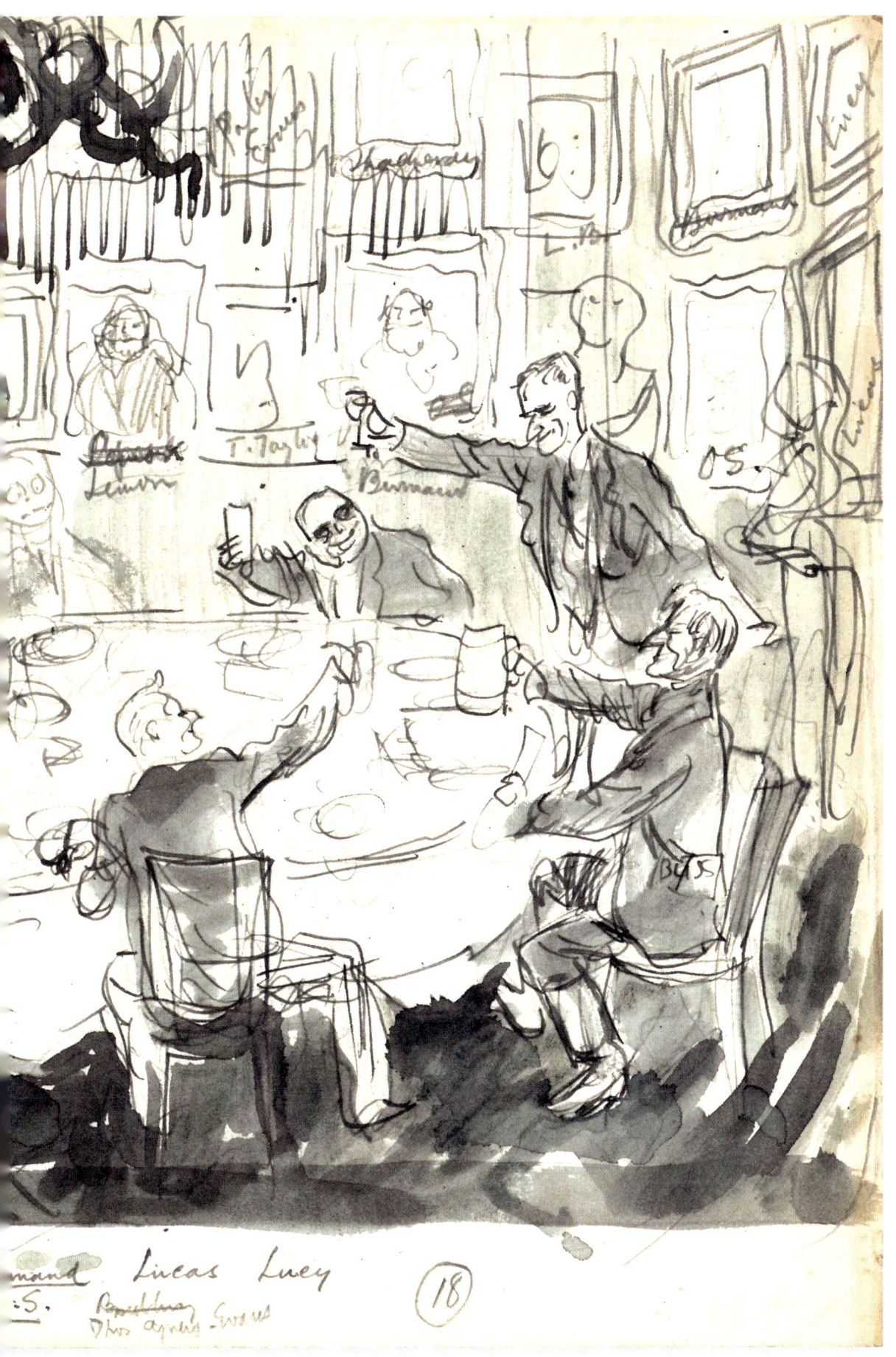

Lucas Lucy
(18)

World War. Milne and Shepard, active with *Punch* from the mid-Edwardian period to the early 1950s, were therefore contributing to the most popular English publication in the world in its heyday.

Punch was distributed around the British Empire and, in places like British India, was seen as a vital connection and lifeline with 'home'. The fact that copies did not arrive until weeks, sometimes months, after publication did not seem to matter. Whenever they arrived, they gave readers on distant shores a feeling of still being a part of the British character: self-deprecating, not taking oneself too seriously, willing to laugh and to find humour in everyday situations, and yet being serious about the things that really mattered – honesty, probity, conscientiousness and dressing for dinner.

In 1904, the year that Milne started to try to establish himself as a writer in London, and in which Shepard got married and worked even harder to develop his freelance career as an artist and illustrator, *Punch* was riding high. Now with offices in Bouverie Street, just off Fleet Street and so in the very heart of the London newspaper and publishing world, with a professional staff, an efficient publishing and distribution machine, and the authority to attract the brightest and the best in British journalism, *Punch* had an unrivalled reputation. The magazine's offices contained a separate dining room containing the famous *Punch* Table. Here senior staff meetings were held over the course of a weekly dinner, and favoured guests and contributors were invited to participate. Essentially, if you were invited to be a regular part of *Punch*'s Table it meant that you were part of the magazine's inner circle.

With some private means at his disposal Alan Milne had the opportunity for a while to be able to try his luck as a writer. He took rooms near Bouverie Street, within a stone's throw of the *Punch* offices, began to write both verse and prose, and sent these pieces unsolicited to a variety of publications. And there was a great variety on offer at the time. There were many small magazines and periodicals, and no less than eight London evening newspapers, so it was hard to choose where to send his speculative work. In his last year at Cambridge, he had been encouraged to write some pieces and to send these to Owen Seaman, at that time deputy editor of *Punch*. Milne was pleased when Seaman responded with suggestions on how to improve his work, and the pieces went to and fro until, finally satisfied, Seaman sent them on to the editor of *Punch*, Frank Burnand. But that was the end of that. No more was heard of them until, months later, they were returned to Milne. In desperation, he sent them to another, much less distinguished publication, which took them with alacrity and then went bust. Hardly an encouraging start.

Encouraged by his father, Milne decided to see whether intervention from more influential connections might help him with a step onto – at this stage certainly not up – the ladder. First he tried his father's old pupil, who had always seemed so complimentary and kind, Alfred Harmsworth. Harmsworth had not yet become Lord Northcliffe, but he was certainly accelerating ahead in his successful career as a newspaper proprietor. Alas, this did not go according to plan, as Milne was brushed off by Harmsworth's minions and, even at a second attempt, was simply passed on to subservient lackeys who clearly had no intention of extending any favours towards a young man who was not already a protégé of the great publishing magnate. It was another ignominious failure.

Milne's next venture into patronage was to approach the former Henley House assistant master, H. G. Wells. In the years after leaving teaching, and while Milne was educating himself at Westminster and Cambridge, Wells had become, in a short space of time, a phenomenally successful writer. But he also had a reputation as something of a maverick, with unconventional views and practices not only in literature but also in personal behaviour, including – in hushed tones – sexual matters. Consequently, the literary establishment regarded Wells as 'suspect'. Wells did at least answer Milne's letters, invited him to stay, and introduced him to a few possible contacts, including the writer William Archer, who turned out to be dry, humourless and unapproachable. It was all very disappointing.

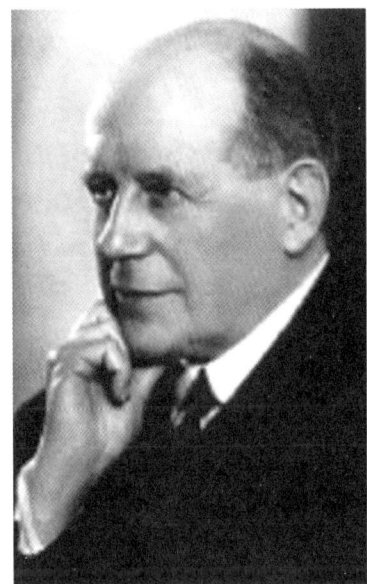

Perseverance, grit and determination gradually won through, and at first a trickle of pieces were accepted, often seemingly randomly, by a variety of lesser-known publications. But *Punch* remained the Holy Grail for Milne. The problem was that *Punch* at that time was so much head-and-shoulders above all the rest that every literary Tom, Dick or Harry was trying their damnedest to get published

Owen Seaman, editor of *Punch* for the early years of the twentieth century.

in the magazine. Having their name in *Punch* was the equivalent of hitting the jackpot for any aspiring writer's CV. *Punch* was therefore overwhelmed with unsolicited contributions, and it was often a lottery as to who might or might not be successful in getting accepted.

Nonetheless, Milne continued to persevere, sending in speculative writings one week, and receiving them back the next, when sometimes he would then adapt them and send them off again to another publication. Slowly, however, he made progress, and in May of 1904 he had his first piece accepted in *Punch*, a poem. Very grateful that this was not just a flash in the pan, shortly afterwards he had another piece of writing accepted. While this was exciting and demonstrated that he could achieve his ambition of contributing to the magazine, there was another problem. Being published in *Punch* was so attractive that the magazine was besieged by freelancers, and was able to pay minimal rates to its contributors. For his first two pieces published in *Punch* Milne received only sixteen shillings and sixpence for both, a paltry sum, whereas other publications would have paid three or four times that amount.

Money was a problem, as his income from his writing was insufficient to sustain even a modest lifestyle. The remainder of his private means was ebbing away, and so he had to give up the rooms near *Punch*, and at the end of 1904 Milne moved to cheaper lodgings in Wellington Square, Chelsea, at that time a largely working-class area, low-lying and too close to the smelly river Thames. It was essentially a boarding house, with rudimentary washing facilities in an outhouse, and where he could only afford to pay for his rooms and breakfast. With little disposable income, and nowhere really to go, there was no alternative other than to knuckle down and focus on his writing.

On the advice of H. G. Wells, he developed some of the articles he had previously published in the *St James's Gazette* newspaper into a book titled *Lovers in London*. Wells had also introduced him to his agent, J. B. Pinker, who perhaps surprisingly, agreed to take Milne on. (Pinker may well have just wished to do a favour for Wells, who must have been a very profitable client.) In any case, Pinker guided Milne through the process of preparing a book for publication and then managed, with some surprise, to get him a contract for the book with an advance of £15, at a time when Milne's total financial resources amounted to some £20.

Published in 1905, this first book sank without much trace, even Milne failing to keep a copy of it. However, this turned out to mark the low point in his early career as gradually, slowly, but inexorably, matters were to improve.

Having started to make his mark at *Punch,* some of Milne's prose pieces about a girl called Lilian, written in a light, frothy and amusing style, caught the imagination of readers and soon became a regular feature. Within a year or so he had contributed over thirty articles to the magazine. However, what came next was totally unexpected. Milne received a summons from Owen Seaman. It seemed that Frank Burnand was at last retiring as editor of *Punch*, to be replaced by Seaman himself, and Seaman had a proposition for Milne. He wanted to delegate the burden of sorting out the unsolicited contributions, dealing with the contributors, and managing the general administration, and for this he was willing to pay £250 a year, plus double the usual fee for Milne's own contributions, which would henceforth be expected weekly. Surprised and delighted, on this basis Alan Milne was appointed assistant editor of *Punch* in February 1906 at the age of just twenty-four. It was a remarkable turnaround in fortune.

Ernest and Florence Shepard – Kipper and Pie – were meanwhile establishing themselves in Arden Cottage in Shamley Green. It was a simple dwelling, with a kitchen and sitting room downstairs, two bedrooms upstairs, a scullery and outside WC, with a cottage garden and water drawn from a well. It had not been lived in for some time, and Shepard, with the help of his brother and sister, had put it in order, using some of the furnishings from the Blackheath house and with wedding presents largely making up the rest. The rent was £6 a year, and they had £70 in the bank.

Both were working artists, and both were keen to earn what they could from their art. Pie had recently completed a prestigious commission of a mural for the nurses' dining room at Guy's Hospital in London, and Ernest was buoyed up by selling his two oil paintings. His success at the Royal Academy's Summer Exhibition had another important consequence. At the viewing he met the American artist and illustrator Edwin Abbey, who took Shepard to meet a friend of his, Linley Sambourne. Sambourne was at this time the chief cartoonist for *Punch*, having taken over from John Tenniel a few years earlier, and thus was an important ally to make. He was friendly and helpful, suggested how Shepard might make progress in his submissions for *Punch*, and encouraged him to persevere.

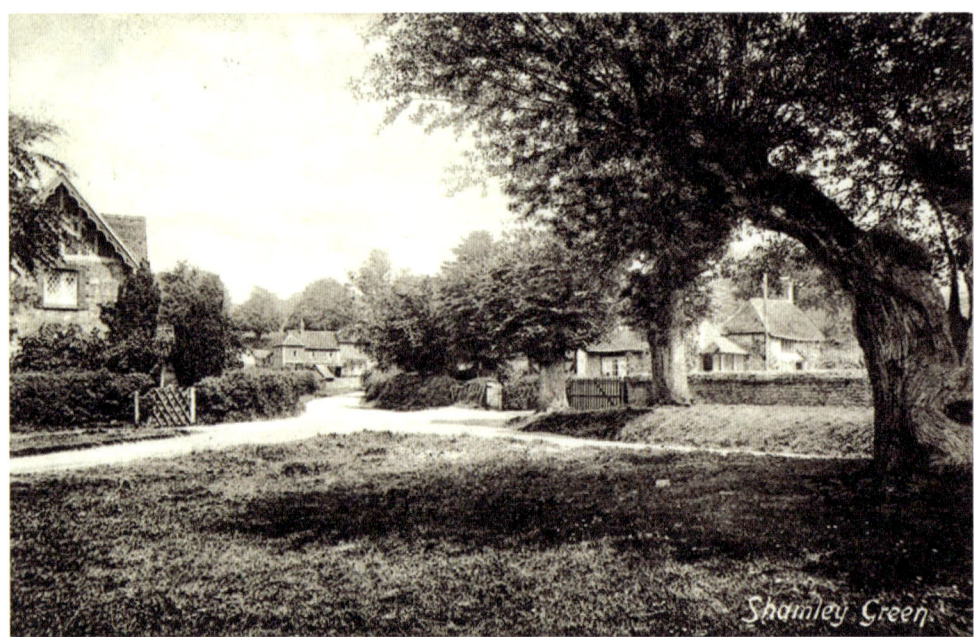

The picturesque village of Shamley Green in Surrey, where Ernest and Florence Shepard –
Kipper and Pie – lived from 1905 until 1927.

It was good advice and, in the meantime, Shepard touted his portfolio to art editors working for publishers and publications. This speculative approach started to bear fruit. Gradually commissions came his way, mostly for dust jackets for books, with the occasional frontispiece and book illustrations in black and white, which suited him well. His work was well received and Shepard started receiving better commissions, including offers to illustrate new editions of some classics of literature such as *Aesop's Fables*, *David Copperfield* and *Tom Brown's Schooldays*. All these jobs gave him more confidence, raised awareness of his talent and skill among the reading public, and increased his income.

In 1905 F. H. Townsend, a well-known artist and illustrator in his own right, became art editor of *Punch*. It was no coincidence that the following year Shepard had his first drawing published in the magazine, the start of an association that would last more than fifty years and take Shepard from occasional freelance contributor to chief political cartoonist and long-standing member of the *Punch* Table. So, for both A. A. Milne and E. H. Shepard, 1906 was a pivotal year in their respective relationships with *Punch* magazine.

Milne took to life as assistant editor of *Punch* like the proverbial duck to water. He and Seaman complemented each other perfectly. Seaman was dry, reactionary, conventional and stolid, while Milne was amusing, radical, pacifist and

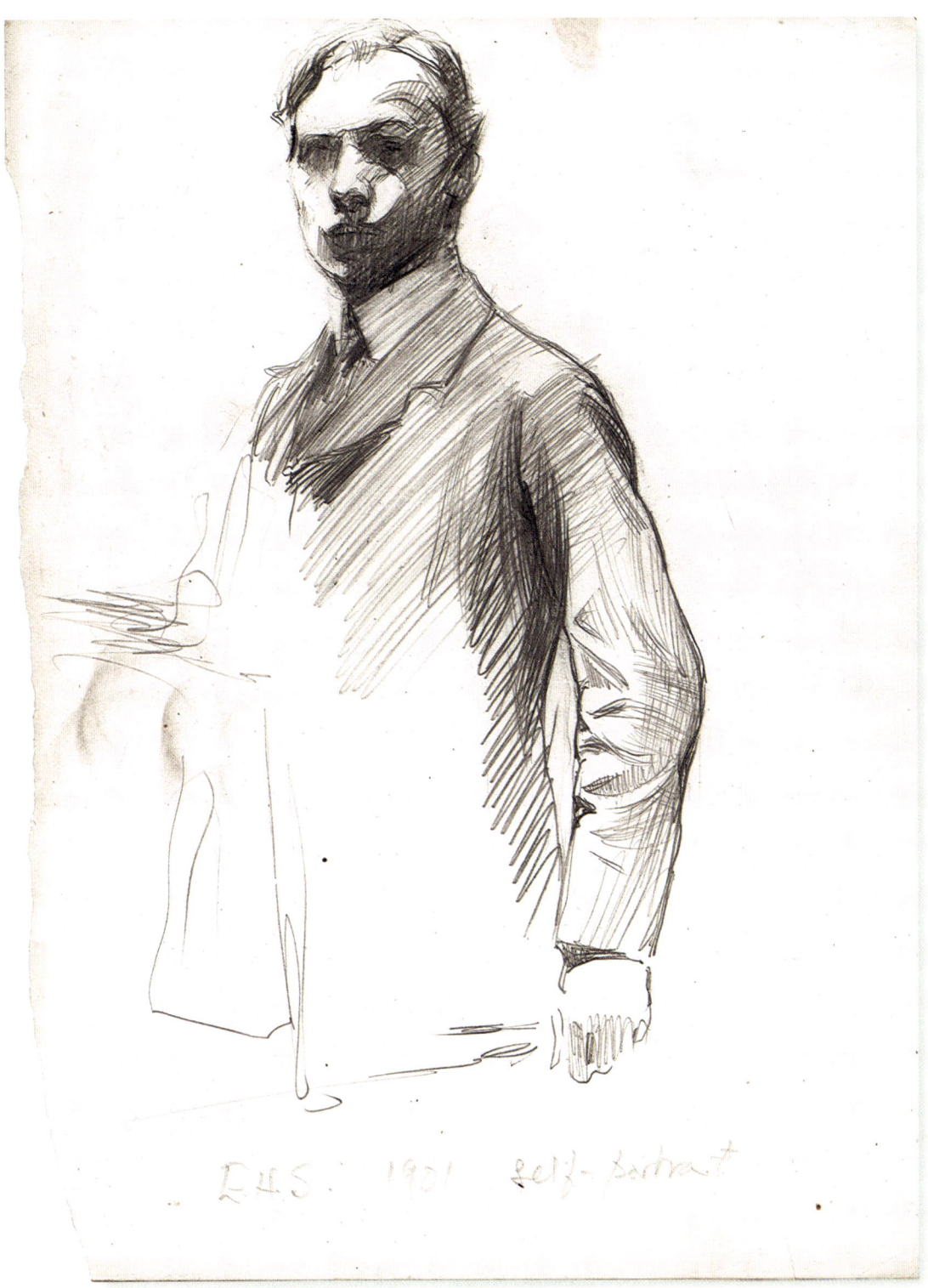

Self-portrait by Ernest Shepard, 1901.

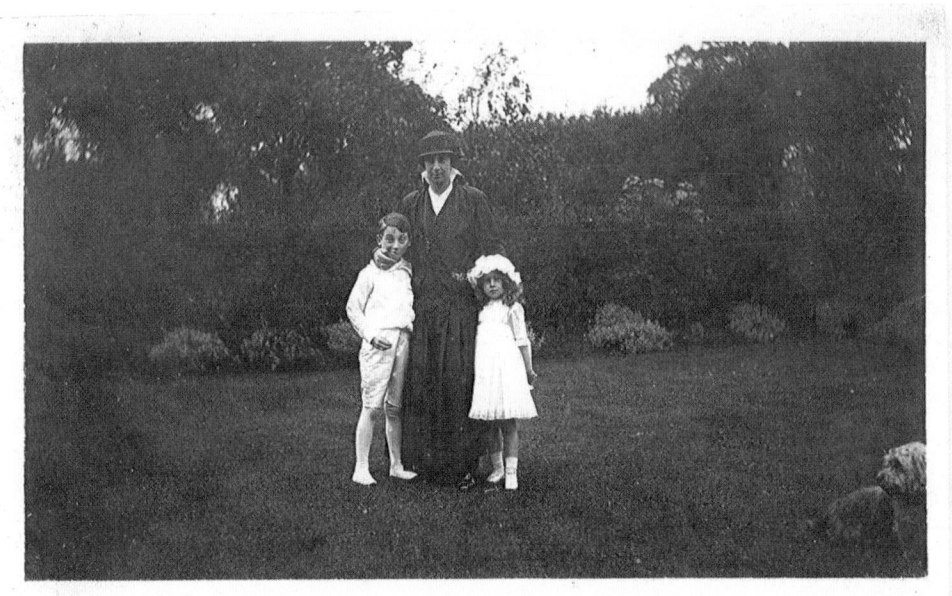

Florence Shepard – Pie – with their children Graham and Mary.

represented a post-Victorian generation. *Punch* had become rather too conventional, too respectably middle-class and too predictable under Burnand, and Seaman did not really seek to change this. After all, circulation was booming and the profits were rolling in. But the magazine had lost its radicalism, its cutting edge, its ability to cock a snook at the 'establishment'. Milne, only in his mid-twenties, was gradually able to influence and shape a sharpening of tone and begin a transition to more contemporary content for the rising generation.

As well as taking some of the dull administrative burden off Seaman, he also reviewed novels and plays, wrote his own pieces, and introduced 'paragraphs', where paragraphs from other publications were critiqued and given *Punch's* crisp and amusing commentary. This was an innovation much enjoyed by readers, where pomposity was punctured, orthodoxy challenged and the status quo questioned, and Milne very much enjoyed doing it.

He later recalled that in 1907 he was standing with F. H. Townsend, the *Punch* art editor, who was looking over a cartoon submitted by E. H. Shepard, and said, 'What on earth do you see in this man? He's perfectly hopeless.' Townsend's reply was, 'You wait.' And although Shepard contributed increasingly to *Punch* over this period, so that by the outbreak of war in 1914 he was a regular freelance cartoonist, the two men never met in person during that time.

Milne's own pieces were usually about contemporary life, again often reflecting his own experiences and those of his generation. They were nothing too serious, just gentle observations about the goings-on of the younger set as life transitioned through the Edwardian period. On a personal basis, financial stability made a significant impact on his life. He was able to move from the lodging house in Wellington Square to bachelor's chambers in Queen Anne's Gate, hard by St James's Park, a much more salubrious area. He was able to accept and return hospitality, and to see more of those mentors who had supported him, including H. G. Wells, Eddie Marsh and E. V. Lucas.

While he remained outwardly gregarious, he was more open and expansive with his male acquaintances on a one-to-one basis, enjoying lunches with male friends and colleagues more than large dinner parties and country house weekend parties. He nonetheless often stayed with the Lehmanns at their country home on the Thames at Marlow (near Cookham Dean where Kenneth Grahame had spent much of his childhood and which was the inspiration for *The Wind in the Willows*). Milne clearly enjoyed these visits to the country, but in a semi-detached manner. While he joined in the fun and frivolity of an Edwardian house party, he was noted for often being quiet and simply observing what was going on. He would sometimes get inspiration for his weekly contributions to *Punch* from what he was seeing and experiencing at these gatherings.

Owen Seaman, while appreciative and grateful for Milne's practical support in the *Punch* office, and for relieving him of so much of the regular drudgery which came with the responsibilities as editor, nonetheless found his assistant editor somewhat of an enigma. Milne presented well as an upright, well-educated, well-behaved young man, who got on well with the *Punch* staff and contributors, and was punctual, reliable and efficient. However, he was considered to be 'unsound' in his personal beliefs, judgements and political convictions. A late-Victorian in his own outlook, beliefs and conservative values, Seaman could not understand Milne's non-conformist views on politics, religion and the changing values of society. It was this anxiety, not any concern about Milne's practical or administrative suitability, which caused Seaman to delay and delay the younger man's expected place at the *Punch* Table. It became increasingly awkward for the members of the Table who assembled weekly to discuss the editorial stance of the magazine for the following week, and the political cartoon to lead it, when the assistant editor was not a part of the discussion and was instead sitting in his office nearby. It was to be more than four years before Seaman finally capitulated and allowed Milne to join the Table, but he only did so after intense pressure from others already there, who could see the benefits that Milne, representative of a new generation of readers, could bring to their deliberations.

It was also not unreasonable for Milne to expect some personal acknowledgement as a regular contributor to *Punch* since 1904, and so in 1908 Seaman allowed the initials A. A. M. to appear after Milne's articles. He continued to develop a style that would later (to his lasting irritation) be called whimsical, that was light, amusing and captured the imagination of a generation of readers of his own age. Between 1909 and 1914 he wrote a series of more than forty tales of the doings of a group of high-spirited young people who called themselves the 'Rabbits', which particularly enchanted readers. It was a clever series. The characters were not part of London 'Society', and the humour was often self-deprecating and restrained: very English and appealing strongly to the aspirational middle classes who were driving the increasing circulation of *Punch*.

Milne sometimes struggled to find inspiration for his weekly contributions to the magazine, often not sitting down to actually write his article until dangerously close to the print deadline. A book of his collected writings from 1908 to 1910 was successfully published as *The Day's Play*, and a follow-up collection, *The Holiday Round*, was published in 1912, bringing renewed interest in his work. It seemed that re-reading his pieces all together enhanced the enjoyment of them.

Shortly after being finally elevated to the *Punch* Table, Milne was taken by Seaman to the twenty-first birthday party of Seaman's goddaughter, Dorothy de Sélincourt. Dorothy, who later preferred to be called Daphne, was the daughter of a wealthy man who had made his fortune in business, initially in the garment trade, and later in retail investments. It was an innocuous invitation as Seaman simply took his young protégé to meet some of the younger generation of his acquaintance. Alan Milne and Dorothy de Sélincourt saw each other occasionally over the months that followed, and developed a light friendship based on mutual friends and interests so that if an extra person was needed for a party or a play, they would be in touch, or if they needed advice about a present for a friend, or a recommendation for a restaurant or a book, they would call each other. It was nothing more than a casual, pleasant and undemanding friendship. More than two years passed until they discovered that, by coincidence, each was going to Switzerland to ski, to the same resort, Les Diablerets, and even the same hotel. Naturally enough, they arranged to meet up. When they returned to London they were engaged to be married.

Alan Milne, at thirty-one, had not previously come even close to marriage, or indeed to a relationship with a woman which might have culminated in marriage. On the face of it, he was superficially comfortable with women: he could make himself amusing and good company for the young ladies he met socially at dinners, dances and house parties, but they were ephemeral connections, never liaisons. He had a distant relationship with his mother as there had never been a close bond between Maria and any of her sons, and his closest female connection was with his sister-in-law, Maud, Ken's wife, with whom he kept up a loving correspondence. He retained his inner prudery and distaste for any conversation or banter about sexual or bodily functions, and he recoiled from any attempt to engage him in any personal conversations about his romantic or sexual proclivities. He quietly deplored personal behaviour in others which fell below his own high bar, although he kept these views to

Les Diablerets, the ski resort nestled in the Swiss Alps at which Milne and Dorothy de Sélincourt (soon to be Daphne) cemented their friendship, returning to London engaged to be married.

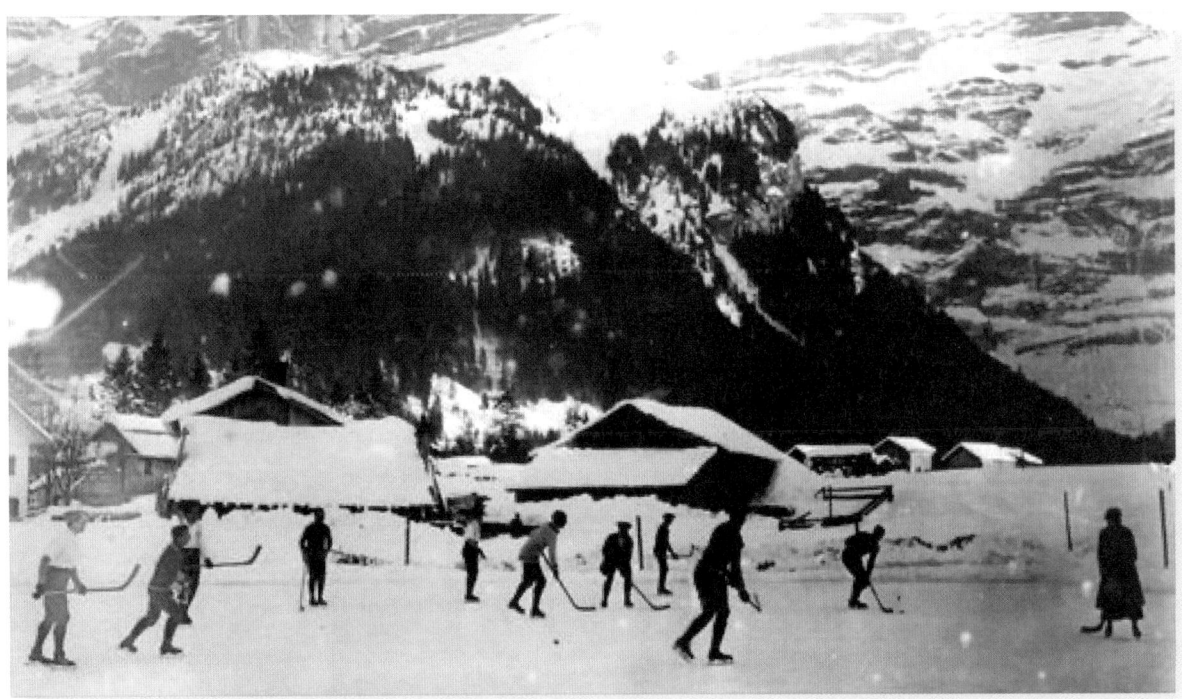

himself. H. G. Wells' unorthodox views on marriage and sex, or Seaman's various mistresses, were simply not subjects he was willing to engage with. He was shy and undemonstrative with women and struggled to express any emotions which might lead him into a romantic relationship. And yet, by the time he was thirty, he seems to have wanted to get married.

However, perhaps it may have been principally for practical rather than romantic reasons. He was frustrated by the disorganized housekeeper who looked after his chambers, and by the problems of how to deal with his laundry, do the cleaning and organize eating in or out. He had reached the age where he wanted to settle down, to focus on his career at *Punch* and his writing while free of other distractions.

Dorothy de Sélincourt was twenty-three years old in 1913, a dangerous age for a young woman who had been brought up to expect an early, suitable and successful marriage. In her own mind, if she did not find a husband soon, she could all too likely find herself on the shelf, and she did not want to remain in her parents' household as the unmarried spinster daughter, all too soon to become an 'old maid'.

During that fateful skiing holiday in Les Diablerets it was likely that Dorothy and Alan were thrown together by proximity, by the pleasure of the skiing and the picturesque mountain scenery, and by the whole ambience of winter sports. Milne later said that he was attracted to her because she laughed at his jokes, and that she read his pieces in *Punch* (along with virtually her whole acquaintance). However they came together, the arrangement between them seems to have been one of mutual convenience, rather than any great romantic passion. Life together as a partnership would be much better than the solitary alternative for both.

The engagement was announced on their return from Switzerland, and the reaction appears to have been one of relief from the de Sélincourts that Dorothy had finally found a husband, and a perfectly respectable one, if not quite who they might have chosen. However, at her age, beggars could not be choosers. Meanwhile, the Milne family were surprised but pleased that Alan had found his life's soulmate. This feeling did not last for long. Dorothy, soon to be Daphne, while delighted to have secured a fiancé who was presentable, solvent and malleable, clearly felt that she was marrying beneath her socially, and, beyond the niceties, she was unwilling to embrace her new family. Maud,

Ken's wife and Alan's close correspondent, was distinctly uncomfortable about the match, although she sensibly did not express her views directly to Alan. He in turn did not take his fiancée to meet his parents for some time after the engagement was announced, possibly because he was aware that their position in life, and particularly their antecedents, would not match Dorothy's sense of social position.

Their short engagement was predictably busy with the practicalities associated with a large and fashionable wedding, which took place at St Margaret's Church, Westminster on 4 June 1913. Alan and Daphne's three-week honeymoon was spent in Dartmoor and does not seem to have been a great success. The initial and major problem between them was sex. Daphne apparently came to the marriage completely innocent and ignorant about sexual matters in every way. It might be thought that at thirty-one years old, Alan Milne would have had at least some sexual experience but if so, it would have been likely to have been fleeting and inconsequential, and it is quite possible that he had none at all. Her ignorance and his embarrassment about such matters almost certainly meant that they had no meaningful conversation about sex prior to their marriage. What is clear is that, initially at least, their sexual relationship was, if not disastrous, certainly unsatisfactory, and this failure on both their parts was a cloud which hung over their marriage.

Their first home was a flat in Embankment Gardens, Chelsea, close by Wellington Square and even closer to the river. They chose this together, perhaps surprisingly on Daphne's part, as Chelsea was perceived in that period to be artistic, bohemian and somewhat raffish, and Daphne's spiritual home would definitely have been in more respectable neighbourhoods. From the start, Daphne took over the domestic side of their life together and proved an excellent homemaker, creating a warm and comfortable home for her husband, with an efficient routine, good meals and the feeling that he need no longer worry about domesticity.

They still did not know each other very well and over time found that there was rather more which divided than united them. His pleasure in sport, in following football in the winter and cricket in the summer, and playing golf all year round, was a surprise to his new wife. At first Daphne tried to share these interests, taking golf lessons and allowing herself to be taken to sports matches, but after mistaking the Marylebone Cricket Club ground at Lord's for a football field, this initial enthusiasm gradually waned. As for Alan, Daphne's love of parties, entertainment and society bored him quite soon, as did interior decoration, clothes and gossipy lunches. They were soon operating in their own spheres. Daphne did not encourage close contact with his family, and some of his old friends were also kept at arm's length. There was no breach with his parents, but visits to and from them and their connections became brief and irregular, and increasingly Milne would maintain these relationships on his own. Daphne's failure to even attempt to build a rapport with Maud, her new sister-in-law, was probably his greatest disappointment. But for Daphne, this was exactly what she had feared: being forced into contact with in-laws who shared neither her interests nor her social position. After all, Ken was simply a civil servant, and he and Maud lived in Croydon! Say no more …

Daphne had great ambitions for her husband and meant to support him in achieving them. It was a pity that her husband did not share these. Daphne had married a successful writer, an assistant editor of *Punch* at an absurdly young age who, in addition to his responsibilities at *Punch*, was a freelance journalist in great demand by other well-known publications. He was also a published novelist. She was now determined that in due course he should succeed her godfather and family friend Owen Seaman as editor of *Punch*, and consequently would be knighted for services to literature (as Owen Seaman was to be in 1914). She would thus become Lady Milne, and from there, she expected that Milne would progress to even higher things, with her at his side as his loyal wife and helpmate.

It did not quite work out like that. Daphne was in no way Alan's intellectual equal, nor was she really interested in the things which interested him. While her own education had been 'finished' in France, her son would later point out that no one seemed to know how, or if, it had actually begun. What Daphne was really interested in was herself. Her appearance was critically important to her, so she spent a substantial amount of time at the hairdresser and beautician and with those who could enhance her natural elegance. She was never a real beauty, but was a highly polished product of the best that money could buy, and she greatly enjoyed buying clothes and hats. She loved the process of having them made, the choice of fabrics, and the endless fittings to achieve the perfect look.

The early part of their marriage, the eighteen months before Alan went away to join the army, was a period of learning from each other, of getting to understand their mutual preferences and perspectives, and coming to sensible decisions about their lives together. But it all comes across as rather forced, rather transactional. Daphne did not do disagreements or arguments. Instead, she looked for a romanticized view of marriage and simply turned away from anything disagreeable. She had abhorred the scenes she had witnessed in her own parents' marriage, usually connected with her father's infidelities, and was determined not to repeat such embarrassing and undignified behaviour. For Daphne, it was always about how it looked, the face

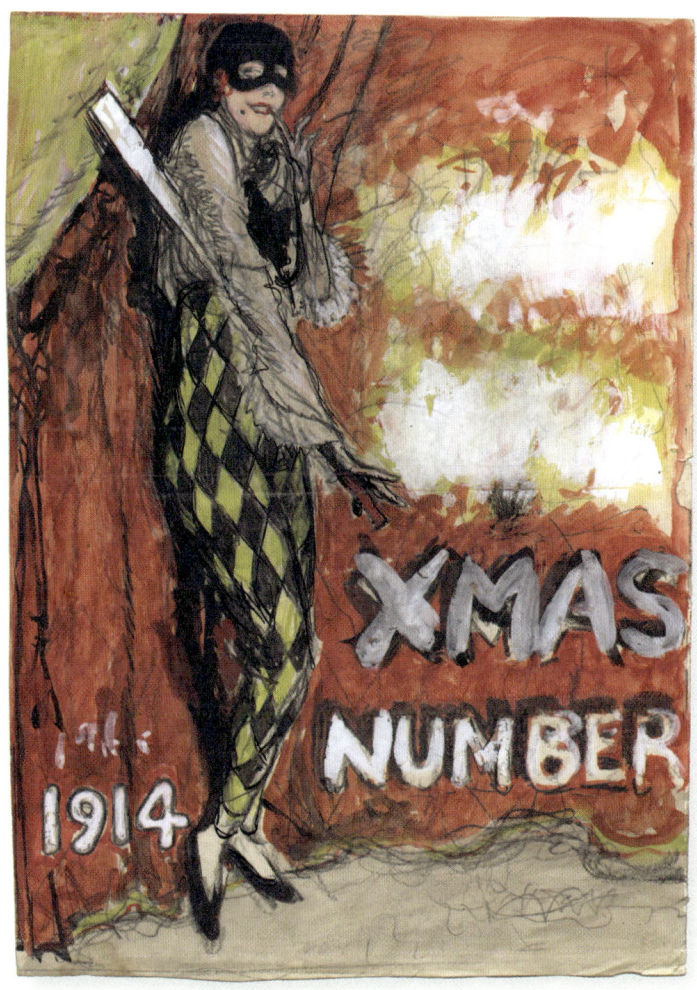

Colour sketch by Shepard for *Punch*'s 1914 Christmas number.

that was shown to the world. She ignored anything that threatened to destroy that ideal, and simply got on with what she thought was important in life.

In the year or so between his marriage and the outbreak of war, Milne became increasingly discontented at *Punch*, largely due to the widening gulf between him and Owen Seaman. Seaman was frustrated by Milne's failure to adopt the orthodox views of his class and background, and by his satirical pieces in *Punch* which laughed at the pretensions of the middle and upper classes or challenged their conservative values – a topic that particularly irked Seaman. After all, Milne had been to a highly respectable public school and to Cambridge University, and now had a senior position in an establishment publication with expectations to succeed to the job of editor. Yet, after nearly eight years in the post, Milne still believed and expressed radical and, indeed, what Seaman saw as unpatriotic views, especially his pacifism. If Seaman had hoped that a grand marriage to his goddaughter and the increasing presence in Milne's life of highly respectable, conventional and conservative in-laws would change the young man's viewpoint, then he was mistaken. And so, in the run up to the conflict in 1914, there was increasing unhappiness at *Punch*.

The ten years between 1904 and 1914 embedded *Punch* into the lives of both Milne and Shepard forever. At the start of this period *Punch* did not make it easy for either of them, despite their personal connections with the magazine. They both had to work hard, experiencing frequent and ongoing disappointment as submission after submission was rejected and returned, and even when occasional articles and drawings were grudgingly accepted, these were few and far between, paid little and guaranteed nothing.

Slowly but surely, as the months and years went by, their perseverance and the quality of their work prevailed. They both learned from *Punch* many of the practicalities of the creative life: how to manage deadlines and last-minute changes, and to be flexible, tolerant and patient. Looking back, although Milne and Shepard did not actually meet in person until 1922, they had both learned the structures, processes and procedures of the magazine, which meant that they were quickly able to establish a productive and profitable professional relationship which was at least in part due to their shared experiences at *Punch*.

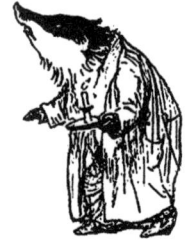

CHAPTER THREE

The First World War and its Aftermath

By 1914 Alan Milne had been married for a year, was living comfortably in London, and had been assistant editor of *Punch* magazine for eight years. He was a pacificist, with unconventional views for a person of his background and situation and found the concept of war as a mechanism for the resolution of national disputes quite bizarre. It seemed extraordinary to him that a major conflict between European powers could be brought about by the assassination of a relatively obscure Austrian archduke in the Balkans, and that nations would go to war for little other reason than a fragile network of alliances which bound random countries together, often for spurious and obscure reasons. As the European political crisis accelerated during those summer weeks of 1914, he struggled with the jingoistic rhetoric and naïve assumptions about the impact of war that he heard around him. It had been barely a decade since the horrors of the Boer War in faraway South Africa had been unsatisfactorily concluded, and yet memories seemed all too short.

In this whirlpool of emotion and confusion as Britain geared up for war, some of Milne's circle were determined to stick with their pacifist principles and register as conscientious objectors, and Milne no doubt toyed with this idea. He discussed what to do, and how to react, with his acquaintances and close friends. He increasingly became persuaded of the argument, much promoted by Owen Seaman, that Britain's reaction to the ridiculous shenanigans on the continent should be to put a stop to this pointless and bellicose posturing and bring the whole sorry mess to a permanent conclusion by taking decisive action. The first aim should be to stop the current tawdry dispute in its tracks, and the second aim would be to conclude matters in such a way as to ensure that it could never happen again: the war to end all wars, in fact. This narrative became widespread, and seemed, at least for a time, to assuage Milne's conscience and to convince him that the short, sharp war that was being suggested would be to the longer-term benefit of all nations and peoples.

The war was not triumphantly concluded by Christmas – as so many of the gung-ho brigade had predicted – and by early 1915, it was clear that it was going to be a protracted struggle. Milne, aged thirty-three and without any children, managed to get a commission as a second lieutenant in the 4th Battalion of the Warwickshire Regiment. He was sent immediately to join his battalion on the Isle of Wight, where his initial training was predictable and tedious. He was appointed a signals officer in August 1915 and was sent to Weymouth for a nine-week course to equip him for his new role, at the end of which he was confirmed as a qualified instructor and returned to his battalion on the Isle of Wight to train his fellow soldiers. By November 1915, having been separated for nearly a year from Daphne, he was pleased to be able to rent a cottage at Sandown where they could be reunited. In this more domestic environment, and with his army work generally completed by tea-time, he felt able to start writing again. Encouraged by Daphne, who had become friendly with the wife of the colonel of the regiment, he started with a short play to be acted by the colonel's children as a Christmas entertainment for the troops. This was a significant moment, as it was the first time that Alan Milne wrote specifically for children. This play apparently encouraged Milne, who then, in his spare time, dictated to Daphne a children's book, *Once on a Time*, which was eventually published in 1917. But at that stage of the war it failed to resonate with the reading public and sank without trace. Later, however, after the success of the Winnie-the-Pooh books, it was republished as a forerunner of those later works.

In July 1916, just after the start of the Battle of the Somme, the blow fell, and Milne was given his marching orders for France. When he arrived there, to his good fortune, the battalion had just retreated from the front line for a period of rest and recuperation before returning to the heat of the battle. There was an initial muddle about his role, there being a signals officer already

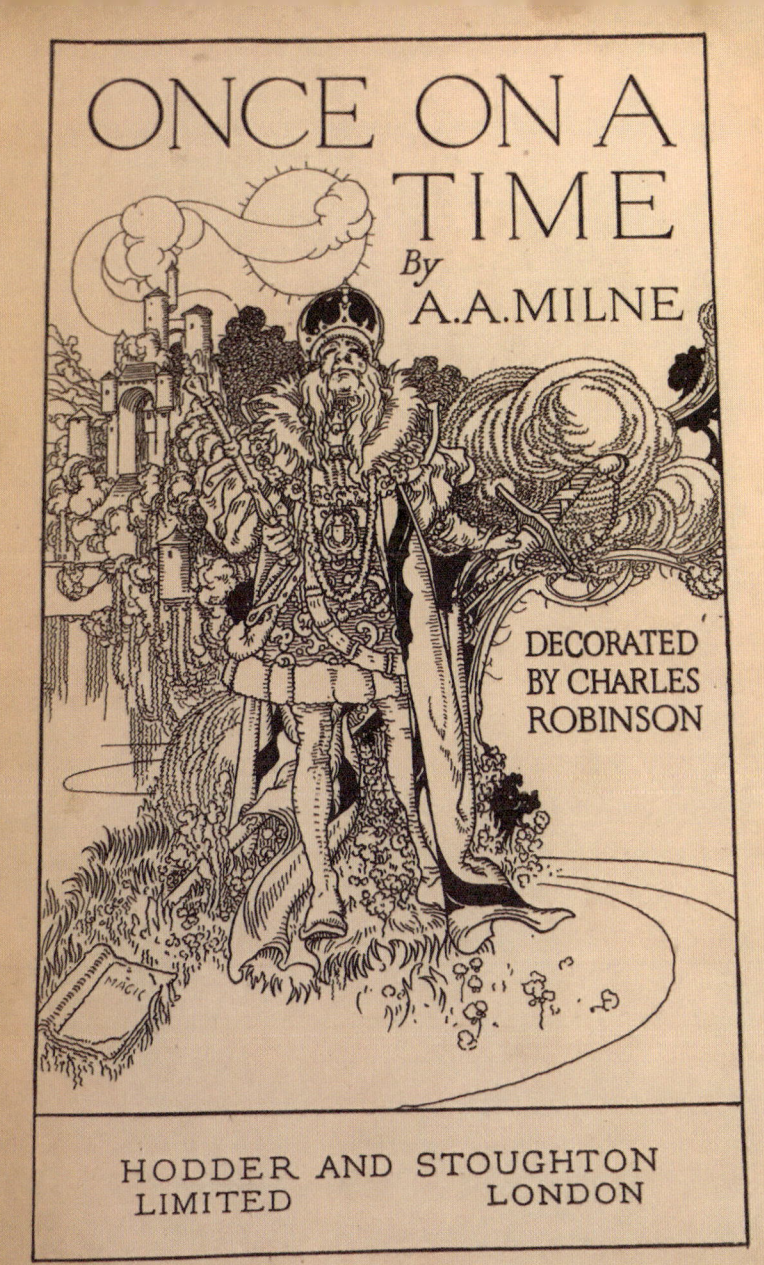

Alan Milne's first book for children. Published in 1917, it was, Milne admitted in his introduction, ' …an odd book'. In a later Foreword he said, 'Read in it what you like; read it to whomever you like; be of what age you like; it can only fall into one of the two classes. Either you will enjoy it, or you won't. It is that sort of book.'

in position, and so he was given a temporary post as a platoon commander, which Milne wryly commented meant he was more likely to be invalided home. But soon he was at the front line, and in the thick of it, seeing at first hand the reality of war. He went through the horrors of the Somme, experiencing things which would haunt him for the rest of his life. Amid the muddle and confusion of battle, he did what he had been trained to do, usually in challenging conditions and circumstances. Working with the senior signals officer, Milne was constantly busy trying to keep the battalion in contact by repairing and maintaining communication lines while coming under heavy enemy bombardment.

In November he became ill with a fever, which did not respond to the medical officer's stock prescription of two aspirins. His temperature rose, and he was moved to a field clearing station and then, as his fever, diagnosed as trench foot, failed to improve, he was repatriated to England, finding himself in hospital in Oxford as the inconclusive Battle of the Somme ground to a winter halt. He had served four months in France. After some weeks in hospital Milne was discharged, and early in the new year of 1917 he was well enough to rejoin his regiment and to resume his responsibilities as signals officer in training new recruits.

His recent experience on the front line gave him added understanding about the practicalities of communication under fire. But by the early summer of 1917 it was clear that he had not recovered from the fever. He was constantly exhausted and dangerously thin, and Daphne became seriously worried. He went back into hospital in Portsmouth and was later transferred to convalesce at Osborne House at East Cowes, yet again back on the Isle of Wight. This was Queen Victoria's seaside retreat where, rather incongruously, he was billeted in the night nurseries where the Queen's children had slept. The Army Medical Board decided that he should be restricted to 'sedentary work', and so, after a further period of rest and recuperation in Hampshire, he briefly returned to his regimental training duties in September, while he applied for a post at the War Office in London. His application was successful, and from the autumn of 1917 until the end of the war a year later he worked there principally on propaganda, where he seems to have had a relatively free hand and was content with his contribution to the war effort. He certainly seemed to find a lot of spare time for playwriting, at least in part because there was so little social life to distract him.

His first 'proper' play, *Wurzel-Flummery*, a one-act comedy, was produced in 1917, sandwiched between two one-act plays by J. M. Barrie of Peter Pan fame. *Wurzel-Flummery* received perfectly respectable reviews, but his second play, *The Lucky One*, failed to make it into production until the following decade. Milne followed this with *Belinda*, a light-hearted romp in a style which recalled Oscar Wilde. It received favourable reviews when it was produced in the spring of 1918 in London, largely due to the performance in the title role of the celebrated actress Irene Vanbrugh. Even so, it came off after only nine weeks, and the New York production, with Ethel Barrymore as the leading lady, lasted barely four weeks. But it meant that by the end of the war, when further employment at *Punch* was no longer an option, Milne could legitimately call himself a playwright. He would have three plays under his belt, two West End productions and a slew of reasonable reviews.

Later on, Milne was criticized for having had what was perceived to be an 'easy' war. Some was overt, although most was muted. Despite being in the army from February 1915 to November 1918, virtually the duration of the conflict, he had spent only four months on active service at the front. The majority of his time had been spent training on the home front, ill, or in what was seen by some to be a cushy desk job in Whitehall. He had also had sufficient 'leisure' time to develop his burgeoning career as a playwright.

As is so often the case, the truth was somewhere in between. After some internal anguish, Milne had volunteered at the earliest opportunity to serve his country, had followed orders and undertaken exactly the same path as other officers, and had no choice when he was selected for a signalling role and subsequently appointed as a signals training officer. He went to the front when instructed to do so, served to the best of his ability, and there was no doubt at all about his ill health when he was invalided back to Britain. In addition, it was an Army Medical Board which restricted his work to desk duties. As Milne himself later recognized, one of the issues his critics had was that when most other servicemen were off duty, they relaxed by playing sport, drinking with colleagues or taking advantage of whatever amusements were available. In contrast, Milne devoted almost all of his limited free time to his civilian day job, with the practical help and support of his wife. This enabled him to complete a substantial body of work, which by its nature was relatively high profile.

After the armistice in 1918, as further propaganda work was clearly unnecessary, Milne was quickly demobbed and was able to return to civilian life. However, his anticipated return to his pre-war role proved to be much more complicated than he had imagined.

When Milne had volunteered for the army it was his clear understanding that *Punch*'s editor, Owen Seaman, would accept him back as assistant editor at the end of the conflict. Seaman did not see it this way. In the period leading up to the war he had felt that Milne had become increasingly out of kilter with *Punch*, and he thought that Milne's decision to enlist was a relatively simple way out of a difficult situation for the magazine. It was further felt that Milne's contributions to *Punch* during the war were fewer than could have reasonably been expected, and that although he had had the opportunity to write more for the magazine, he had instead prioritized his playwriting over his obligation to his employer. And, after all, that employer had been paying him half wages all through the war.

Essentially, Seaman no longer had confidence in Milne, due to the younger man's continuing lack of alignment with editorial policy and a perceived lack of personal commitment, and so was very reluctant to see him reinstated. He felt that when Milne had left the magazine in 1915, there had only been a very vague – and reluctantly given – hint that he might be able to return, and the situation should have been quite obvious to Milne. Milne thought otherwise. While acknowledging their different positions, he felt there had been a 'gentleman's agreement' that he could return to *Punch* at the end of his army service. How the apparent misunderstanding between the two men arose is unclear but suffice it to say that Milne was more than disappointed at not being able to return to his former post as he had expected. After a pause, Milne continued to submit material to *Punch* for publication, and he was far too good a writer for the magazine to let go completely, but the emotional connection was broken and would never be fully repaired.

From an early age Ernest Shepard had an interest in military matters. During his summer holidays, he would sometimes cycle around the countryside following and observing soldiers on exercises and drawing them. At school, an older boy introduced him to guns, artillery and heavy weapons, and he became particularly interested in this aspect of modern warfare.

Nonetheless, in August 1914 he was torn between what he felt was his patriotic duty and his anxiety about his personal situation. He was an enthusiastic supporter of the war effort, and like most people he was convinced that the British position was right and justified, and that Germany needed to be checked. However, he was understandably concerned for his family and the need to provide a steady income for them. At this time, although Shepard was forging a satisfactory freelance practice, money was still tight. He had scarcely any savings, and there was no family money on either side as a buffer for hard times.

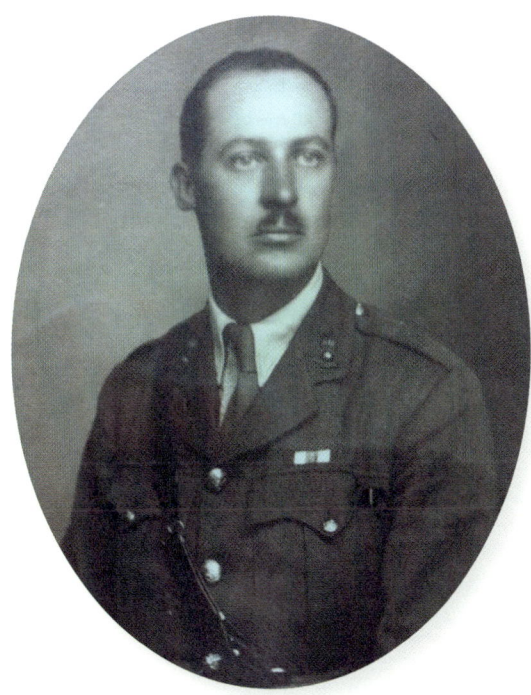

Shepard enlisted in the army in 1915 and was assigned to basic officer training. Throughout his military service he continued to record his experiences in sketches and larger drawings.

In the early days of the war there was a profusion of men of fighting age enthusiastically trying to enlist. Shepard therefore continued to work as usual but tailored his cartoons and contemporary illustrations to suit the mood of the country, which was at first very gung-ho towards a war widely perceived to be one of right against wrong, with God on the side of Britain and her allies. He was asked by Owen Seaman to introduce some humour into the somewhat gloomy tone of the magazine as the war started. So, from the autumn of 1914 onwards, Shepard conjured up a succession of amusing cartoons which managed to strike the right balance between being entertaining, but not offensive. These tended to focus on exaggerating perceived characteristics of the combatants, from the pomposity of British army officers to the gluttony of the Germans, the incompetence of the Italians, and the intellectual deficit of the Irish. These cartoons undoubtedly succeeded in their aim of raising a smile or a chuckle in the readership of *Punch*.

By the summer of 1915 the restrictions on volunteering for the army were relaxed. Shepard, with his old friend Bruce Ingram, editor of the *Illustrated London News*, enlisted in the army and was assigned to basic officer training. With his interest in guns and artillery, he applied to join the Royal Artillery, and was assigned to a siege battery being formed at Dover prior to moving over to the front in France. From January 1916 to the end of the war in 1918, Shepard was on active service as an artillery officer, starting his war as the most junior officer in his battery and ending it as the most senior.

Throughout his war service Shepard recorded his life and experiences, always carrying a small pocket sketchbook in which he quickly pencilled drawings of anything he thought of interest. In his downtime, which was necessarily limited, he would review these pocket sketches and, when time allowed, work them up into larger drawings, initially in pencil but sometimes, particularly if he felt he wanted to record an image for posterity or for potential future publication, in pen and Indian ink.

After a time, his artistic activity was noticed by his fellow officers and men. They were impressed by the accuracy with which Shepard recorded not only technical details, as in his drawings of specific guns, but also the landscape around him, which was increasingly the front line. In due course, word of his skill reached the Intelligence Corps, which got in touch and asked Shepard if he would work informally for them. He agreed to this, taking on responsibilities mainly connected with mapping and drawing future targets, adding estimates of distances and other elements. This was to improve the accuracy and efficiency of artillery bombardments.

As if all this military activity was not enough, Shepard managed to keep up a semblance of his freelance illustration work. Liaising through his agent in London – the wonderfully named H. E. Hassall – he worked on projects for clients back home as and when he could from the field, and in frenetic bursts of activity when on leave. He felt that it was critical for his future career to maintain at least some limited work and keep his name in front of commissioning editors. Also, the additional income was welcome, since his army pay, as a second lieutenant, was hardly sufficient to maintain a growing family.

Shepard managed to juggle these various commitments by being extremely disciplined and organized, traits which were engrained in him from early on, and which stood him in good stead throughout his long life. His army responsibilities were obviously his priority; his role as artillery officer his primary duty, followed by his work for the Intelligence Corps. Only when he had discharged these responsibilities would he turn to any outstanding civilian work.

In terms of Shepard's development as an artist, there was a gradual change in his style, particularly with cartoons and illustrations. This was largely due to the time constraints now imposed on him, meaning that he had much less time available and needed to work faster. Before the war, his style could be somewhat ponderous, with significant areas of heavy hatching and shading, and a great deal of detail in certain areas, such as on faces. With time at a premium, he had to

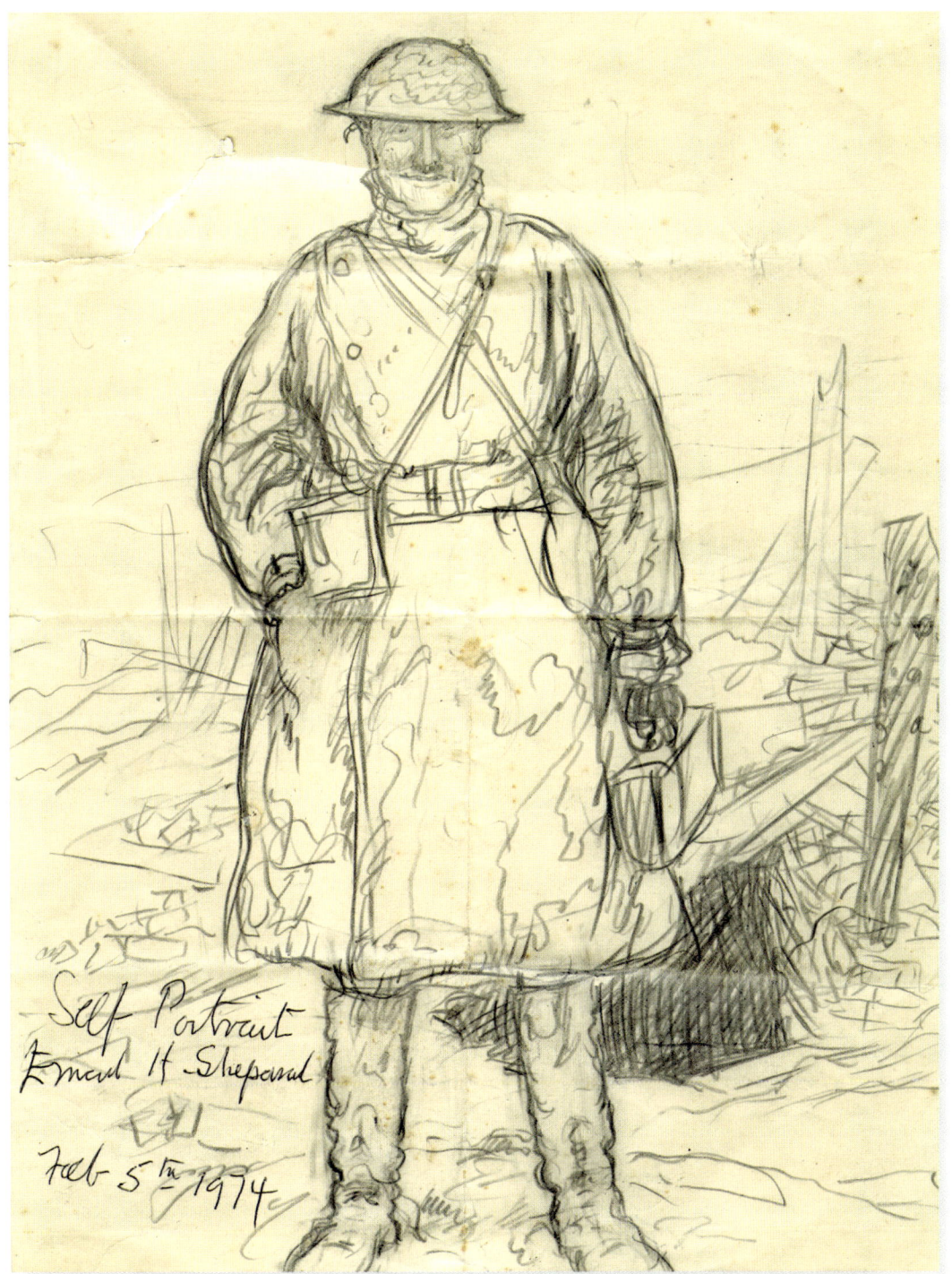

Self-portrait drawn on the Western Front, later annotated by Shepard just two years before his death.

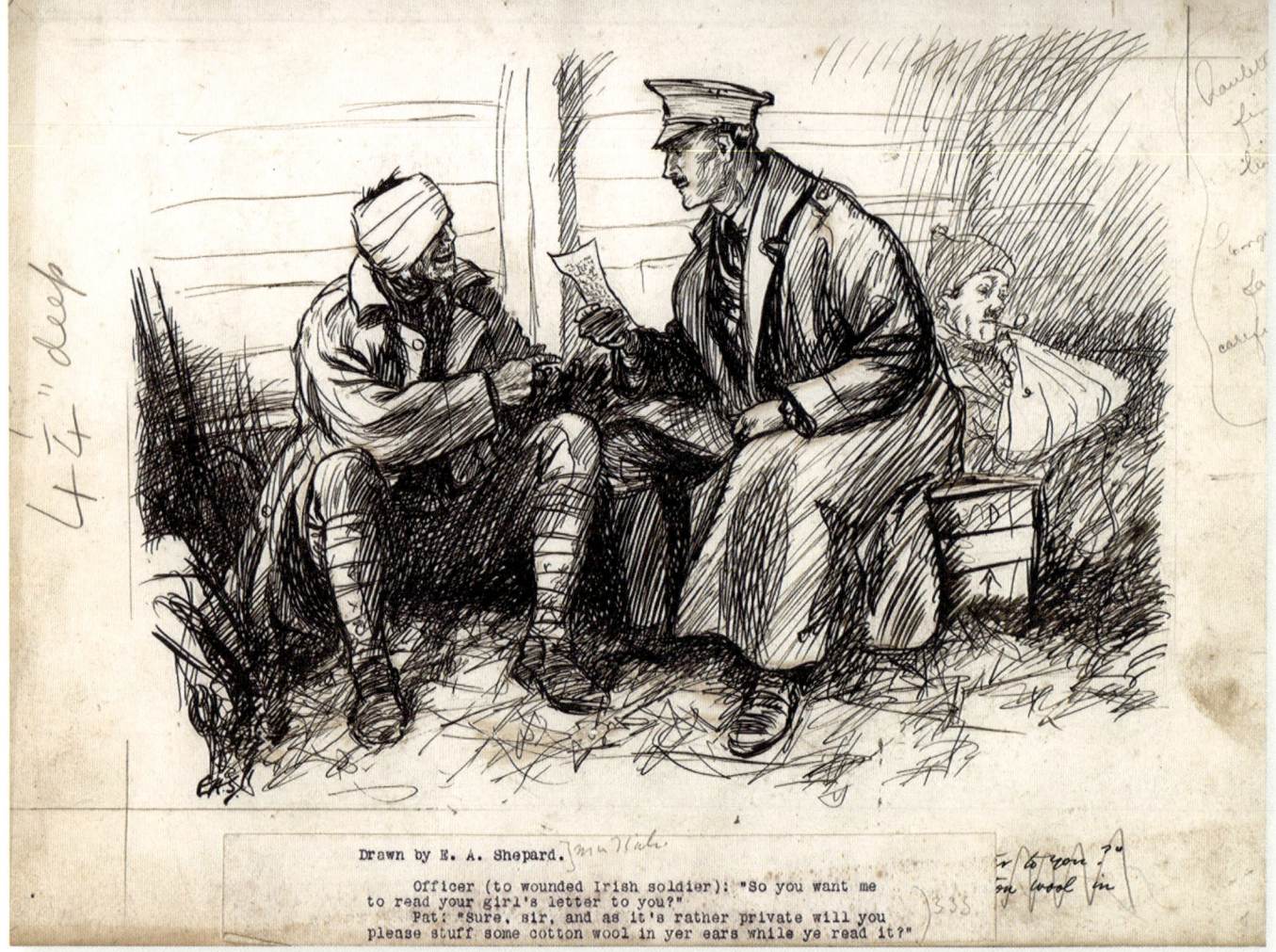

Drawn by E. A. Shepard.

Officer (to wounded Irish soldier): "So you want me
to read your girl's letter to you?"
Pat: "Sure, sir, and as it's rather private will you
please stuff some cotton wool in yer ears while ye read it?"

Shepard's style evolved from cartoons and illustrations with heavy hatching and great detail to a simpler but no less evocative approach.

speed up, and so Shepard moved away from more intricate work and segued into a greater economy of line and simplicity of approach. This transition developed from about 1916 onwards and can clearly be seen in both his wartime drawings and his civilian work. The change in style would have a significant impact on his later work, including his best-known illustrations for *Winnie-the-Pooh* and *The Wind in the Willows*, for later, particularly in his drawings for the Pooh books, he managed to convey a wonderful array of characteristics in seemingly just a few simple lines. But all this was in the future.

Shepard travelled to France with the other officers and men of the siege battery in January 1916, but unfortunately their guns, on which they had been trained, were left behind in England due to an administrative muddle. The battery was nonetheless moved forward towards the front line, and the French artillery generously lent them some armament so they could practise for the forthcoming Battle of the Somme. But nothing really prepared Shepard for the reality of a major battle.

The horrors of warfare were brought home almost immediately through a personal tragedy. Shepard's elder brother Cyril, who was in the reserves of the Devonshire Regiment and had been married just a month before, was killed in the first infantry advance on the first day of the Battle of the Somme. Shepard remained on the Western Front throughout the Battle of the Somme and was later actively involved in the battles at Arras and, later on in 1917, at Passchendaele. He suffered several near misses. On one occasion he was supervising the operation of one of the field guns, then moved away towards another gun. The first gun was then hit directly by an enemy shell, killing the gun-crew, destroying the weapon and wounding a number of other men who were near it. Shepard himself was wounded during this period, although not seriously, but what he saw and experienced, as with so many servicemen, affected him for the remainder of his life. His personal courage was never in doubt, and for his bravery he was awarded the Military Cross in 1917.

At the end of the Battle of Passchendaele in November 1917, when Shepard had been looking forward to long-promised home leave, he and the siege battery were sent urgently to northern Italy to support the Italian army, which was facing an unexpectedly strong attack from Austrian and German forces. For the remaining eleven months of the war he was in almost constant action as the enemy made repeated attempts to break the Allied lines and, in particular, to capture Venice.

During this time, when camped out in woods above the river Piave, Shepard was asked to look after a young wounded American ambulance driver. They got on well, enjoying each other's company. Shepard later managed a rare weekend's leave in Milan with his new friend, and he wrote to his wife about it, ending his letter with the words, 'His name is Hemingway'. With a little more time on his hands, Shepard was able to do more drawings of the end of the war in Italy. He showed the confusion and muddle as the advance and retreat of forces on both sides became normal, while fighting continued right up until Armistice Day in November 1918. The siege battery was finally disbanded in Calais early in 1919 and Shepard was formally demobbed from his army duties in May that year. He returned with relief and gratitude to his wife and children in Shamley Green and set about re-establishing his civilian life and practice.

On his return home, and after the practicalities of his war service had been resolved, Shepard appears to have dealt with his feelings, thoughts and

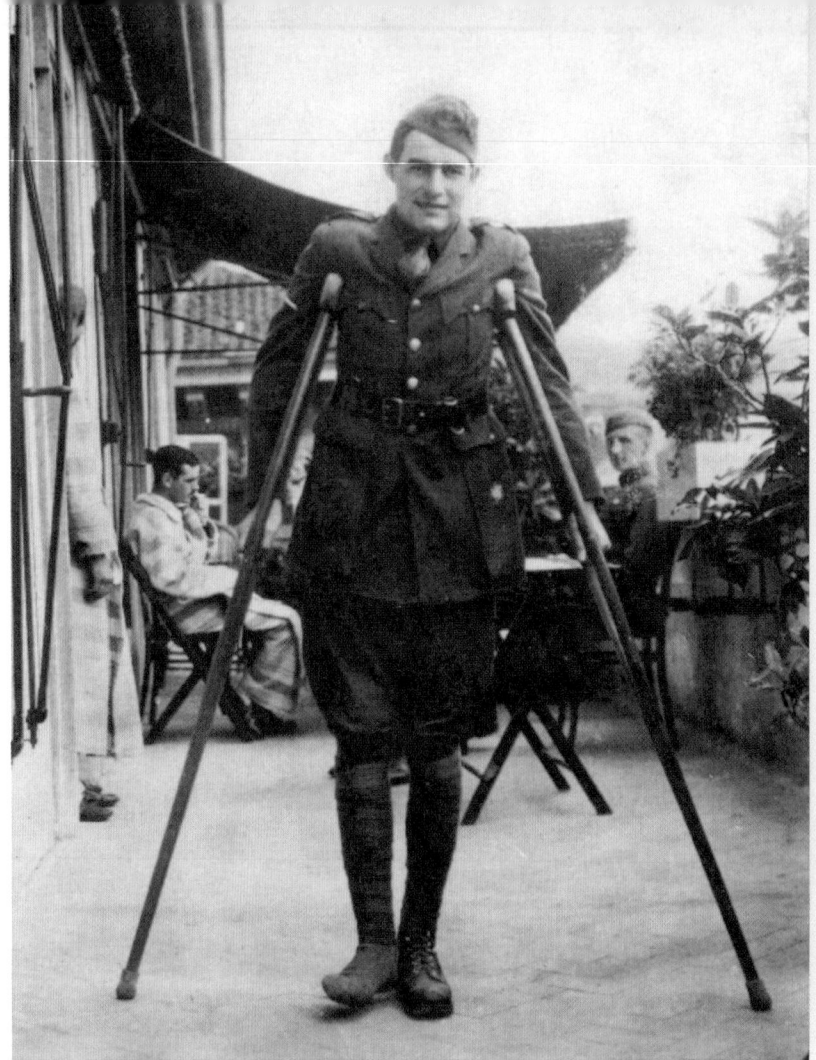

Ernest Hemingway in Milan in 1918, at the time of his meeting with Shepard.

emotions to do with the war in a manner very typical for a man of his upbringing and time. He simply packed everything connected to his time in the army – his uniform, equipment, technical documents, photographs, document case, and thousands of drawings, sketches, paintings, cartoons and illustrations, both loose and in countless bound sketchbooks – into boxes and put them away. Out of sight and out of mind. And, according to his family, although he remained interested in military matters, and was very supportive of army charities, regimental reunions and so on, he never spoke of his own personal experiences of the war. And so these records and possessions remained hidden for nearly a hundred years, until in the first decade of the twenty-first century organizations interested in commemorating the centenary of the First World War approached the Shepard family to ask for the loan of relevant material. The boxes were eventually located and opened and were found to contain a treasure trove covering Shepard's own very personal journey through that long-ago conflict.

Alan Milne had a more complicated war than Ernest Shepard. He was an intellectual and someone who thought deeply about human issues. He was unconvinced about the ethics of conflict, the relevance of the nation state and the competence of politicians and leaders. His trajectory from Cambridge University through literary London and the comfort of a civilized existence put him in a position of privilege. He felt strongly that a more collaborative approach to resolving differences, particularly at strategic levels, with less nationalistic aggression, would result in a better way of life for all concerned. Milne was distressed by the build-up to war and its outbreak in 1914.

His experience of the war left him permanently scarred and a confirmed pacificist for the remainder of his life, even when this, both personally and professionally, was challenging for him. Unsurprisingly, he was conflicted by his views. He felt that his personal experience of war, particularly the horrors of the four months he had spent on active service in France, gave him the right to comment and judge on its futility. On the other hand, he could be scathing about those who had avoided war service: the conscientious objectors, those in protected occupations, men exempted by spurious health issues, and in particular the 'profiteering skrimshankers' who exploited the war for personal gain.

Shepard, by contrast, acknowledged the horror of the conflict but felt very differently about its outcomes. He thought from the start that Germany was an aggressor which needed to be challenged and stopped, otherwise worse would come. He was conservative by nature, and believed that God, in whom he had an implicit faith, was on the side of right, and was thus undeniably on the side of Britain and her allies. Shepard also supported the democratic process of an elected government taking the country into war, feeling that this represented the views of the majority. He did not recoil, as did Milne, from the crowds cheering on the prospect of war in the summer of 1914: he understood the sense of nationalism and patriotism which led so many to volunteer and to commit life and limb to a cause which they felt instinctively was right.

Clearly their separate experiences in the First World War affected Milne and Shepard significantly, but in different ways and they had differing reactions. It certainly seems to be the case that their wartime experiences impacted the way they created the Winnie-the-Pooh books. For Milne, the war was a period of horror, anxiety and confusion. His experiences shattered his previously

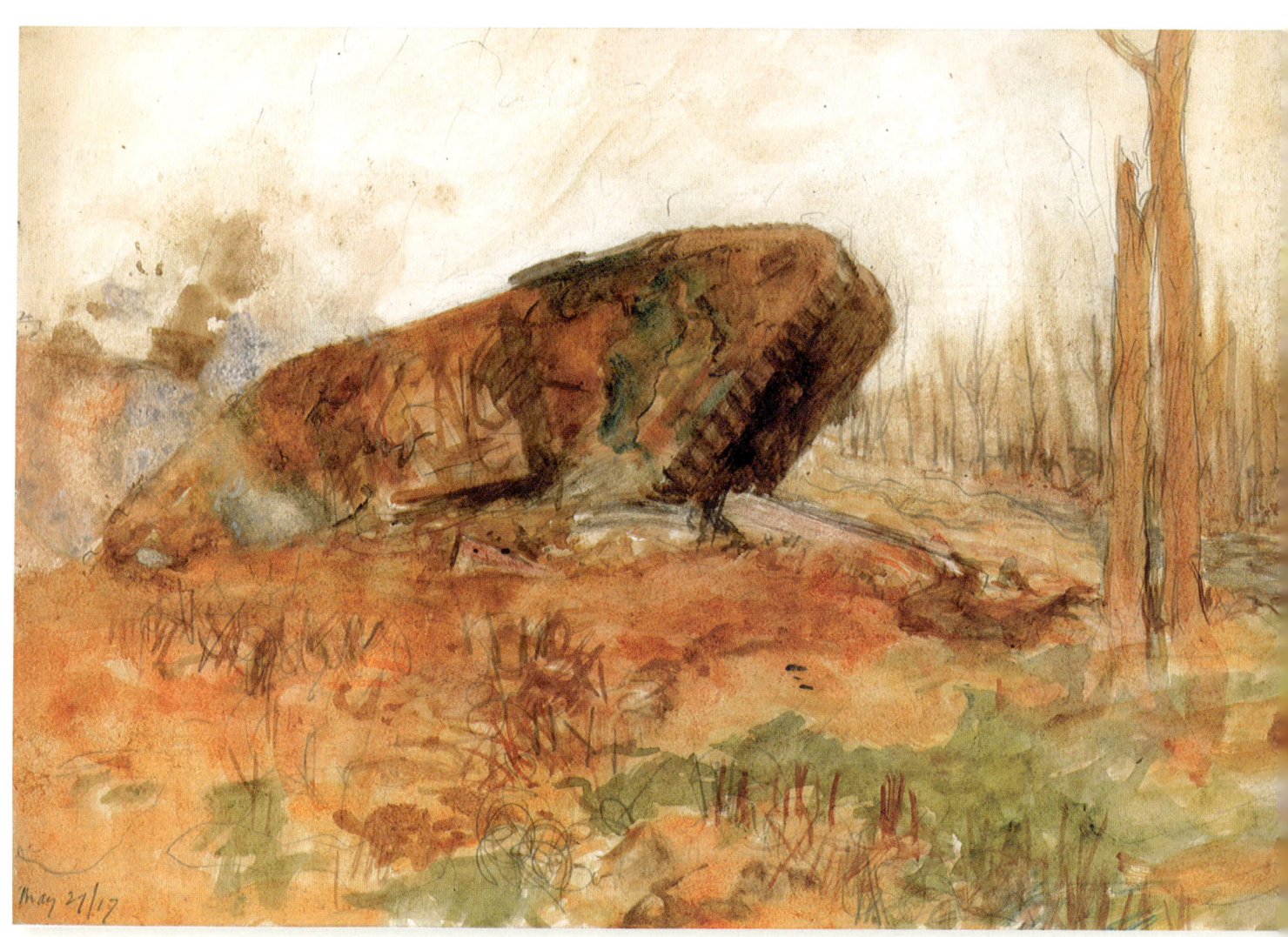

These three wartime watercolours show the breadth of Shepard's interest in his experiences. The quick sketch of the tank (above) shows the movement of the vehicle through the landscape of the front line; while (above, opposite) Italian forces prepare an artillery gun for battle; and (bottom) an Italian landscape.

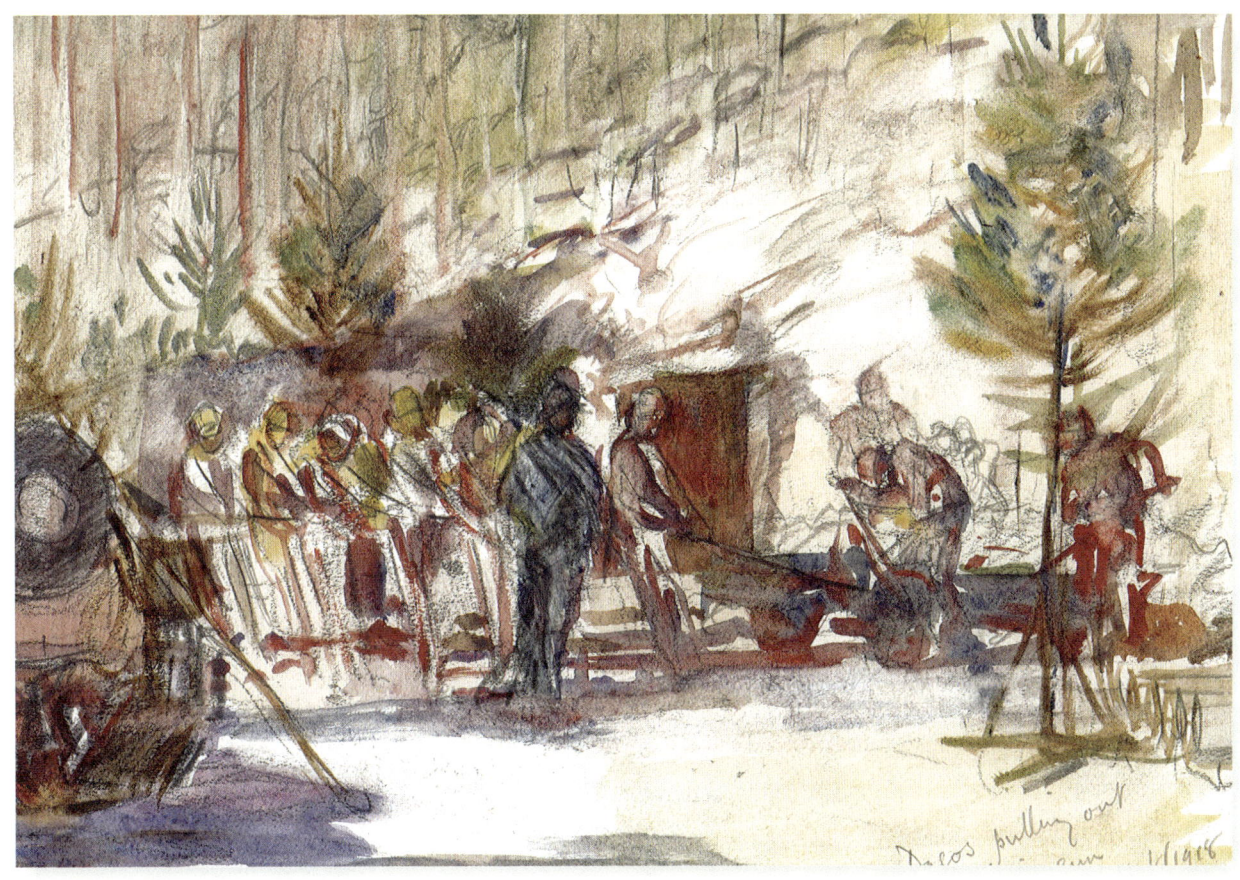

Dacos pulling out 1/1906

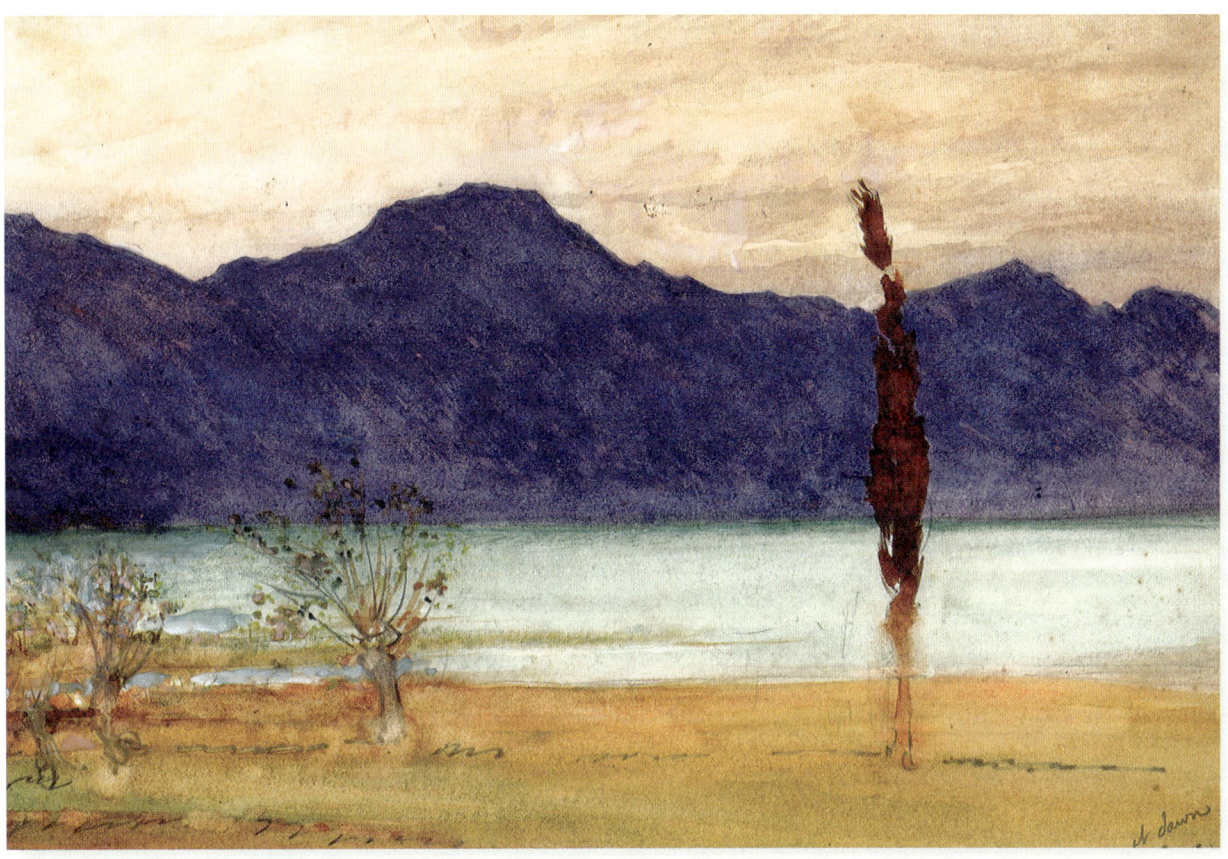

N dawn

comfortable existence and his beliefs. The nursery stories he told his young son in the immediate post-war period were an antidote to the horrors of war. He deliberately created an idyllic world of peace and enchantment, blocking out any discordant or inharmonious matters and concentrating on simple pleasures. While these were nursery stories, created for a much-loved young child, banishing anything uncomfortable or unreasonable and focusing solely on concepts of essential goodness, they resonated strongly with an adult generation traumatized by the war years.

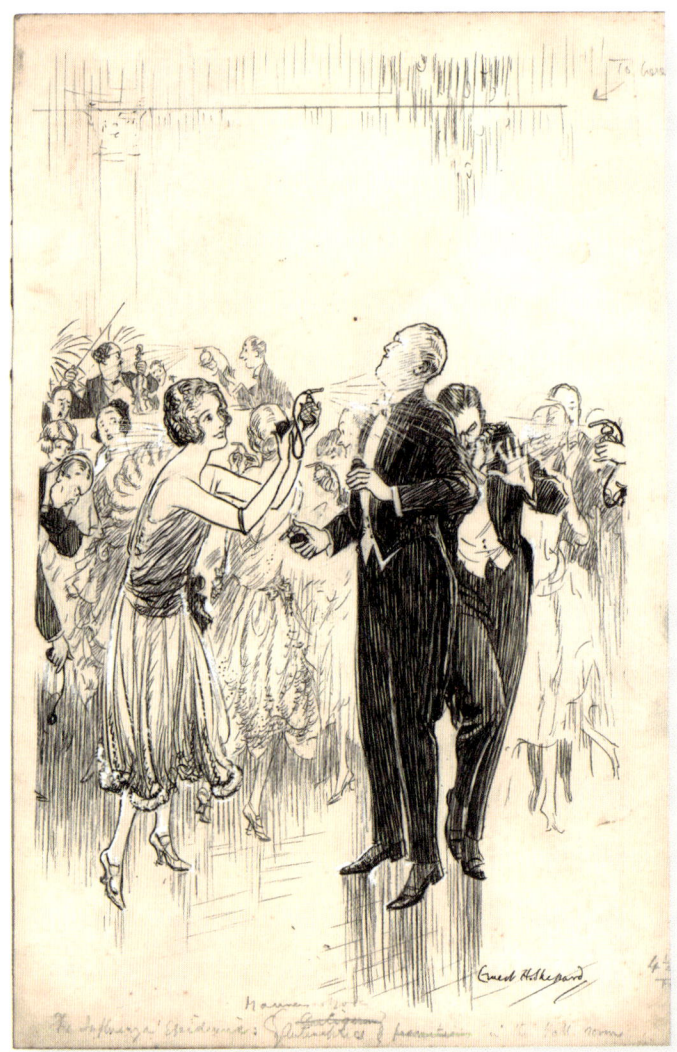

Shepard's cartoon about the Spanish flu epidemic of 1919–20 has striking parallels with Covid-19 a hundred years later.

Shepard freely admitted that the commission to illustrate Milne's poems and stories gave him an opportunity to revisit his own and his children's happy childhoods. Those late-Victorian and Edwardian eras were comfortable and secure, at least for the middle and upper classes. With his drawings he recreated a fantasy of innocence and charm, untrammelled by harsh realities which he deliberately swept away or ignored. Shepard drew from models and from life, but he ensured that those models and the contexts in which he placed them reflected the naïve innocence and charm of Milne's writing, and as such he was complicit in Milne's make-believe. Both men wanted to exorcise the memories of the horrors of the war from adults, who would be as much the audience for the poems and stories as actual children.

In February 1919 Milne finally severed his contractual relationship with *Punch* and with it his place at the *Punch* Table. He was inevitably disappointed at the formal ending of a relationship on which he had set so much store back in 1906 and was saddened by the way his bond with *Punch* had dwindled away in a welter of politely articulated mutual recriminations. Perhaps even more upset was Daphne. She saw all her aspirations now evaporate in front of her eyes. This change in circumstances was a bitter blow to her social ambitions and Milne was all too aware of this.

In 1919, it seemed quite clear to Milne that his principal literary activity would be playwriting. His first plays had given him a taste for what he thought he could achieve, matching his light and whimsical touch with contemporary dialogue and creating settings which would attract theatre-goers after the war years. The four years of the war had accelerated a change in the public mood, attitudes and behaviours such that society was almost unrecognizable from that which it had been in 1910. There was an increasing generational divide between those of an age to have fought in the war and their contemporaries, and their parents' generation. The latter struggled to maintain the standards and values of former years, while the former pushed the boundaries to create a more relaxed, informal and less judgemental world. It was the Owen Seamans as opposed to the Alan Milnes. And in this environment, the theatre-going public wanted to be amused and entertained.

Probably Milne's best-known play after, inevitably, *Toad of Toad Hall*, is *Mr Pim Passes By*, started at the end of the war and completed by the spring of 1919. The play can best be described as a social commentary on the new morality of the post-war years and a challenge to the conventional orthodoxy of a seemingly traditional marriage and contrasts the attitudes and behaviours of the pre- and post-war generations. *Mr Pim Passes By* received good reviews from the London critics as an amusing and well-crafted light comedy: 'gossamer', 'slender', 'delicate' and 'subtle' were among the words used to describe it. While some more traditional and stuffy reviewers railed against this pot-shot at the social status quo, audiences clearly enjoyed the play. The themes of family and marital relationships, and the consequences of blindly following convention, were to run through much of Milne's work over the next decade, and not just on stage. *Mr Pim Passes By* was a great success in London, running for virtually the whole of 1920, and then opened in New York early the following year.

In August of 1919 the Milnes moved to a much larger home, a townhouse in Mallord Street in Chelsea, and later that autumn they were thrilled to discover that Daphne was pregnant. The baby was born on 21 August 1920, and both Alan and Daphne had hoped for a girl, to be called Rosemary, so it took some adjustment for them to be the parents of a boy. Although formally named Christopher Robin, he was always known as Billy, and later as Billy Moon, after his early attempts to pronounce 'Milne'. While Alan was in an afterglow of happiness and contentment with his new son and sense of family, neither he nor Daphne were overly demonstrative in their affection for their new son, Alan particularly expressing in letters his feelings in a way he seemed unable to do in person. Daphne liked the idea of a baby and the management of all that went with it, organizing and decorating a nursery, recruiting a wonderful nanny, Olive Rand, who looked after and really brought up Christopher Robin for the first ten years of his life, making sure the baby was appropriately clothed, creating a routine with the perambulator leaving promptly for the park at the correct time, and showing off the baby at tea-time in the drawing room. Maternal affection did not seem to be a high priority, but she did later enjoy sitting on the nursery floor with Christopher Robin and his toys before bath-time. And although it was the fashion of the time for boys to have long hair and wear loose shirts that were similar to dresses, she allowed his hair to be slightly too long and his smocks to be slightly too feminine, so that he was easily mistaken for a girl.

Meanwhile, *Mr Pim Passes By* had propelled Milne into a new league of fame and popularity, one where he was feted by his contemporaries as well as by the theatre-going public. The Milnes became extremely popular. Invitations poured in, interviews were sought after and the publicity machine rolled into Mallord Street. Milne was initially amused by the sudden interest, hoping that it would encourage theatrical producers and funders to be more confident about putting on his plays. Daphne was delighted by the publicity. With the nursery routine established, she helped to answer the deluge of correspondence, with the important proviso that she would decide which invitations to accept and which to decline. Her work as her husband's informal secretary was extremely helpful to him, since she acted as a gatekeeper and manager, allowing Milne to focus on his own work, distracted as little as possible by the administration and management of his increasingly public life. An ongoing irritation at this time was the behaviour of Daphne's brother Aubrey, who was constantly asking the Milnes for 'loans', which inevitably were never repaid. This situation drew to a close when Daphne simply refused to speak to Aubrey and his wife, Irene, a family breach which lasted for more than twenty-five years.

After the great success of *Mr Pim Passes By*, Milne turned the play into a novel. He also entered the world of detective thrillers with *The Red House Mystery*. It was a good time to be doing this. As the twenties were settling down, there was an increasing public interest in crime and mystery stories. Two years after Milne finished writing *The Red House Mystery* (although it was not actually published until 1922), both Agatha Christie and Dorothy L. Sayers entered the field, and the stage was set for an explosion of crime thrillers. In fact, *The Red House Mystery* turned out to be Milne's most successful book (other than the Winnie-the-Pooh books, of course), based as it was not on whimsy, but on an intellectual challenge. Readers had to follow the plotline, absorb the clues, and solve the mystery. At the time this was quite a change from the more usual thrillers where the story was more about the thrills and spills than identifying the murderer. Milne's literary agents, Curtis Brown, recognized this original approach and urged him to write a follow-up to *The Red House Mystery*. Indeed, two more crime novels were proposed and planned, but in due course these came to nothing, mostly due to constraints on Milne's time and capacity.

But for Milne the early 1920s were to be dominated by plays, playwriting and productions. He wrote plays prodigiously quickly, starting the next before the current one was even in production. In 1921 *The Dover Road* was first produced in New York. It was a moralizing tale about a house close by the port of Dover, where the proprietor intercepted unmarried couples who were on their way to the continent to indulge in the illicit pleasures of infidelity and persuaded them to remain on the marital straight and narrow. It was very much of its time. In the immediate post-war years the number of marriages failing as a result of the war was rocketing, and the increasingly relaxed morality in certain quarters of society made infidelity and divorce much more acceptable. Almost simultaneously, his play *The Truth about Blayds* was also produced in New York, so that by January 1922, J. V. Milne was proud to be able to say that Alan had five plays running simultaneously: three in America, one in London and one in Liverpool. Alan's stock was running high, and he was confident that he had found a successful formula. But pride comes before a fall, and his next play, unluckily named *Success*, proved the point. While Milne thought it was his best play, the critics gave it a mauling and it lasted barely six weeks. Milne reacted badly to this unexpected setback and aimed his fire on the critics, who he felt were unfairly over-critical of *Success* and were responsible for its short run (he had not, of course, objected to their praise for his previous plays). It was early evidence of Milne's increasing sensitivity to criticism. He had been unusually fortunate that up until that point he had not been on the receiving end of much negative criticism. Perhaps because of this, he had a very thin skin and found it very hard to take criticism at all, let alone constructively. He wrote directly to critics to berate them, which did not endear him to those whose very support he needed. He came across as petulant, self-entitled and arrogant, and there was more than a hint of truth in those descriptions.

Milne was a quintessential club man, beginning with membership of societies and clubs at Westminster School and Trinity College. He enjoyed the company of other men with similar interests and of a similar disposition. In 1919 he was put up for the Garrick Club, frequented by precisely the sort of society he sought, men of letters, like-minded companions in a masculine society safe from women. He took to the Garrick immediately, finding comfort and solace within its portals and when in London he usually lunched there several times a week.

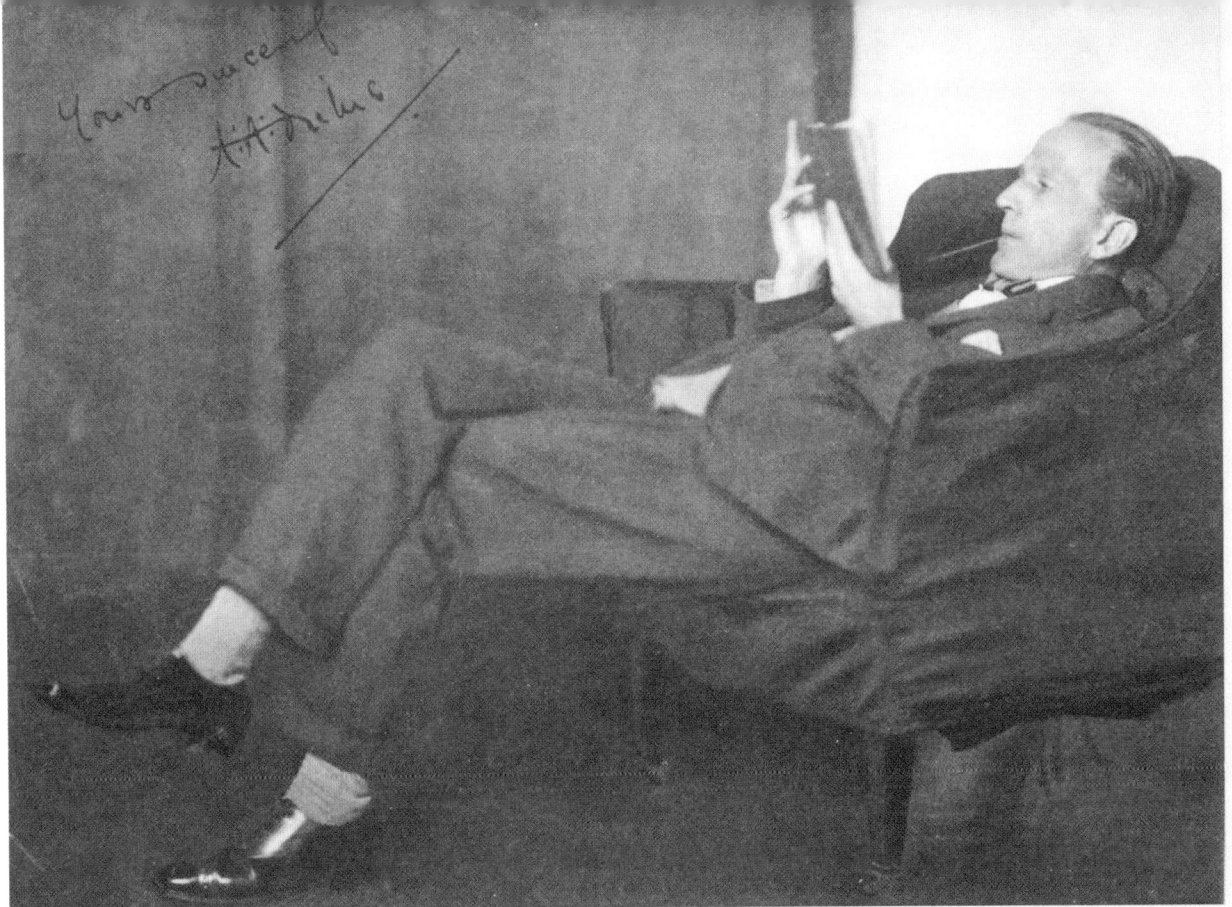

Alan Milne in relaxed mode.

After his return from Italy in the spring of 1919, Shepard set about re-establishing and reinvigorating his freelance practice as an artist and illustrator. From his studio in the garden at Shamley Green, he began renewing contacts with publishers, art editors, magazines and periodicals, and of course with *Punch*. His initiative was soon rewarded. Some of the drawings that he sent to *Punch* were accepted and printed, and other work also started to come in. He was invited to illustrate a new, abridged edition of *The Diary of Samuel Pepys*, *Everybody's Pepys*, with a large number of drawings, for which he asked £600. This was a bold move, as this was the equivalent of a year's salary, but he felt it was justified by the quantity of work involved. This was too much for the publisher, who was nonetheless keen to retain Shepard, and so offered him a lower lump sum but also a percentage of the profits. Shepard had never been remunerated in this way before, and he was rather nervous about the risk involved. However, eventually he agreed to accept a down payment of £150 and a ten per cent royalty. This contract made him think differently about how he might be more flexible about payment options going forward. Fifty years later he was still receiving royalty payments from Pepys' *Diary*.

More commissions started to come through, and so increasingly did his work from *Punch*. He was delighted, and flattered, when he was invited to join the *Punch* Table in 1921. To sit at the same table as so many luminaries, and follow in the footsteps of such distinguished company, was a high honour. This usually meant that he now attended the Wednesday evening dinner, drew up the following week's cartoon on Thursday for circulation and comment, then finalized it on Friday morning before delivering it to the printers. The subsequent scramble for the last train to Guildford on a Wednesday, and then the commute into London on Thursdays and Fridays as well, became very onerous, especially in winter weather. So he took a room in Holland Park Avenue in west London as a studio and bedsit, sleeping there on Wednesday and Thursday nights. He later progressed to a couple of rooms in Cleveland Square near Bayswater, in a flat owned by his old friends Michael and Chattie Salaman. Shepard retained these as his London base until 1934, when he bought a house in Melina Place in St John's Wood, as his London house.

Shepard's wife, Pie, suffered periodically from asthma, and at that time there was little that the medical profession could provide to alleviate this. She found that the damp climate in England, particularly in the winter months, tended to make her condition worse, so she chose to spend time in warmer countries where the air was better for her asthma. This gave them an opportunity to travel, which they both enjoyed, especially since they now had the money to do so in comfort. The regular change of air certainly seemed to improve Pie's asthma, and in due course her doctor, Eric Sheaf, a friend of them both, suggested that the damp situation of Shamley Green, low in the valley of the river Wey, was probably not helpful to her condition. So they decided to move to higher and healthier ground, and in due course they found a plot of land high up on Pewley Down, on the southern outskirts of Guildford, well-placed to catch the sun and the prevailing breezes, and away from the damp valley below. It seemed ideal, and they commissioned a handsome brick house, named Long Meadow, to be built, with a special studio for Shepard. It was to be his home for many years, but, sadly, he was never to share it with Pie.

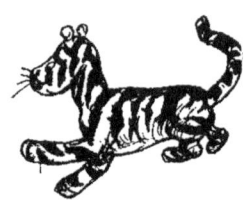

CHAPTER FOUR

The Start of Winnie-the-Pooh

Since the end of the war Alan Milne had worked from home, first in the flat in Embankment Gardens and, from August 1919, in Mallord Street. Here he had his own study where he wrote undisturbed while Daphne ran the household and ensured that her husband was not interrupted. He was a Londoner who enjoyed walking, and often these expeditions gave him inspiration for his work. He would come in, settle down in his study, put pen to paper, and work steadily, principally in the mornings. He would usually lunch out, after 1919 frequently at the Garrick Club. His afternoons were usually spent in meetings or on the golf course.

In the happy afterglow of the birth of Christopher Robin in 1920, Milne started to write snippets of poetry and doggerel in a light-hearted, whimsical style, ostensibly for children but aimed at resonating with grown-ups as well. At first, he did these for his own amusement and for the pleasure of writing for his precious son, but gradually he took some of these scribblings and started to work them up into pieces which he thought might, at some point, be suitable for publication.

In the summer of 1922, Milne and his friend, the actor and impresario Nigel Playfair, took a holiday house, Plas Brondanw in north Wales, family home of the architect Clough Williams-Ellis. They were looking forward to a summer vacation with congenial friends in a beautiful part of the country rich in opportunities for walking, sea bathing and enjoying the scenery. Alas, the weather eluded them and it rained non-stop, and so with little to do the house party became fractious. In addition, the food was poor, the staff were surly and the Milnes were bored and irritated that Christopher Robin was banished to the nursery wing and not encouraged to make an appearance downstairs. In the midst of this gloom an envelope arrived for Milne from Rose Fyleman, author and editor of books and magazines for children, mostly about fairies. She had commissioned a poem from Milne for a new children's magazine, *Merry-Go-Round*, and now sent him the proofs to check and correct.

Milne was only too pleased to excuse himself from the party and the rain, and to ensconce himself peacefully in a summerhouse in the beautiful garden to review the poem, which was to become 'The Dormouse and the Doctor'. The work was soon done, but Milne did not want to return to the irritable party, so he began scribbling ideas for other poems. He knew that what he ought to be doing was working on his second thriller but he was very willing to be distracted by something else. And although he had previously been rather disdainful of whimsical works for children, fashionable baby talk and fairies, he embarked on a series of poems for children in the vein of 'The Dormouse and the Doctor'.

It proved an ideal escape from the house party, but Daphne was not amused at being abandoned by her husband in these uncongenial surroundings, and so arranged for them to leave a week earlier than had originally been planned. Nonetheless, as they drove away from Plas Brondanw, Milne had completed about a quarter of the poems which would eventually form the collection *When We Were Very Young*, destined to be the first of the four Winnie-the-Pooh books.

What next? Milne had written these poems speculatively, partly as an escape from the dismal house party, partly as a distraction exercise and as an excuse to further postpone work on the promised thriller that he did not want to write, and partly to see whether he really could write for children. And now that he thought he might have done so, he pondered over the way forward. To start with, he sent the proofs of 'The Dormouse and the Doctor' back to Rose Fyleman for publication and waited to see what the reaction would be.

At this point he had not considered whether the poem would be illustrated or not, nor that he might be in any way involved in this decision or its consequences. At that time authors had little connection with artists, as the question of illustrations was left entirely to the publishers, whether of books or magazines, to decide. Publishers' decisions were based on sales potential, and

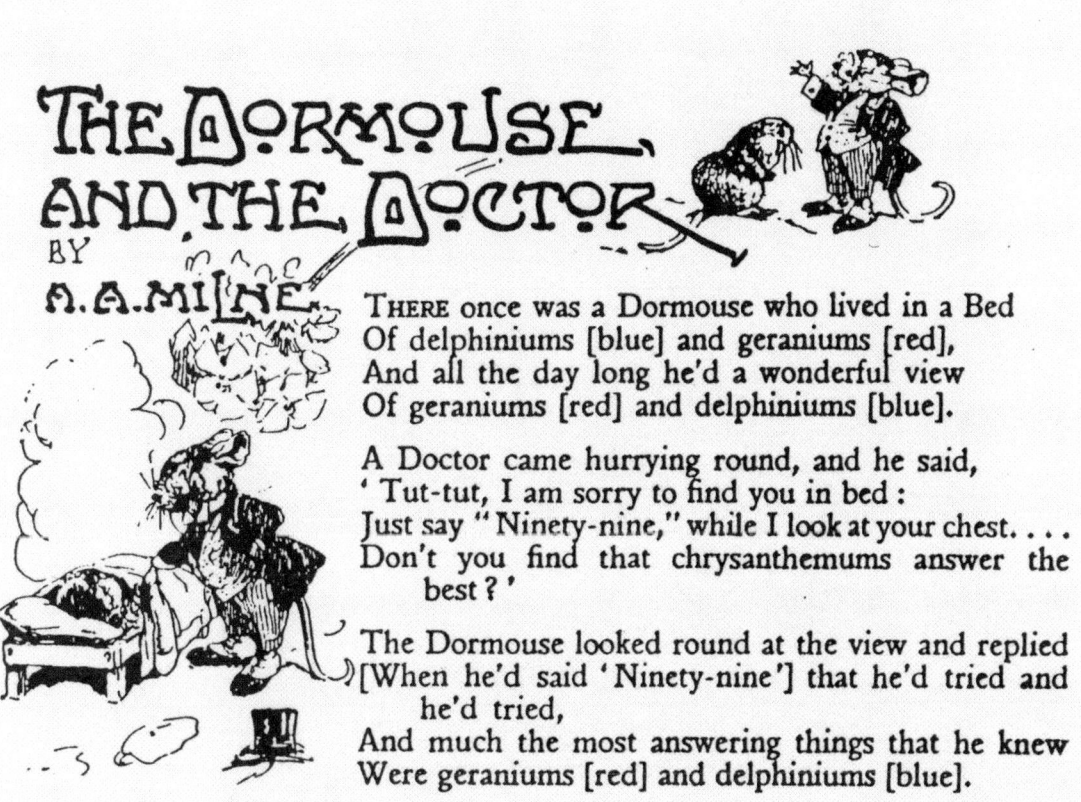

THERE once was a Dormouse who lived in a Bed
Of delphiniums [blue] and geraniums [red],
And all the day long he'd a wonderful view
Of geraniums [red] and delphiniums [blue].

A Doctor came hurrying round, and he said,
' Tut-tut, I am sorry to find you in bed :
Just say "Ninety-nine," while I look at your chest. . . .
Don't you find that chrysanthemums answer the
    best ? '

The Dormouse looked round at the view and replied
[When he'd said ' Ninety-nine'] that he'd tried and
    he'd tried,
And much the most answering things that he knew
Were geraniums [red] and delphiniums [blue].

Harry Rountree's original illustration for 'The Dormouse and the Doctor'.

whether the addition of illustrations would enhance sales of books or magazines sufficiently to justify the extra cost. This was not just the artist's fee, but also the additional typesetting and printing costs. Very often, authors were unhappy at a publisher's decision not to commission illustrations, and occasionally would suggest paying for these out of their own royalties. Even more often, authors were unhappy with the illustrations that were produced, usually feeling that they failed to adequately represent their work. This, famously, was the case with Kenneth Grahame and *The Wind in the Willows*, first published in 1908, where the author did not like any of the illustrations until the eventual arrival of E. H. Shepard more than twenty years later.

After his return to London Milne decided that the poems might form the basis for his next project and continued to work on the collection. It was a very personal endeavour as he knew that his publishers were lukewarm about the idea. They wanted him not only to cash in on the success of *The Red House Mystery*, but also to carry on with his increasingly successful plays. *Mr Pim Passes*

By had been a huge hit in London in 1920 and later in the USA, and so there were pressing demands on Milne to write more in this genre. Children's verse seemed to Milne's publishers to be an unnecessary diversion from this 'real' work. More to the point, Milne had no track record in writing for children, which was already a highly competitive market, and so they resigned themselves, rather reluctantly, to await the manuscript. And to a large extent, Milne agreed, as he himself described it:

'I am writing a book of children's verses. Like Stevenson, only better. No, not a bit like Stevenson really. More like Milne. But they are a curious collection; some *for* children, some *about* children, some by, with or from children.'

One day in the autumn of 1922, he watched from the landing in Mallord Street as Christopher Robin knelt by his bed, saying his prayers supervised by his nanny. Milne then went, chuckling to himself, down the stairs to his study and, in due course, presented Daphne with the poem 'Vespers', with the suggestion that if she wished, she could see if she could make any money from it. Daphne sent the poem to *Vanity Fair* in New York, where it was published in January 1923, and Daphne received fifty dollars. To Milne's surprise, the reaction to the poem was generally positive, and he decided to develop further some of these musings about childhood into poems for possible publication.

E. V. Lucas was to be highly influential in the writing, illustration, publication, and successful promotion of the four books soon to be known collectively by the title of the second, *Winnie-the-Pooh*. Lucas was a prolific writer in a range of genres, had worked for *Punch* from 1904, for the book publishers Methuen from 1908, where he was to become chairman in 1924, was a distinguished member of the *Punch* Table, and knew both Milne and Shepard well. In the late autumn of 1922 Milne sent Lucas a selection of the verses written so far, in the hope that Lucas, as a friend as well as publisher, would give him an honest appraisal of their merit. Lucas realized almost at once that the poems would appeal to a wide audience and should be published in book form once there were enough of them. He also felt that it would be a good idea to do a 'trial run' by first publishing a selection of the poems in *Punch*. He thought this would test the market and show whether readers had an appetite for this type of new work from Milne, already established as a *Punch* contributor for adults as well as a successful playwright.

'The Dormouse and the Doctor' had been illustrated for *Merry-Go-Round* by Harry Rountree, commissioned by Rose Fyleman. He was a skilled animal artist, regularly drawing from life at London Zoo, and unsurprisingly, having read the poem, he represented the characters as animals, but dressed in currently fashionable human clothing. The illustrations were adequate and seemingly acceptable to Rose Fyleman, but they conveyed little of the charm and dexterity of the poem and the story it described.

E. V. Lucas understood that Milne's collection of children's poems would need illustrating to broaden and enhance the sales appeal, but that Harry Rountree would not do. So, he cast through his extensive contacts in London's artistic and literary circles and one evening, at the end of the *Punch* Table dinner, he turned to Ernest Shepard, who was sitting next to him. Lucas casually mentioned that he had received some charming verses from Alan Milne, which were to be published in *Punch* and would need illustrating, and asked Shepard if he would be interested in producing some initial sketches. Always pleased with a new challenge, and keen to be accommodating to Lucas, who was highly influential in his world, Shepard agreed. Shepard was by no means the only choice; there were plenty of other potential illustrators for Milne's verses, a number already being published in *Punch*. But Lucas had a hunch that Shepard could not only draw well enough, but was also temperamentally suited to working with Milne, whom he recognized would not necessarily be the easiest of collaborators.

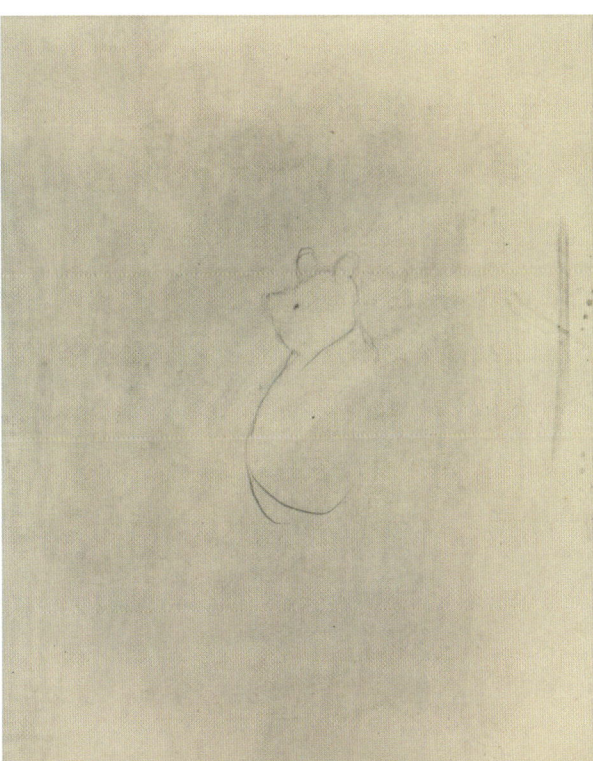

The earliest known (and very faint) drawing of 'Winnie-the-Pooh' in a sketchbook by Shepard.

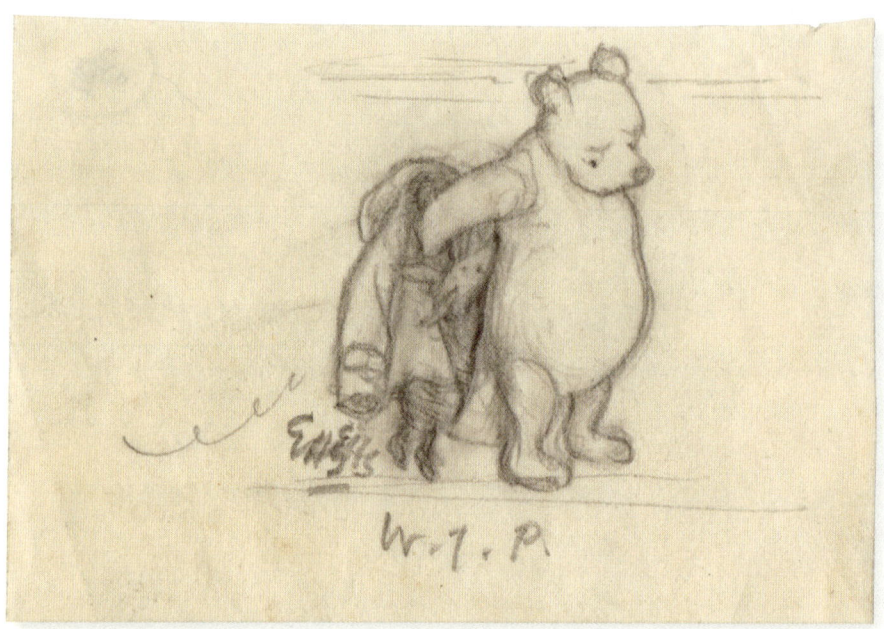

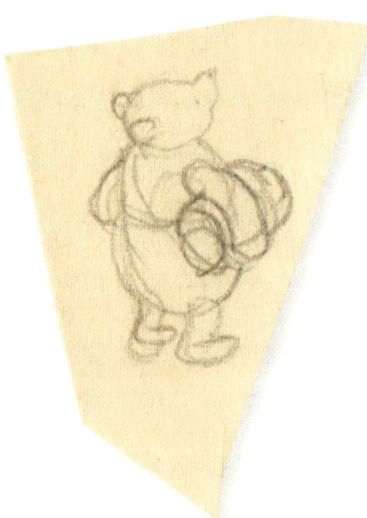

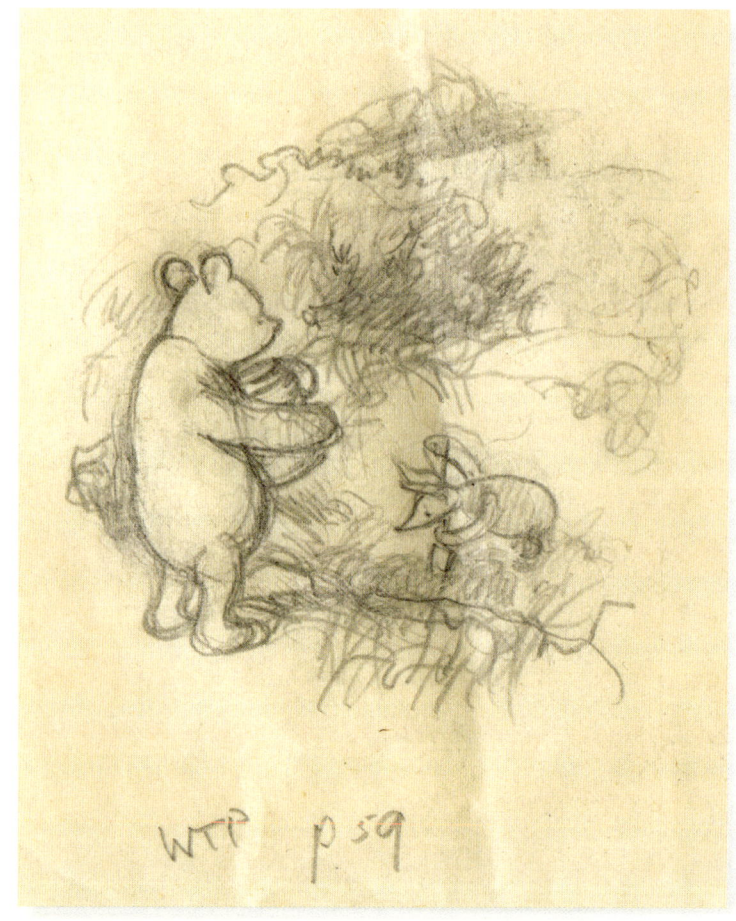

Shepard started drawing Winnie-the-Pooh in 1923. He would begin by sketching in his studio in Shamley Green, using pencil on thin paper, experimenting with positions and scale, and then transfer successful images onto larger sheets as he worked these up towards the final illustration. Here are three very early drafts – you can see the paper fold in the flimsy sketch of Pooh and Piglet, and the tiny drawing of Pooh with an oversized jar of honey is on a mere scrap of paper, while the sketch of Pooh struggling into his duffle coat is initialled – indicating that he would probably share this with A. A. Milne.

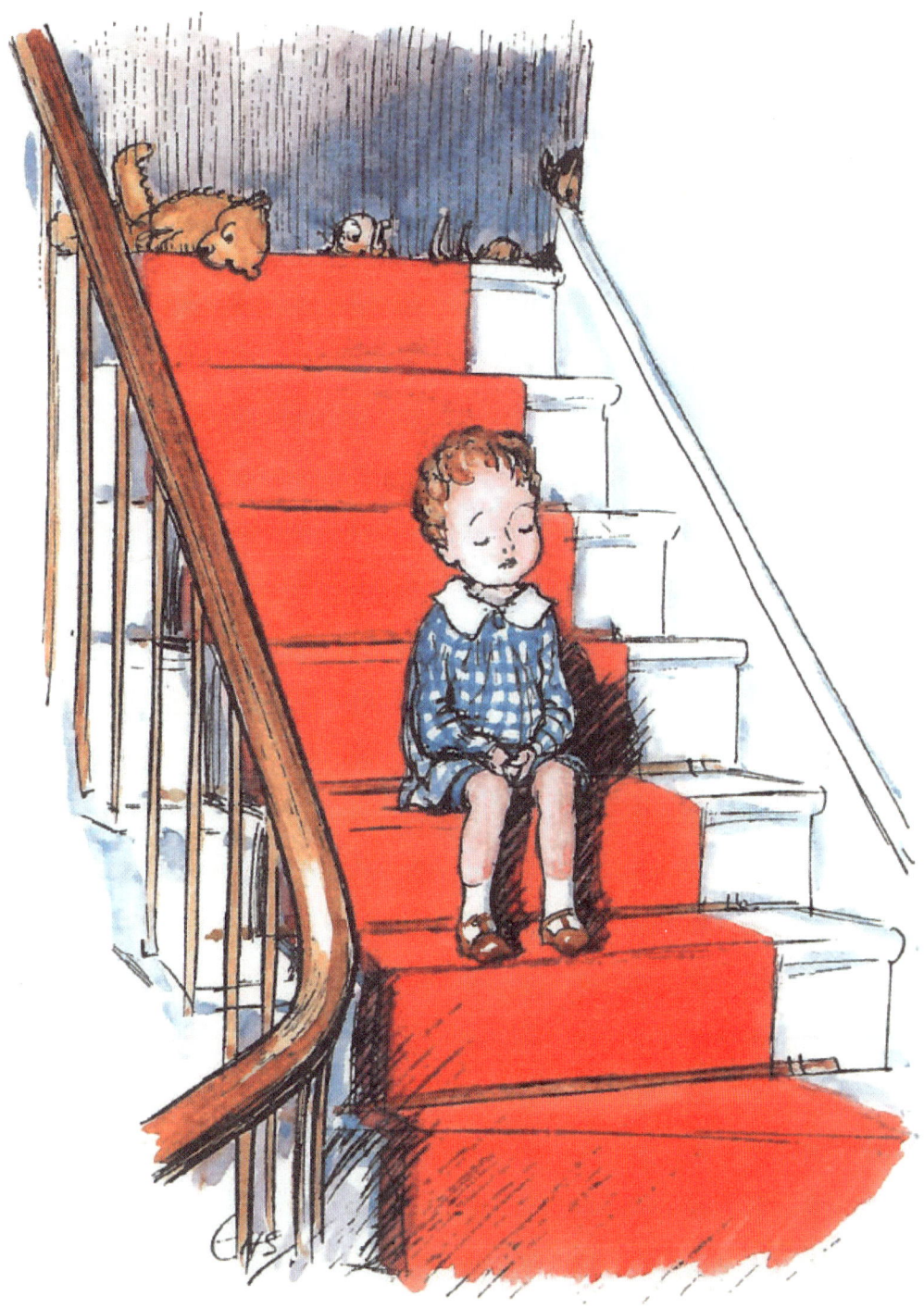

In the first volume of poems by A. A. Milne, *When We Were Very Young*, published in 1924, there are only a few fleeting images of the bear who would become the star of the next book of stories, 'Winnie-the-Pooh', and so in this illustration is simply known as 'Teddy Bear'. This illustration is exciting because it is one of the earliest published 'decorations' of what was to become the most famous bear in the world, and it was one of the first pictures that Shepard coloured in from the original black-and-white.

Alan Milne was initially less enthusiastic. He had known Shepard's work from his period as assistant editor of *Punch*, when Shepard first started submitting drawings to the magazine, and had not been particularly impressed. Indeed, he struggled to understand what *Punch*'s art editor saw in Shepard and was confused when commissions continued to go Shepard's way. There was also some collateral damage from Milne's attempted return to his post at *Punch* after the First World War. This had been mishandled by *Punch* and led to Milne feeling poorly treated, while at almost exactly the same time Shepard was moving up the *Punch* hierarchy. In due course Shepard had joined the *Punch* Table, where Milne had previously sat for many years but was now denied a place. Nonetheless, respecting Lucas's professional judgement, he was prepared to look at Shepard's sample drawings with a relatively open mind.

Ernest Shepard saw his initial work on the poems as a standard commission. He had received the approach informally at dinner from Lucas, and he understood that the offer was essentially as an 'extra' to his existing contractual work for *Punch*. It was a gentleman's agreement and there was no specific discussion as to fees or terms at this stage, nor was there any suggestion that Shepard would need to see Milne before starting work. This situation was confirmed later in April 1923 when Milne's publishers issued a completely standard contract for the first book of verse which stated that the illustrations would be provided by the publishers at their expense.

Shortly after that conversation at the *Punch* Table, Shepard received the poems to be illustrated for the magazine and in short order produced initial sketches to run across full pages in *Punch*, as he was asked. Milne was pleased when he saw the first drawings for the poem 'Puppy and I', which was apparently his own favourite of the collection. Indeed, almost everyone who saw Shepard's initial drawings thought that he had absolutely captured the liveliness and charm of the poems. Lucas was delighted, both by the drawings but, perhaps more importantly, by Milne's enthusiastic agreement that Shepard was indeed the man for the job.

It was now confirmed that the project would go ahead. A selection from the original set of poems written at Plas Brondanw would be published first in *Punch*, and Milne now searched for a title for the collection, which appears to have been somewhat of a struggle. He eventually settled on *When We Were Very Young*, in part because no one could think of anything better. And so, on

9 January 1924, under that title, three short poems, without illustrations, were published in *Punch*. The following week there was a single poem across a full page, 'Puppy and I', with the Shepard illustrations which Milne had so admired set around the text of the poem.

This was also a significant innovation, as usually there was a definite division between text and illustrations in magazines and books. The editor of *Punch* was unenthusiastic about this change to usual practice, and questioned whether it was really necessary. But *Punch*'s art editor was insistent. Despite the misgivings of his editor, the additional complexities of setting the pages and the extra expense, he was sure that this innovative integration of words and pictures would elevate the image substantially in the eyes of the magazine's readers, and he was proved absolutely right.

Over the following weeks further poems, with and without illustrations, were published, including 'The King's Breakfast' and, significantly, 'Teddy Bear'. The illustration for 'Teddy Bear' was the first one to show the bear who was to become Winnie-the-Pooh. At this stage simply referred to as Teddy Bear, and later on in the collection as Mr Edward Bear, the bear was shown in no less than seven separate drawings. These marked the start of the journey for the world's most famous bear.

Initially, Shepard had drawn the first sketches of the bear based on Christopher Robin's teddy bear in the nursery in Mallord Street, as he had with the boy's other toy animals. The future importance of this toy bear and the accompanying illustrations in the poems 'Teddy Bear' and 'Halfway Down', was not at all clear at the time. Neither Milne nor Shepard put any particular emphasis on a bear, or teddy bear, within *When We Were Very Young*. There is no mention of a teddy bear in the verse for 'Halfway Down', whose illustration shows a teddy bear lying across the top of the stairs. For the illustrations of 'Teddy Bear', the bear is first seen lying with other soft toys on a nursery chaise-longue, later in front of a mirror, and then meeting an elderly gentleman. But this bear is quite small compared to his surroundings. (We assume, as he is referred to as Edward Bear, that he is male.) In addition, the bear's snout is slightly more elongated than we see in the later books. It is probably a reasonable assumption that at that stage the bear was just one of the many characters that were introduced and illustrated.

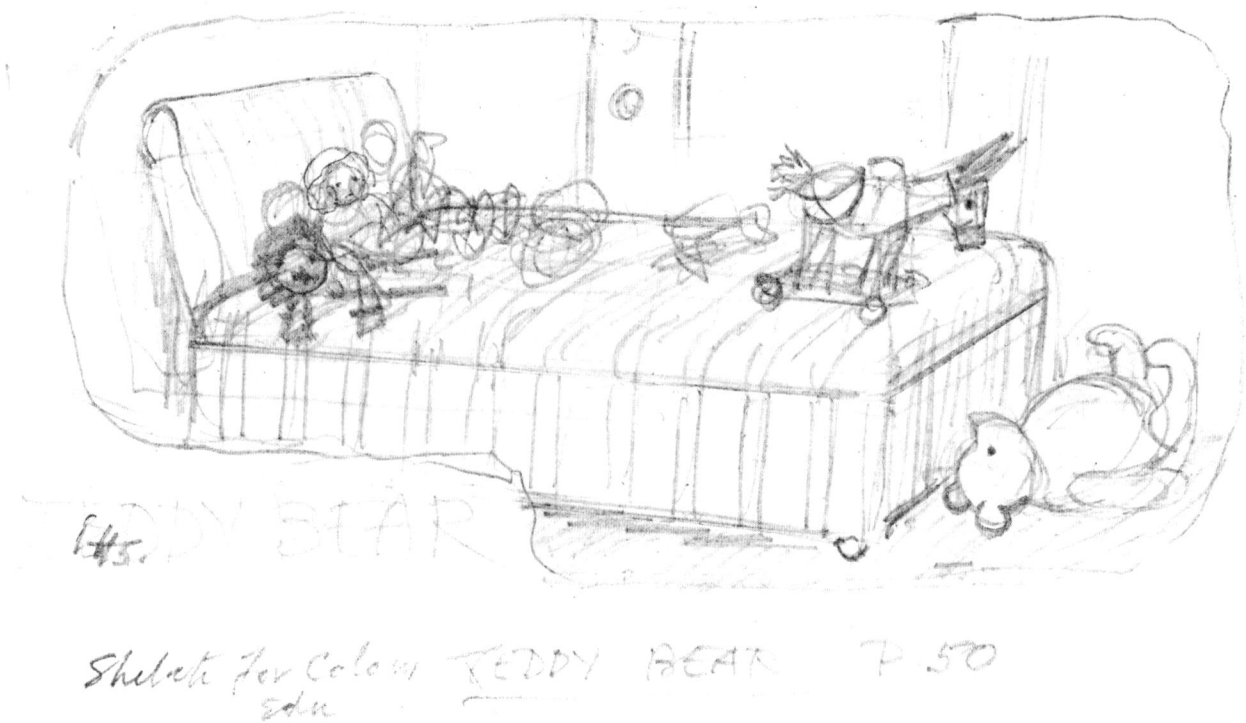

The sketch above is for the colour edition of 'Teddy Bear' in *When We Were Very Young*.
It is one of the earliest versions of Winnie-the-Pooh (as he was to become).

It is also likely that when the first poems were being written, although Christopher Robin had already received his toy teddy bear, which came from Harrods, he had not yet reached the stage of being taken on regular outings to the zoo to see the famous Winnie, the brown bear from Winnipeg in Canada after whom 'Winnie' was named. Nor, at this time, was Christopher Robin calling swans by the name of 'Pooh' when throwing breadcrumbs to them. These were future developments which would lead Milne to rename the bear Winnie-the-Pooh.

But for the present, all the players were interested in was how the illustrated poems in *Punch* were received by the magazine's readership. The reception was overwhelmingly positive and confirmed the success of the innovative setting of text and image. Lucas therefore proceeded with plans to publish the full book of poems in the autumn, and Shepard began adapting and redrawing the illustrations, with additions as necessary, to accommodate the smaller page sizes of the book format. For this work, which had been more than he had anticipated, he was paid a single fee of 50 guineas. He had informally agreed this sum with Lucas to cover the extra work, which was over and above what he was expected to do for his regular payments from *Punch*.

The book's dedication was, predictably, to Christopher Robin Milne. It was written in terms which made it quite clear that the book was not only for him,

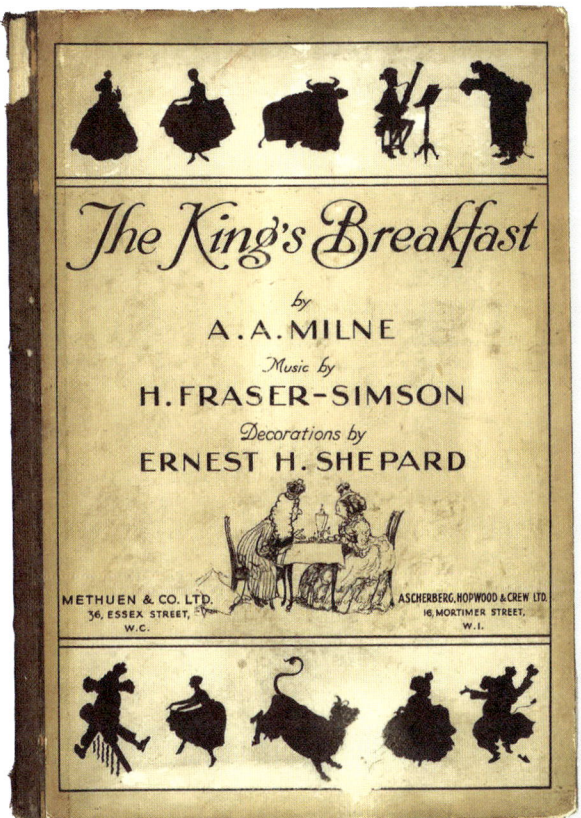

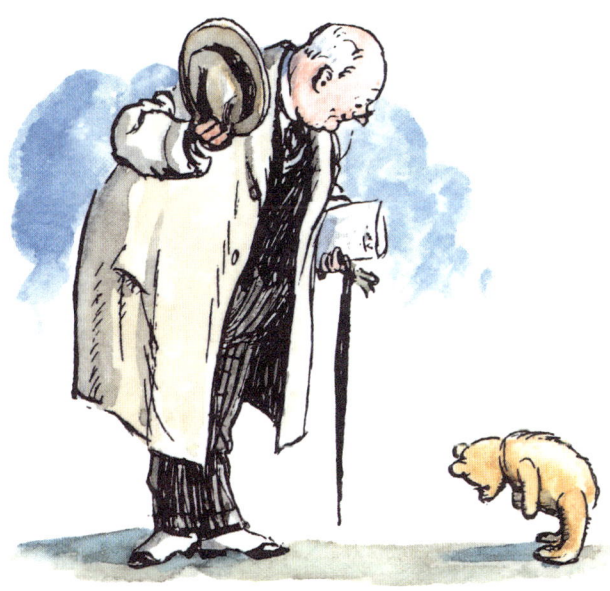

A number of poems were set to music by Harold Fraser-Simson – this is a first edition with special 'decorations'.

A coloured-in version of 'Mr Edward Bear' from *When We Were Very Young* from the 1960s.

but that he was the small boy in some of the poems. It linked him forever with the 'fictitious' Christopher Robin and blurred for the rest of his life the line between the real and the make-believe.

No one seems to have anticipated anything particularly out of the ordinary as publication of *When We Were Very Young* approached. Indeed, there was some anxiety at Methuen as fewer than the usual number of copies they would expect had been pre-ordered by retail booksellers. It was a similar story in America. Even so, on publication day itself, Lucas realized that the 50 guinea flat fee for the illustrations was woefully inadequate and sent Shepard a cheque for 100 guineas as a bonus. This was before the enormous sales which followed.

When We Were Very Young was published by Methuen in London on 6 November 1924, and by Dutton in New York City on 20 November. Methuen's first edition sold out on the day of publication, was immediately reprinted, and continued to be reprinted as demand soared, with over 40,000 copies sold by the end of 1924. It was a similar story in New York, where not only had Dutton

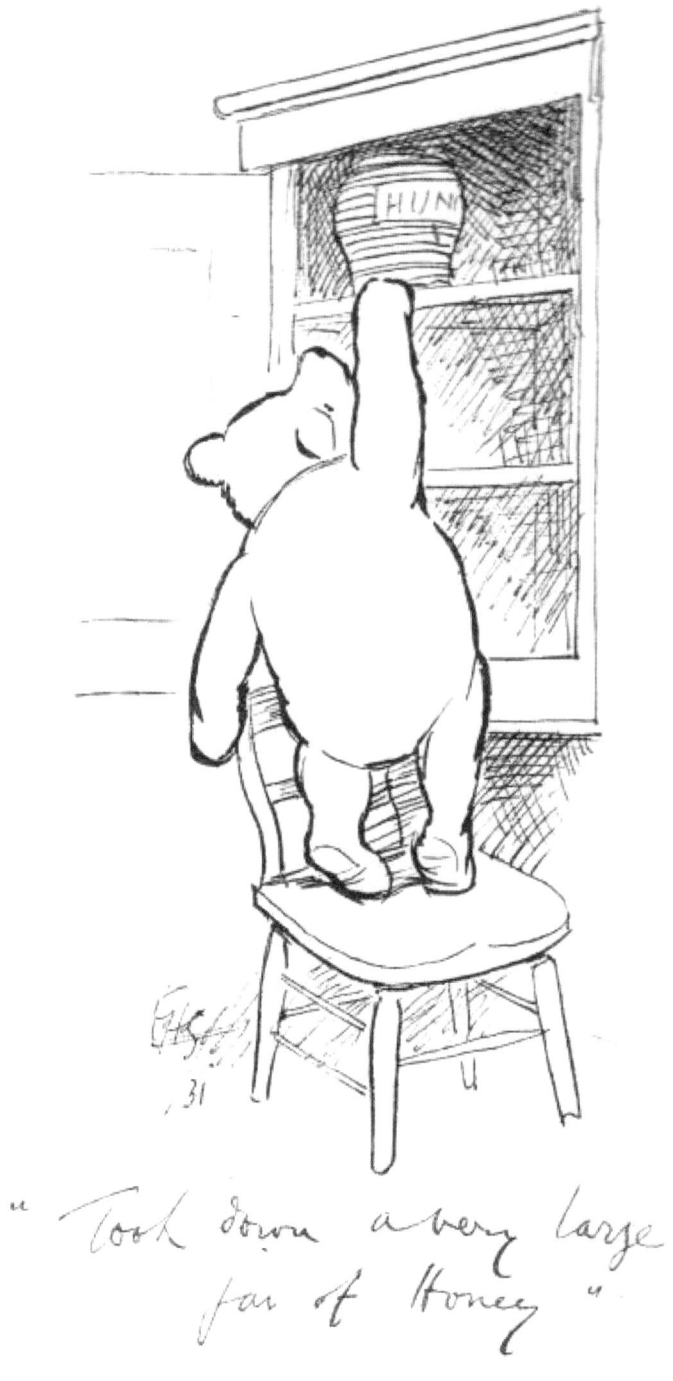

" Took down a very large
jar of Honey "

Above: The final printed version of Pooh reaching for a 'very large' jar of honey.
Opposite: This illustration of Pooh and Piglet wrapped up warm in the snow was
never published.

sold over 10,000 copies by Christmas 1924, but by the time that its successor volume of verse, *Now We Are Six* was published in 1927, more than a quarter of a million copies had been sold in the USA and Canada alone.

The critics, on both sides of the Atlantic, initially focused on *When We Were Very Young* as an interesting sideline by the master playwright of the moment. They were encouraged to do this by the blurb on the original dust jacket, which specifically drew attention to the change of emphasis by the author, and also most unusually name-checked the illustrator as well. Reviews were generally mixed, a number were quietly supportive, some were more enthusiastic, and a few were dismissive. Some drew a distinction between those poems clearly written for and about Christopher Robin, and others which seemed much less inventive and more like standard fairy tales of the time. However, the reviews were all quite irrelevant, as the buying public voted strongly with wallet and purse, and *When We Were Very Young* developed a momentum quite of its own.

From the start it became apparent that adult readers were buying the book quite as much for themselves as for children, a phenomenon which would be repeated as the following three Winnie-the-Pooh books appeared in due course. There seemed to be a resonance in the effect of the verse and the accompanying illustrations which conveyed a timeless charm and connection with people of all ages, and adults were not in the slightest bit embarrassed to be seen with the book but without any children accompanying them. Milne had tapped into a latent demand from the reading public for escapism after the horrors of the First World War, the Spanish influenza pandemic, widespread unemployment and peacetime challenges. He mined this seam highly effectively, applying to his verse for children (of all ages) the same feeling of escapism that he conjured up so successfully in his plays throughout the 1920s.

Once the mounting sales and critical impact of *When We Were Very Young* became apparent, Methuen and Dutton were only too willing to eat their previous words, and began to press

Alan Milne for a sequel. Milne, however, was in no hurry. He was pleased, if surprised, at the reception for *When We Were Very Young* and was quite confident that he could repeat this with a second volume of children's verse in similar style. But for the present he did not feel any sense of urgency, other than for him to secure the future services of E. H. Shepard as illustrator. Milne immediately recognized, as did both critics and the public, that the illustrations, or 'decorations' as they were called, had been an integral part of the success of the first book. In the meantime, and presumably both to flatter him and to secure Shepard's cooperation, Milne wrote to him to ask if he would undertake to illustrate a re-issue of his wartime book *Once on a Time*. It had been first published in 1917 with little fanfare and fewer sales but now, in the afterglow of the success of *When We Were Very Young*, Hodder & Stoughton were reprinting it to catch the public demand for Milne.

Shepard was also soon aware that *When We Were Very Young* was unlikely to be a one-off, and initially he seems to have had mixed feelings. E. V. Lucas was of exactly the same mind as Milne, and attempted to secure Shepard's services as soon as it became clear that there would be a sequel. Shepard was more wary than might have been expected. While delighted at the critical acclaim for his drawings, and pleased by the enormous sales, he seems to have felt that to jump straight into a second volume might start to pigeonhole his work, and his existing heavy workload was a good excuse to put the brakes on as far as he was concerned. And indeed this was quite true. He was on the staff at *Punch* and was increasingly involved not only in producing cartoons and artwork for the magazine, but also in becoming part of the administrative and managerial side of the business, which was almost a full-time job in itself. His wider freelance commissions were also keeping him busy.

With the huge sales bringing in very substantial royalties for Milne, it also seems that Shepard felt that he had perhaps been rather too accommodating to Lucas regarding payment. The 150 guineas he had received was frankly a steal, bearing in mind the extent to which his illustrations contributed to the overall success of *When We Were Very Young*. He decided to pause and to take further professional advice on how to negotiate appropriate remuneration for his work in the future, both with Milne, Methuen and Dutton in particular, and his wider practice in general.

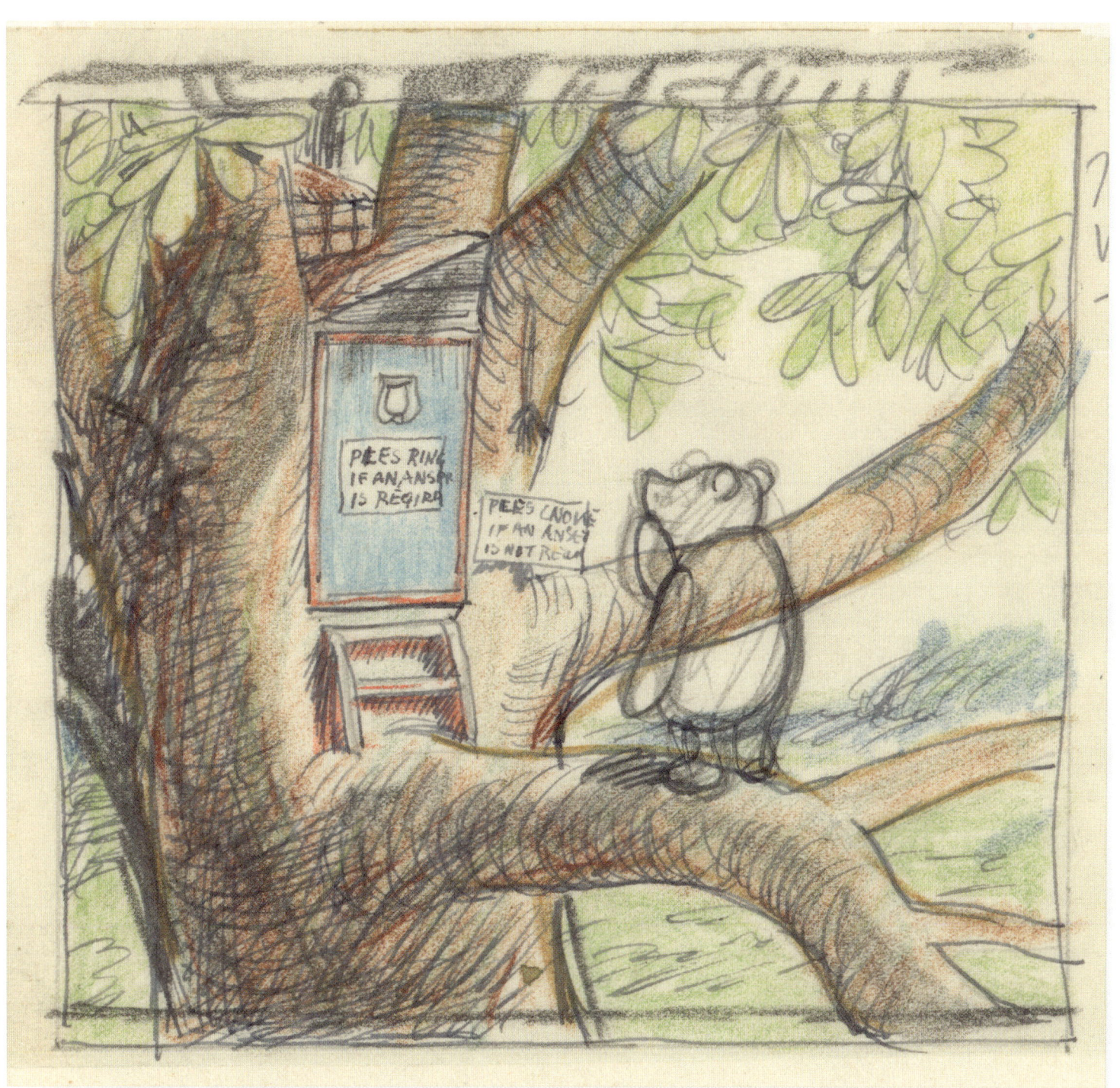

Shepard's way of working was to draw and colour the background and 'drop' the characters in so that Milne – and perhaps the publisher – could see how the finished item might look.

One of the reasons for E. H. Shepard's ongoing success as a commercial artist and illustrator was that he combined, unusually, not only outstanding artistic ability and draughtsmanship, but also a sound grasp of efficient business practice. Shepard responded to enquiries by return, he completed commissions on time and on budget, and fulfilled the brief accurately. There was rarely any need to ask for changes, and publishers and commissioning editors respected him. Shepard at that time had a wooden outbuilding as a studio in the garden of his cottage at Shamley Green in Surrey, and it was his practice to work there alone, undisturbed, going up to London by train from Guildford weekly, usually to attend the *Punch* dinner and to meet with publishers, agents, clients and others. He fulfilled both his artistic and administrative commitments highly efficiently.

Although there had been some wariness on both sides as they began their collaboration over *When We Were Very Young* in 1923, Milne and Shepard developed a long and mutually rewarding professional working relationship over thirty years. It ended with Shepard illustrating Milne's last work in 1952. Over time, each developed a respect and admiration for the other's craft and practice. Shepard would prepare draft sketches for Methuen and, unusually, as this was not normal custom and practice, Lucas would show these to Milne for his comments and observations, which were in turn conveyed back to Shepard, who would make the necessary changes. The two would meet in person rarely at this stage, but their relationship was always professional, respectful and harmonious.

The two were never close personal friends, largely for three reasons. First, although they appeared to have much in common, they had significantly different attitudes to life. For example, on the subject of military conflict, Shepard was a bastion of support for the establishment view, agreeing that war was sometimes necessary. He supported army and regimental charities and associated causes all his life. Milne, on the other hand, was a pacificist, did not conform to upper-middle-class orthodoxy on a number of issues, and was left-leaning in a manner unusual for someone of his background and class.

Secondly, while Shepard was gregarious, enjoying a varied social life and delighting in the company of friends, Milne was inward-looking, with only a small group of close male friends, most particularly his elder brother Ken. Milne best enjoyed a quiet lunch at the Garrick Club with a single male guest, followed by a round of golf with another male friend. He was, by and large, uncomfortable with women he did not know well, and did not enjoy the social round which his wife cultivated.

Finally, Daphne Milne did not consider the Shepards suitable as friends. Daphne was acutely aware of her social position, and tried hard to maintain and, indeed, to enhance it. The Shepards were not in her circle: they lived modestly in a country cottage, they had no obvious social connections, and there was really no reason for any further relationship other than her husband's professional one.

Daphne Milne's reaction to the success of *When We Were Very Young* was one of pleasure and admiration of her husband's talent and ability in yet another sphere of writing and authorship, and one which they could better share as it revolved around their beloved Billy Moon. Daphne was ambitious for her husband, supporting him as a part-time secretary when necessary, which was more often than she would have liked, as Milne was not nearly as organized as Shepard. Not wishing it to be known that she personally stooped to these administrative tasks, she adopted a pseudonym, Celia Brice, for her secretarial duties, and was delighted when, in due course, she was able to surrender the job to a professional employee. Daphne was keen on the social duties falling to the attractive and well-dressed wife of a fashionable author and playwright, accepting with gusto invitations to stylish events and parties which, on his own, her husband would most definitely have refused. She still left Nanny in charge of Christopher Robin in the nursery, but revelled in the reflected glory of his public persona in *When We Were Very Young*.

The reaction of the Shepard family to the success of *When We Were Very Young* is much harder to gauge. Initially, the family probably thought little, if anything, of the book. Shepard had such a busy professional life, producing so much work across a range of commissions in addition to his *Punch* responsibilities, that this seemed just another relatively modest stand-alone commission. They all had other priorities at that time. Pie was suffering from increasingly acute attacks of asthma and was frequently away from home for the sake of her health, while Graham was a boarder at Marlborough College and Mary was at school nearer home in Surrey. So it was likely that other than the unexpectedly huge sales and subsequent publicity for their father, the Shepard family probably took the first book in their stride.

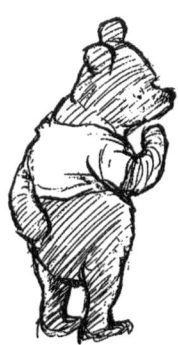

CHAPTER FIVE

And Tigger Joins the Cast

Alan Milne was not to be hurried into writing the next book. He had no need for money and wanted some time to focus on a range of other projects which had been on the back burner since the previous autumn. He also wanted to spend some quality time with his young son, who at the age of four and a half was becoming an interesting and delightful companion. Milne had begun to develop what was to become the most important relationship in his life, particularly after the death of his brother Ken, and his close connection, affection and companionship with his son would sustain him until the Second World War would separate them. Their time spent together, walking to school, on expeditions and on holidays, often without Daphne present, cemented their special relationship.

The year 1925 turned out to be much busier than Milne had anticipated, despite the leisurely start, as he intended to take his time over the new books for children.

Milne claimed that the inspiration for a book of stories specifically about Christopher Robin's teddy bear came from himself and Daphne. Certainly the wonderfully inventive and endearing bedtime stories which Milne made up for his young son delighted Christopher Robin and enchanted Daphne, who seemed often to have been there in the night nursery as the stories were told. She also helped Christopher Robin to play with his toy animals and to develop their individual characters. Milne himself did not join in this play but watched with pleasure and made quiet notes. As Christopher Robin's affection for his teddy bear increased, he demanded more stories about the bear, and Milne began to weave a tapestry of tales with a natural setting based on the Ashdown Forest

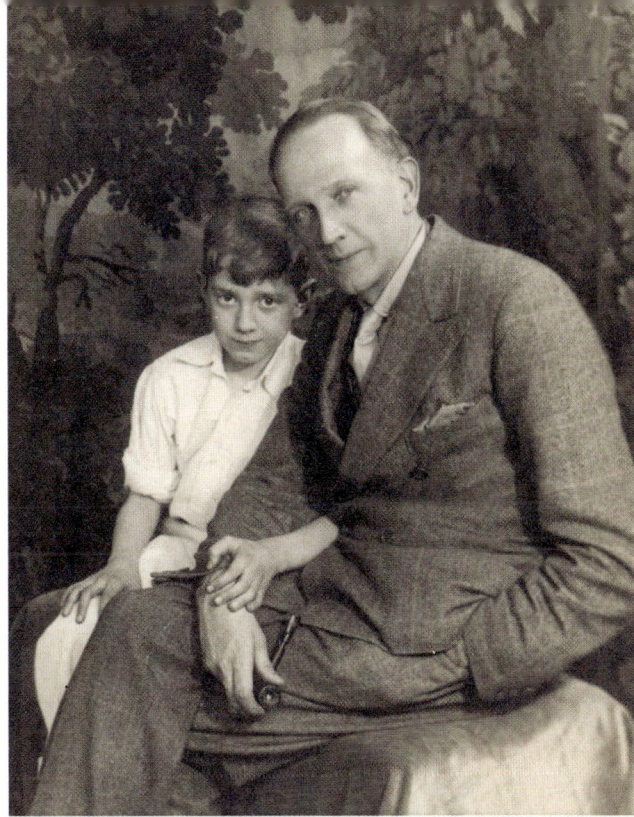

A studio portrait of Alan and Christopher Robin Milne by Howard Coster.

in East Sussex. In 1925 the Milnes had bought a weekend and holiday home, Cotchford Farm near Hartfield on the edge of the Ashdown Forest, so the area was well known to them all.

As 1925 progressed, the ongoing enormous success of *When We Were Very Young* became almost overwhelming, and inexorably the 'real' Christopher Robin became gradually exposed to the public. It started innocuously enough, with studio photographs of the three Milnes together, but gradually his public exposure began to accelerate, largely due to Daphne. Thrilled by the great triumph of *When We Were Very Young*, she was keen to use her husband's raised profile as a stepping stone both for the greater advancement of his career and for her own social ambitions and status. The charming and photogenic little son in the nursery in Mallord Street was a potent weapon to be deployed in this campaign.

Daphne was probably delighted when a neighbour, Harold Fraser-Simson, set to music some of the poems from *When We Were Very Young*. He was a popular composer of the day and arranged for the verses and music to be published. E. V. Lucas wanted a royal dedication for this volume, realizing that, then as now, an association with the British royal family would only further enhance the publication's appeal and with it, book sales. Unfortunately, at that time the only royal children were the grandchildren of King George V by his daughter Mary, the Princess Royal, and her husband, Lord Lascelles, and so, rather tenuously, the fourteen songs in the book were formally dedicated to the Hon George and

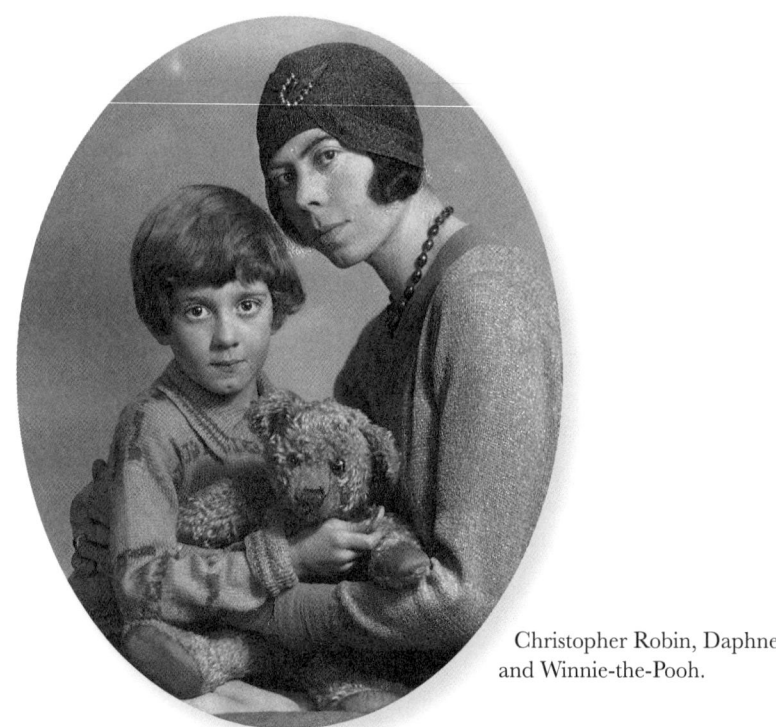

Christopher Robin, Daphne and Winnie-the-Pooh.

the Hon Gerald Lascelles. However, even this semi-detached royal dedication had the desired effect, and Daphne Milne must have been thrilled when they were invited to a private dinner party where the guest of honour was HRH Princess Marie-Louise, granddaughter of Queen Victoria, who had expressed a particular interest in meeting A. A. Milne.

By the autumn of 1925 the bandwagon was still merrily rolling along. Christopher Robin was being photographed again and again, Daphne was interviewed by fashionable publications which included pictures of the immaculate nursery in their articles, while Milne absented himself from this publicity drive, promoted and encouraged by his wife, and kept silent. To get away from this social chatter, which bored him, Milne deliberately spent much of his time on sports, both as a spectator, principally of cricket, and as a player of golf, which he very much enjoyed.

However, he had committed to produce a children's short story to be published in London's *Evening News* on Christmas Eve, 1925. On Christmas Day the story was also to be broadcast on the BBC wireless. The new Milne story, both print and broadcast versions, was heavily promoted and trailed. Milne appealed to Daphne for inspiration for the subject of this story, but she was distracted by her social activities and told him to simply write down one of the bedtime stories he made up for Christopher Robin. And so Milne did, writing a story not about fairies or dragons, but about his son and his teddy bear and their adventures together. This appears to have been completed at rather short notice. Shepard was unavailable to illustrate it and so the accompanying drawing was by James H. Dowd. The bear was now named Winnie-the-Pooh, and Dowd drew him as a very dark bear lying on his back on the ground, with Christopher Robin standing over him with a balloon in one hand and, surely rather incongruously, a rifle in the other. The *Evening News* made a big deal of Milne's new story, splashing a headline across the front page, with further large type headings on the inside pages where the story appeared. It was a huge success and a triumph for the *Evening News* and the BBC. Encouraged by this reaction, in the new year of 1926 Milne sat down to create his next children's book.

As Daphne had suggested, it may simply have been a matter of Milne writing down the stories he had already invented of the adventures of Christopher Robin, his teddy bear and the other toys in the nursery, with the background to the tales being the forest. And perhaps it really was that simple. Milne was an experienced professional writer who worked quickly, and he seems to have set down the fruits of his imagination in the nursery, inspired by his young son's enthusiasm. By the spring of 1926 the majority of *Winnie-the-Pooh* was down on paper.

The original handwritten manuscript for this book, now held in the imposing Wren Library of Trinity College, Cambridge, Milne's *alma mater*, is a fascinating exercise in understanding Milne's process of writing. Generally, the text reads fluently and coherently, as if Milne knew the story exactly, and was simply putting down on paper what was already in his head. What is particularly intriguing about these pages is seeing the particular emphasis which Milne puts on specific words or phrases, sometimes by using capital letters, and sometimes by underlining. These were not replicated in print, and occasionally the particular emphasis in the original seems to convey a different stress or meaning than in the published versions we know so well. For example, the line 'I think Heffalumps come if you whistle' has the word 'think' underlined in the manuscript, but not in the printed text, and the underline arguably gives a different meaning to the line. It brings a feeling of uncertainty, in contrast to the text without the underline, which gives a much more confident feel to the dialogue. Similarly, at the start of the manuscript the name Eeyore is written as Ee-yore, particularly where he appears in Chapter 6. It is only in Chapter 10 (Roman X in the manuscript) that the hyphen is lost and Eeyore appears as we know it. This calls to mind Milne's initial spelling in that story in the *Evening News*, where the bear is first named as *Winnie-the-pooh*, where the 'pooh' has a lower-case 'p', which was later, of course, to be elevated to the capital 'P', giving us the 'Pooh' we know today. Reading the original manuscript right through gives an extraordinary sense of Milne's fluency and confidence as a writer. There are no awkward pauses, or the feeling that the author is struggling to find a connection, a phrase or a specific word. It all flows naturally and easily, and in a way which will appeal both to children on one level and adults on another.

By the spring of 1926 Milne had managed to clear his desk of most of his commitments. It was this workload that made him determined not to be put under pressure to produce his next children's book. So, now he had more free time, his publishers were only too keen for him to focus on what looked to them like an almost guaranteed money-spinner. The only real casualty was his playwriting. Nigel Playfair, his co-host on that wet summer holiday at Plas Brondanw, had been anticipating a Christmas pantomime from Milne, and that expectation was to be dashed. After his successful run of plays in London and New York, Milne perhaps decided that a pause in his playwriting career would be no bad thing. He may have reasoned that if he prioritized what looked likely to be a commercial winner in the book world, it would probably not harm his prospects of having his future plays produced.

So Milne took the opportunity to really focus on *Winnie-the-Pooh*, and in doing so he revolutionized the way in which children's literature would be produced in the future.

When We Were Very Young had been a fairly standard exercise in book publishing, with the exception of the innovative illustrations. Milne had proposed a book, consulted with his agent and negotiated with his publisher. In due course, he had received a standard author's contract, which delegated the production of the book and any illustrations to the publisher, and all had proceeded normally. But after the success of *When We Were Very Young*, Milne wanted a different approach. He had seen from the response to the first book the importance of several factors, which included the balance between text and illustration, relationship between words and pictures on the page, the emphasis on the right-hand page, and the physical feel of the book. He wanted to be an integral part of these decisions. He also made an unusual acknowledgement for

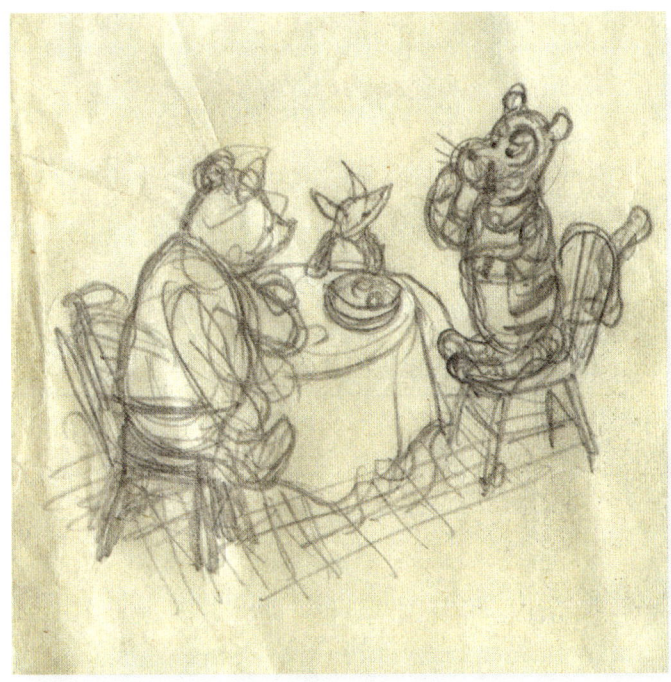

A very early draft – note the thin and crumpled paper – for *The House at Pooh Corner*, showing Shepard's early version of Tigger, with enormous eyes, having tea with Pooh and Piglet. Shepard always started off with preliminary drawings like this, gradually working up towards a final version.

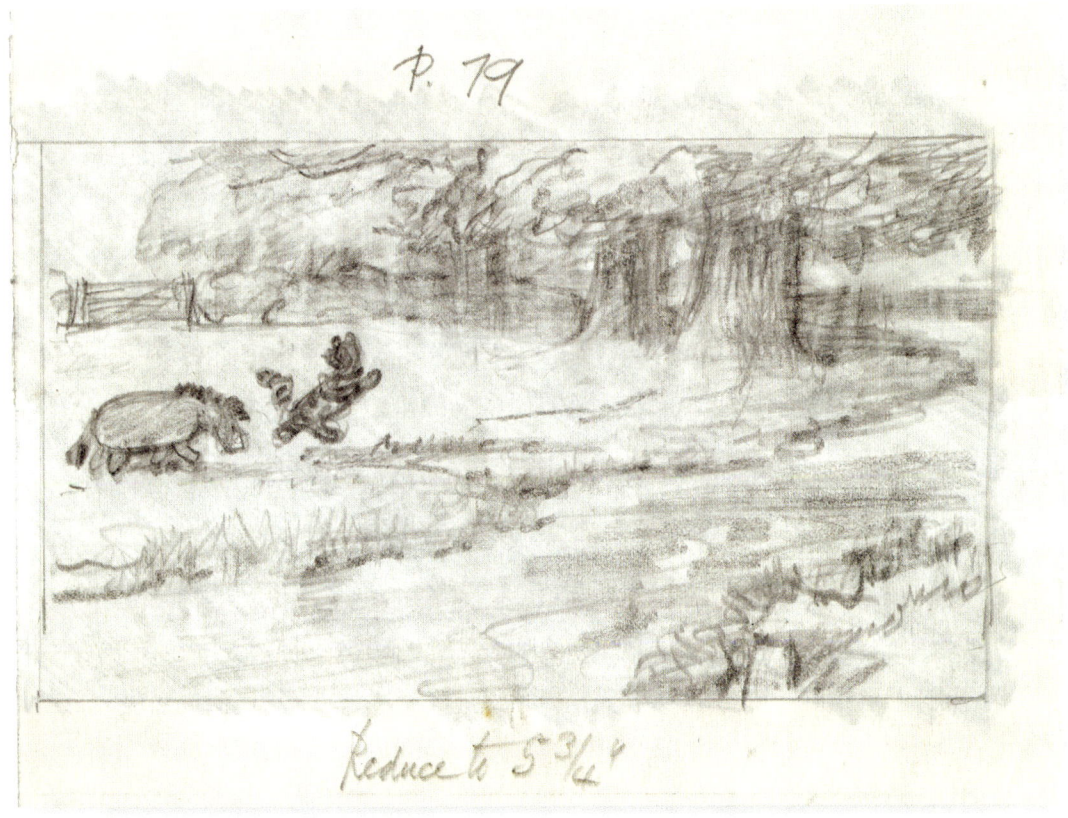

Another very early sketch of Eeyore and Tigger by the bank of the river. Shepard has not got the respective sizes of the two quite right, and while Eeyore ambles slowly, Tigger is bouncing along.

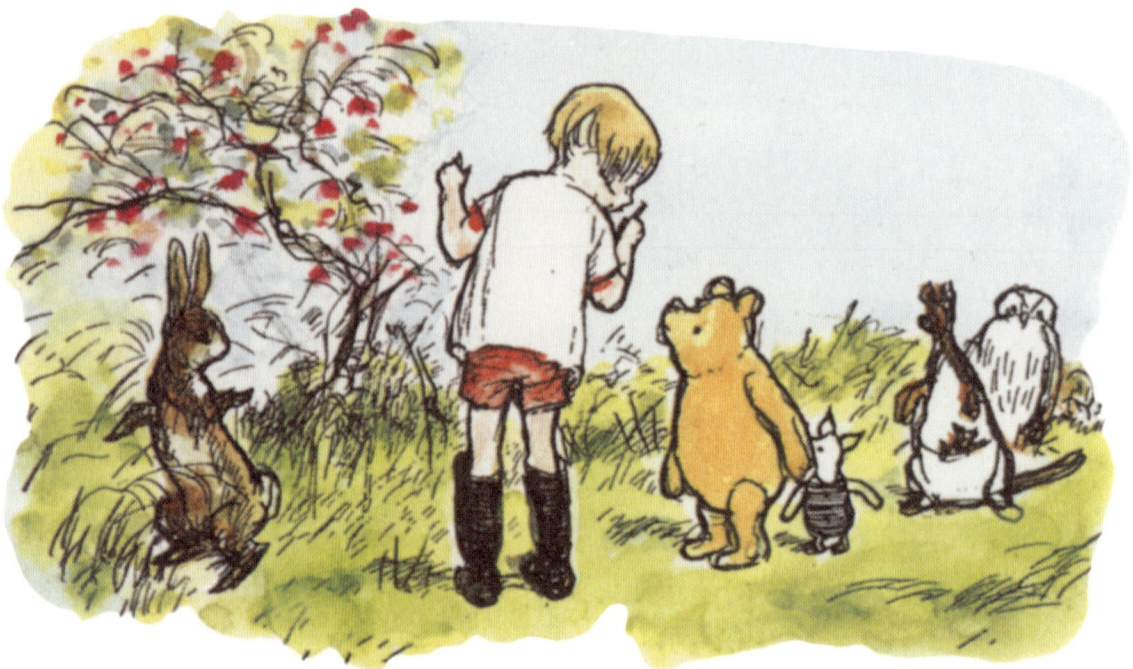

Rabbit, Christopher Robin, Winnie-the-Pooh, Piglet, Kanga, Roo and Owl, some of Milne and Shepard's principal characters.

that time, which was to stress the importance of the illustrations. He had made a reference to this in the Introduction to *When We Were Very Young*, where he wrote that,

> '… *this book is entirely the unaided work of Christopher Robin, Hoo, and Mr Shepard, who drew the pictures.'*

This very public acknowledgement of the contribution of the illustrator was almost unprecedented. But in 1926, having compared the Shepard illustrations with the interpretations of Harry Rountree and James Dowd, Milne was acutely aware of the importance of securing Shepard's commitment to illustrate the further two books he planned at this stage. Milne also wished to be much more personally involved in the process of creating these vital images to enhance the new stories. And thus began one of the most celebrated partnerships of author and illustrator, not only in children's literature, but of all time. For looking back after a century, it is fair to say that to the general public the names of Milne and Shepard are as linked and inseparable as those of Gilbert and Sullivan, Bonnie and Clyde or Laurel and Hardy.

Gradually Milne became personally involved in all aspects of the publication of the new book, including its production and finances. Both Milne and Shepard were aware, as were their agents and the publishers Methuen and Dutton, that the previous financial contract that had been in place for *When We Were Very Young* could not be repeated. But it was apparently Milne who proposed an innovative arrangement in which Shepard should receive a share of the royalties, rather than agreeing to a lump sum payment as was usual (although Shepard and his agent would doubtless have negotiated a substantially increased lump sum than the 50 guineas plus 100 guinea bonus that he had received first time round!). After discussions with literary agents Curtis Brown, who now represented Shepard as well as Milne, and therefore had a strong interest in an agreement acceptable to both parties, Milne wrote to Shepard setting out his new proposal, which was essentially that future royalties would be split eighty per cent to Milne and twenty per cent to Shepard. Having thereby acknowledged the key role played by Shepard and his illustrations in the success of *When We Were Very Young*, and therefore of their future books for children, the question was whether this 80/20 split accurately represented the contribution of each party. Interestingly, the person who put her finger precisely on the issue was Daphne Milne, who told her husband that while she was sure he could explain the rationale behind the proposed 80/20 split, she felt, 'It will want a lot of explaining to *Mrs* Shepard.'

This arrangement formed the basis of the ongoing long-term business relationship between the two parties. However, almost inevitably, it was the cause of difficulties that would occur in the future, long after Milne's death. The first problem was that while Milne spoke of a joint agreement, in reality Shepard had no rights at all over the contract itself. This caused him great distress when, many years later and after her husband's death, Daphne decided to sell her remaining Winnie-the-Pooh rights to Walt Disney. She did not involve or consult Shepard in her plan, even though she was committing his creative work, along with that of her husband, to a third party. The sale left Shepard without any means of retaining control over changes to or manipulation of his original artwork.

The second problem was that the contract took no account of how the world of visual imagery might change in the future. It was an understandable oversight. Milne and Shepard were working in an age when not even television was invented, and films were still silent. However, from the 1960s Disney era onwards, the image began to become more important than the text. More and more, the marketability of the Pooh brand – and the income generated from it – reflected the images rather than the words. Consequently, as Shepard lived through the changing eras of films with sound, TV, video, and so on, the 80/20 words versus images split seemed increasingly unfair to him.

The two families met for the first time in the summer of 1926, as Milne wanted to take Shepard to the Ashdown Forest around Cotchford Farm and show him the settings for the various stories in the book. It would allow Shepard to get a feel for the place. As the Milnes went to Cotchford Farm only at weekends, Milne felt that it would be unreasonable to ask Shepard to break his weekend time with his own family, so he invited the whole Shepard family over for lunch. It was an interesting visit for the Shepards, as Mary Shepard, then fifteen, later recalled in a radio interview. Her elder brother Graham played with Christopher Robin, then aged nearly six, in the stream in the garden at Cotchford Farm, showing the boy how to play make-believe, such as turning a piece of wood into a dragon, and building dams. Mary and Graham got the strong impression that Christopher Robin was not used to playing with other children, and in fact that Graham was in essence showing him *how* to play. This resonates with Christopher Robin's own memoirs, where he recalls his parents being present, but never actually engaging in play with him. Perhaps unsurprisingly, given Daphne's acute sense of social position, Mary found Daphne to be 'very grand indeed', and 'rather alarming'.

Milne sent a series of letters to Shepard giving him exceptionally detailed instructions for the illustrations for *Winnie-the-Pooh*. The artist was amazed by this flow of correspondence, but, appreciating the significance of the commission, he threw himself wholeheartedly into the task, taking immense pains over every detail. He visited Mallord Street and drew from life. He also regularly visited the Ashdown Forest surrounding Cotchford and drew the landscape again and again from multiple vantage points, guided by Milne to the exact spots where the stories were set. He had Christopher Robin photographed, so he could draw his image in his studio, and the resulting sketches flew to and fro between the three interested parties, Milne, Shepard and Lucas. Shepard felt he was certainly earning his increased fees, as he was putting a disproportionate amount of effort in making sure the drawings were absolutely right. The two men continued to

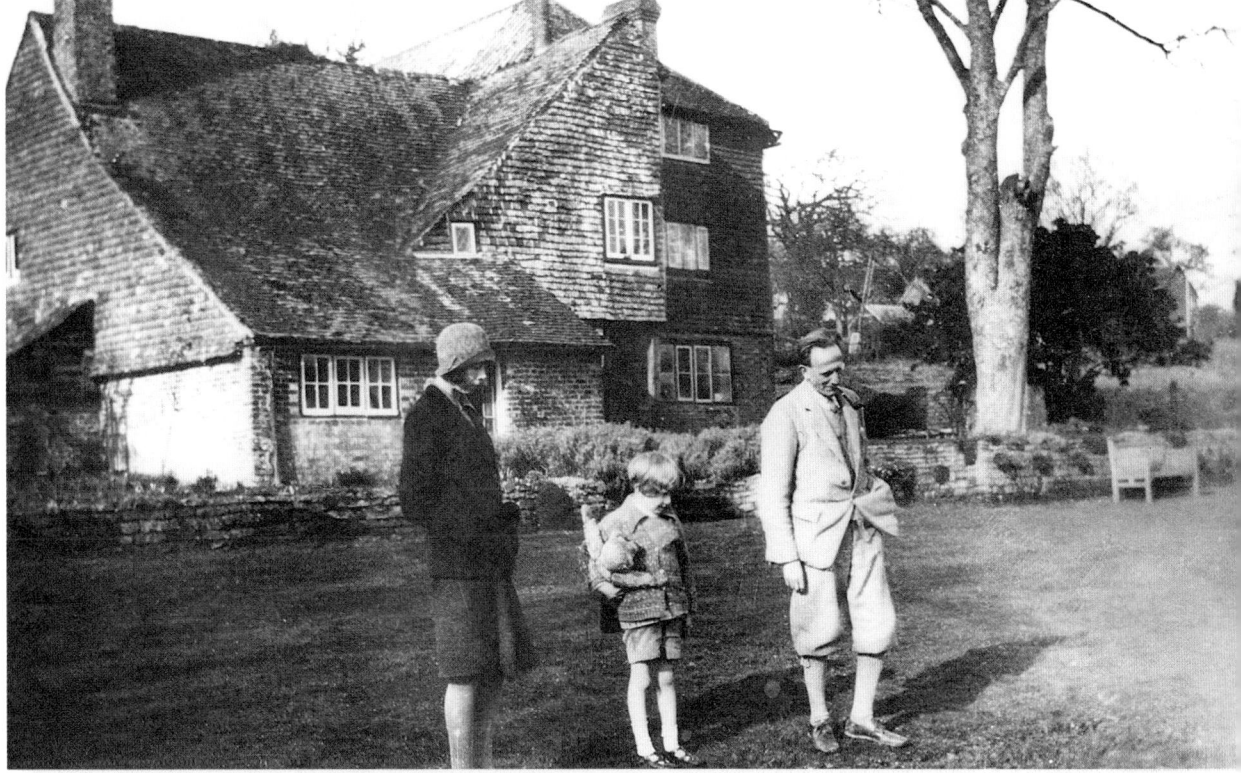

The Milne family at their holiday home, Cotchford Farm, on the edge of the Ashdown Forest, East Sussex, the setting for the Hundred Acre Wood of the Pooh stories.

work harmoniously together professionally, but there was no movement towards a closer personal relationship. 'I always had to start again at the beginning with Milne,' said Shepard later, 'every time I met him.'

Milne's personal reserve was simply a part of who he was, and he behaved towards Shepard as he did to almost all his professional and social acquaintances. He was less reserved with only a very small group of mostly male friends with whom he felt comfortable. While Shepard and Milne did meet in person from time to time, mostly they communicated by letter, which was Milne's preference. Shepard, who usually saw Lucas weekly at the *Punch* Table, would then report back verbally to Methuen. And they were now under pressure: Milne had agreed to a pre-publication serialization of six stories in the monthly journal the *Royal Magazine*, which needed longer print deadlines than had been anticipated. The agents Curtis Brown even interrupted the Shepards' spring holiday in Italy to chivvy him on.

So how did Shepard approach his task of interpreting Milne's inimitable words into a visual image? He almost always drew from models, so Christopher Robin was drawn from life (and photographs) with some minor alterations, Shepard taking as his second model drawings of his own son, Graham, made when Graham was the same age as Christopher Robin. For example, Christopher Robin had rather spindly legs, and so Shepard substituted Graham's. Also, Christopher Robin had rather long hair for a boy, even by the fashion of the

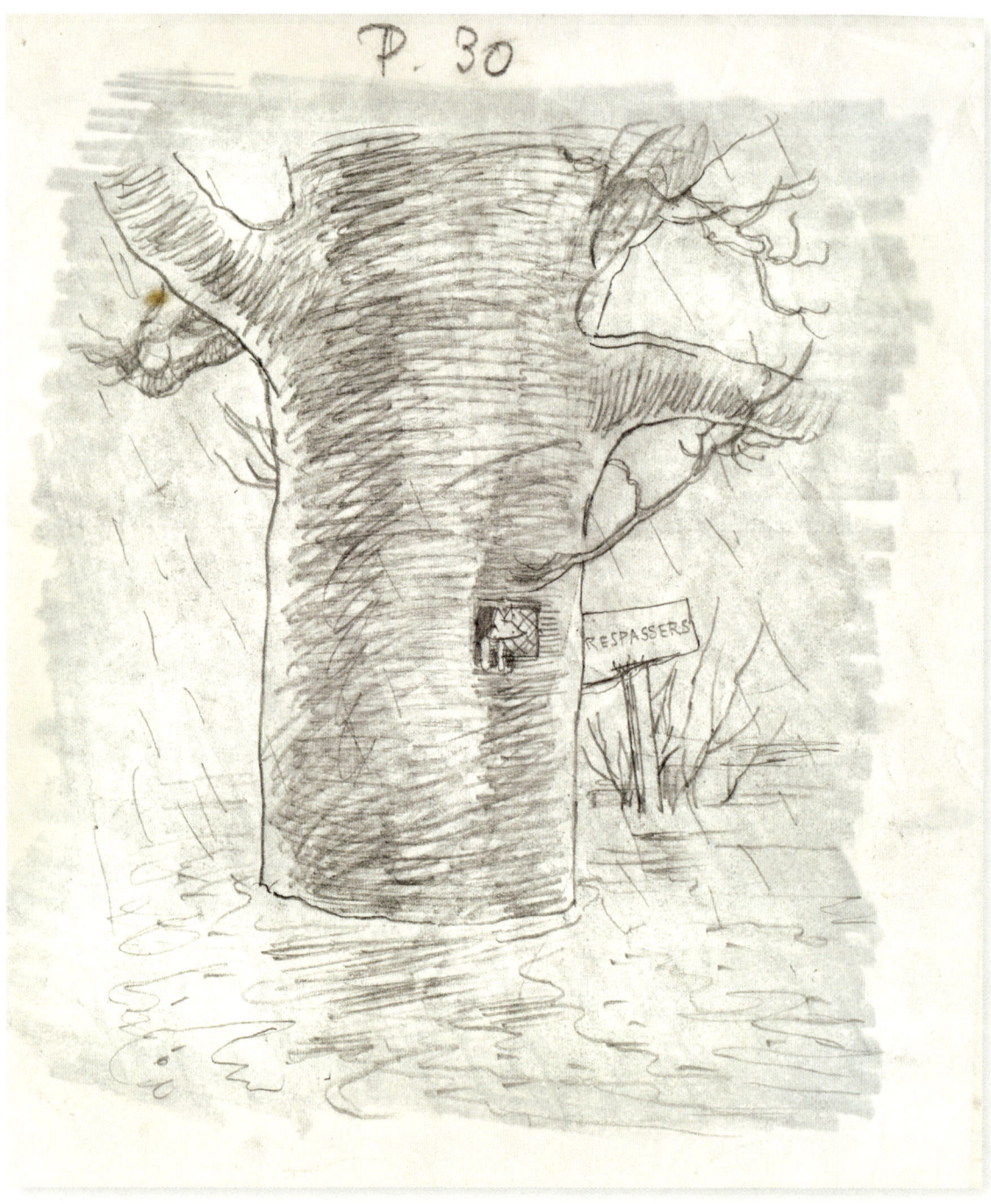

This pencil drawing shows Shepard working up first sketches of the scene where Piglet is caught in rising flood waters into the format for publication. Note the page number at the top of the page, which indicates that he knew exactly where the illustration would sit in the book. See the obviously quick pencil marks, the scribble to create the roundness of the tree trunk and the curved lines to indicate the swirling flood water.

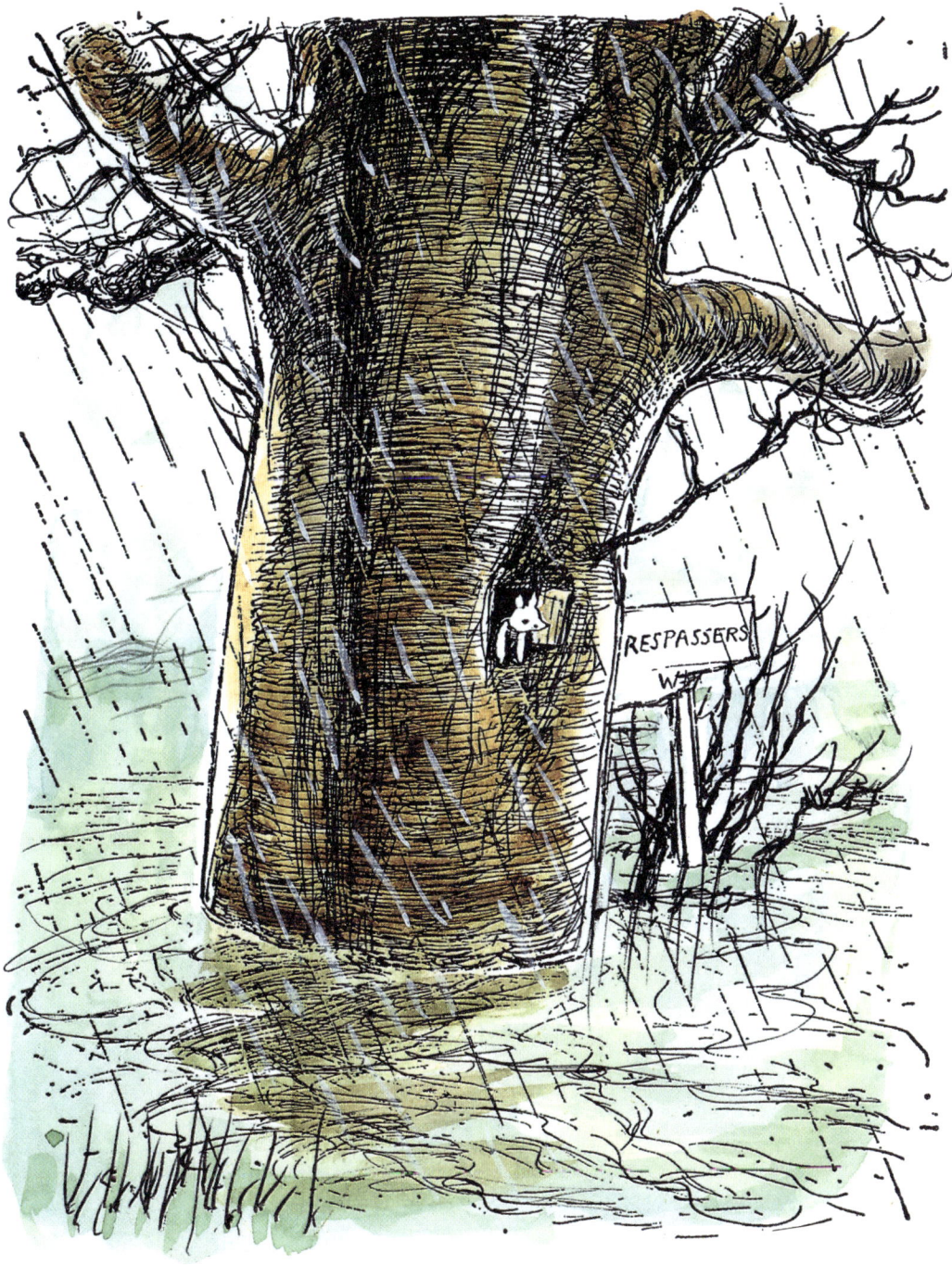

The final coloured version from later editions builds on the earlier pencil drawing. Note the new vertical black lines, giving more definition to the tree trunk, better delineation of the broken 'respassers W' sign, a change to the window beside Piglet in the tree, and the addition of the white marks against the trunk to accentuate the downpour. The green and brown of the water shows both the shadow of the tree and the movement of the water.

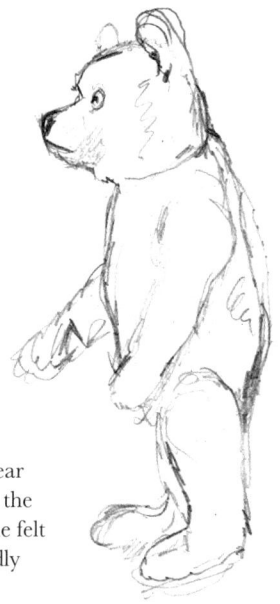

Christopher Robin's Pooh bear
(as he began life) in 1924. In the
end, both Shepard and Milne felt
this bear looked too unfriendly
to be the model for Pooh.

*Christopher Robin's
Pooh bear
(as he began life)
in 1924
EH Shepard*

time, and again, Shepard adjusted this appropriately. Today, seeing photographs
of Graham Shepard and Christopher Robin Milne at the same age, and then
comparing them to the finished drawings in the books, Shepard's pictures seem
to be an amalgam of both boys. There was a similar approach to the bear. Shepard
started off by drawing Christopher Robin's teddy bear, but both he and Milne
felt it looked too gruff and unfriendly. So Shepard turned to Growler, Graham's
old teddy bear, still lying on Graham's bed in Shamley Green, and which he had
already drawn numerous times before. Between the two bears he created the
Winnie-the-Pooh we see in that book, the bear which was to become so famous,
slightly different from the Mr Edward Bear of *When We Were Very Young*.

Shepard then turned to Christopher Robin's other toys which would appear
in the stories. Eeyore had been bought from Harrods for the purpose of being
included in the group of animals. Then there was Piglet, who was a gift from
a Mallord Street neighbour and who was much larger than Milne described in
the stories or Shepard drew: in reality about the same size as Winnie-the-Pooh.
Some other animals, such as the rabbits, came from Milne's imagination.

On one occasion Milne asked Shepard to come to Mallord Street in the late
afternoon to draw Christopher Robin as he played with his toys while Milne
told him a story. Fortunately, this historic visit was independently recorded by
John Macrae from the American publishers Dutton, who happened by chance
to be present and who wrote of the scene, 'Milne sitting on the sofa reading the

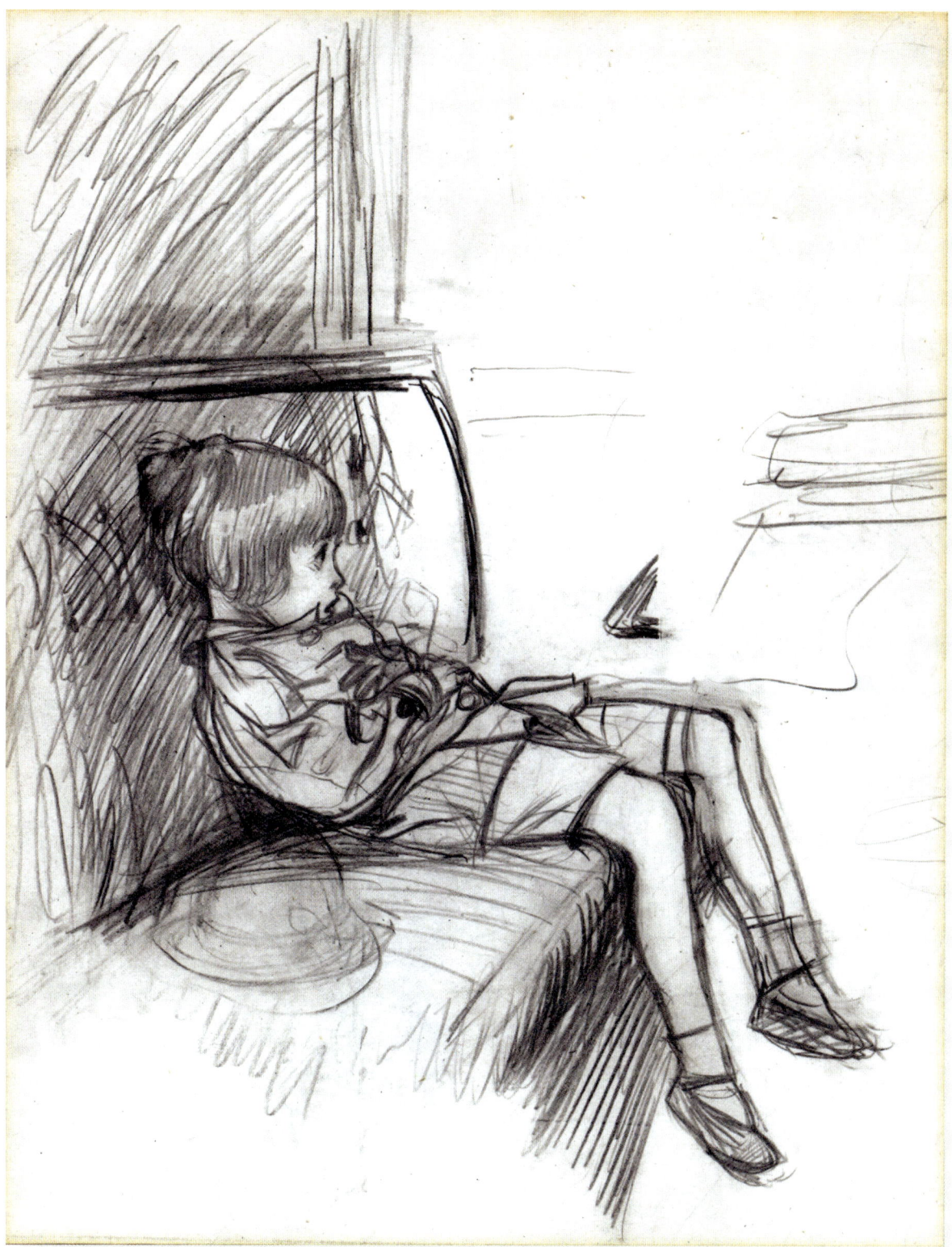

This illustration of a young boy captures the mood perfectly and shows Shepard's gift for figures.

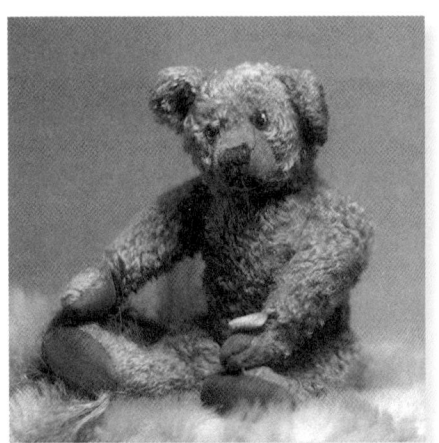

The 'real' Winnie-the-Pooh.

story, Christopher Robin sitting on the floor playing with the characters, which are now famous in *Winnie-the-Pooh*, and, by his side, on the floor, sat E. H. Shepard making sketches for the illustrations which finally went into the book …'

Shepard had the rare ability to marry scenes of the forest with make-believe characters which sit at ease in the real landscape, and to invest in the animals human characteristics that come across as entirely believable.

Having dedicated *When We Were Very Young* to Christopher Robin, Milne now dedicated *Winnie-the-Pooh* in similarly effusive terms to Daphne, perhaps in part to make up for the fact that she had virtually no part in either book.

The new book was published on 14 October 1926 in London and on 21 October in New York. *When We Were Very Young* and the stories published in the *Evening News* and in the *Royal Magazine* had been so successful that everyone involved in the publication expected that the new book would receive a positive reaction from the buying public. What was perhaps more surprising was the almost universal acclaim from critics. Then, as now, reviewers were usually all too willing to find fault with a popular success, but in the case of *Winnie-the-Pooh* they fell over themselves to praise and garland Milne and Shepard. While there were a few who compared it a little less favourably to its predecessor, essentially there was overwhelming agreement that Milne had done it again, creating a book which was magical for children while being equally attractive to grown-ups.

After the sales of *When We Were Very Young*, the publishers were better prepared for high demand for *Winnie-the-Pooh*, so Methuen published a first edition of 32,000 clothbound, with a further 3,000 leatherbound. By the end of 1926, barely ten weeks after the book was launched, Dutton had sold over 150,000 copies. It was another resounding triumph.

Since both Milne and Shepard had already started on the poems and drawings for the next anthology of children's verse, Methuen and Dutton did not have to do much chasing. As with *Winnie-the-Pooh*, Milne threw himself into the production process, spending days at Methuen's offices working on the

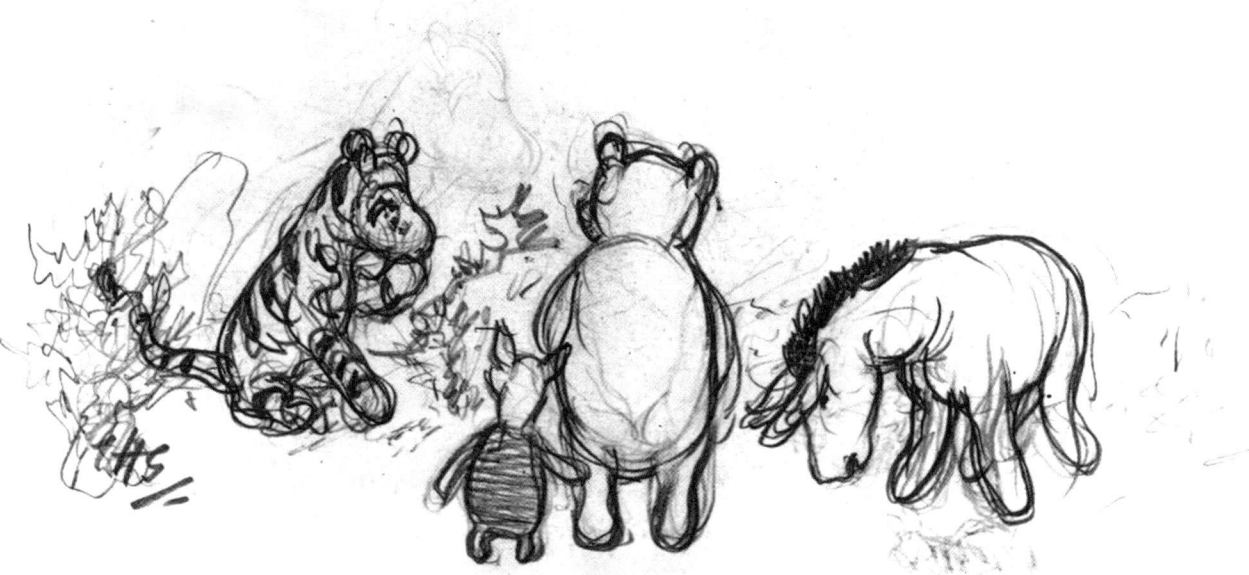

Early pencil sketch, including a new character, Tigger.

layout and setting of the new book. He wrote frequently to Shepard, often with logistics about the space available and the size of the drawings needed. He didn't always get it right. The original plan for the illustrations for the poem 'Forgiven', which featured Alexander Beetle, was that it should be laid out over three pages so that Shepard could draw the beetle scuttling across and over the pages. However, this didn't work out as planned, as, when actually printed, the poem started on a left-hand page rather than a right-hand page, and so the poor beetle appears to be sliced in half between pages one and two, rather than running over the page as it was turned, as originally intended. But these were minor details. Shepard also drew Christopher Robin as older than in *When We Were Very Young* and *Winnie-the-Pooh*, while keeping the other characters the same. This is most noticeable in the poem 'The Morning Walk', which showed Christopher Robin and his friend Anne Darlington on a morning walk in London.

By now, despite Shepard's reservations about having to start all over again with Milne, the two men had established a seamless working relationship, one in which each could often second-guess the other. They became comfortable in suggesting ways in which the other's work could be altered to enhance the final result, with Milne often suggesting a position or size for a drawing which would complement the setting of his text, and Shepard proposing that more or less text in a certain position would improve the visual impact on the page. Many of these exchanges continued to be done by letter. Both men seemed to have a feel for what would work in terms of the reader experience – a novel concept in those days – and the success of the previous two books gave them confidence in their own judgement.

The new book was dedicated to Anne Darlington, a frequent companion of Christopher Robin, and daughter of one of Milne's closest friends, W. A. Darlington, theatre critic of the *Daily Telegraph* and a Chelsea neighbour. Anne and Christopher Robin were, if not inseparable, certainly close friends, as a picture of them both at Cotchford Farm shows. By this time both shared walks to and from school in London, sometimes with Nanny but often with Alan Milne, who regularly made this the start to his day. He used these walks to notice what interested the children, and how they reacted to it. Anne was also considered 'suitable' by Daphne Milne, and the Milnes' friendship with the Darlingtons was close.

Meanwhile, the Shepard family had other concerns to think about than Winnie-the-Pooh. In September 1927, as their new house, Long Meadow, was being finished, Pie went into a London nursing home for a minor and routine nasal operation to relieve some of the symptoms of her asthma. She died under the anaesthetic. This was a totally unexpected catastrophe for the whole family.

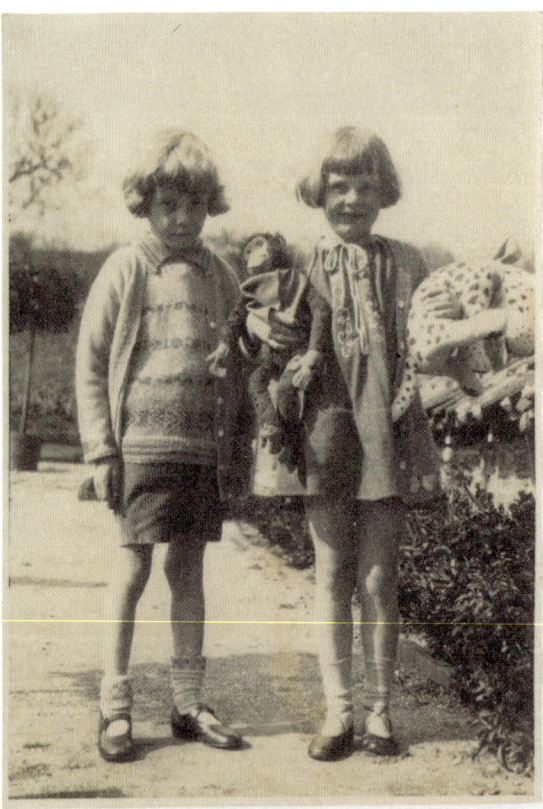

Christopher Robin Milne and his friend Anne Darlington in the garden at Cotchford Farm.

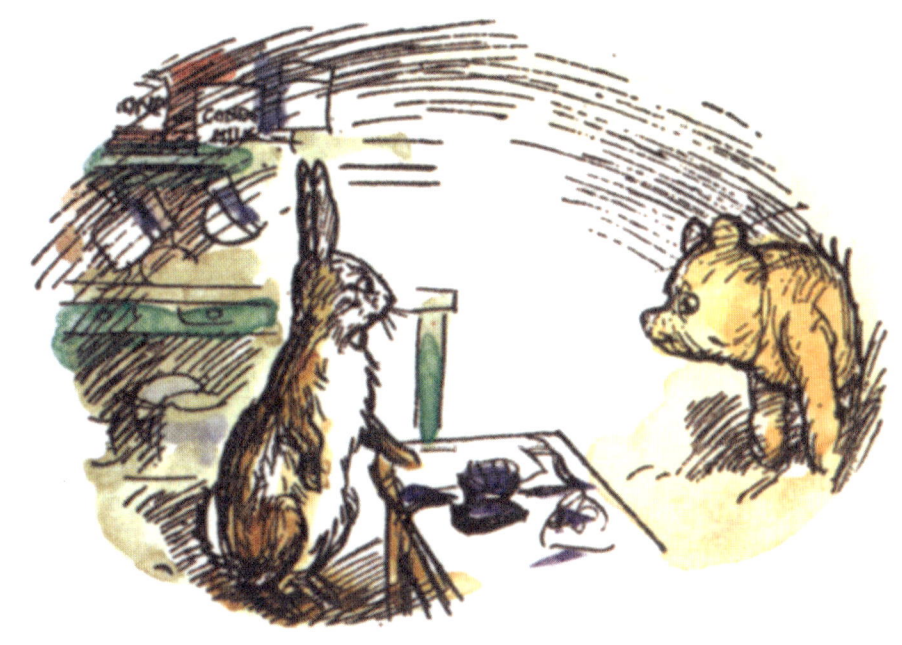

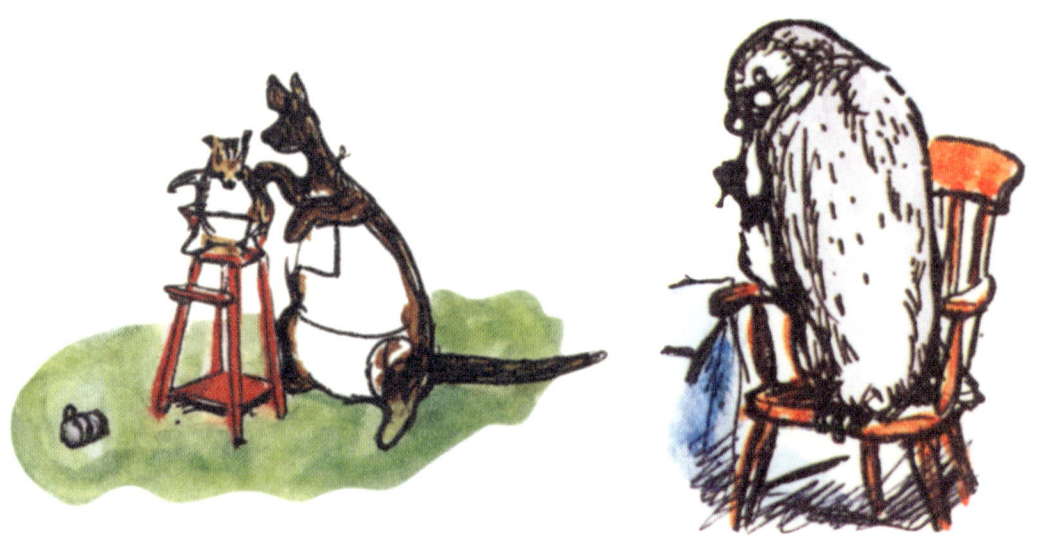

Published illustrations showing Rabbit and Owl, the only two characters not drawn from Christopher Robin's toy box but from the natural world around Cotchford Farm, along with Kanga and Roo, who join Tigger to add some extra fun in the very last book, *The House at Pooh Corner*.

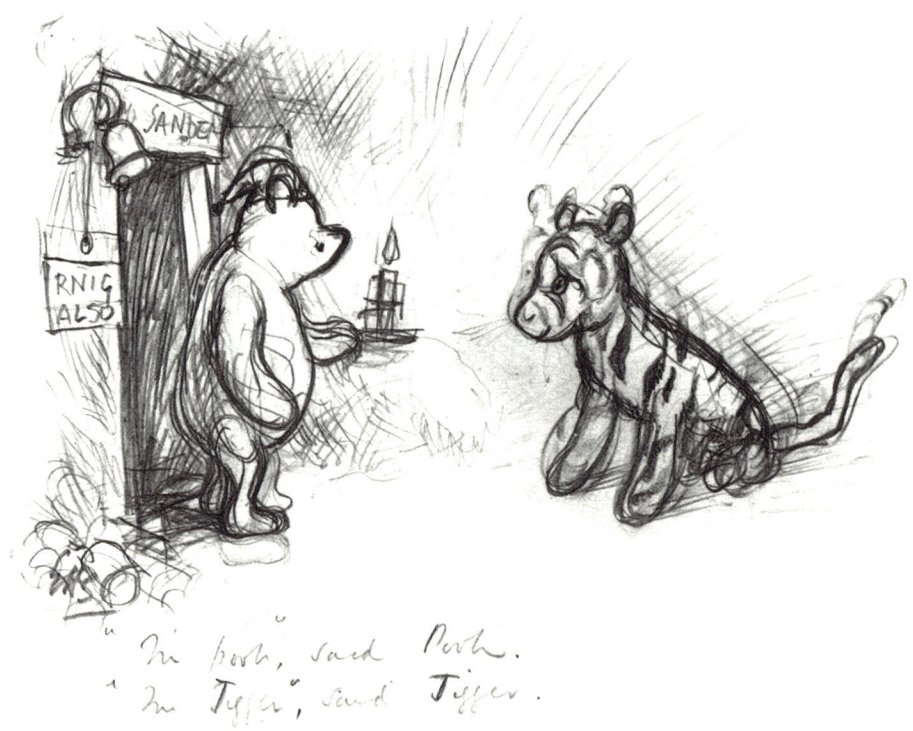

" _Mr pooh_", said Pooh.
" _Mr Tigger_", said Tigger.

Tigger has always been one of the most popular and endearing characters in the Winnie-the-Pooh stories, even though he only appeared in the final book, *The House at Pooh Corner*. Even A. A. Milne got over-excited, telling Shepard that he couldn't wait to see the drawings of Tigger. Shepard usually drew Tigger a little higher than the other characters in a drawing, and often with a paw slightly raised, to give the impression of energy and bounciness, and we can see him experimenting with this in the pencil sketch above. In the final, coloured version, the addition of the horizontal lines conveys this effectively.

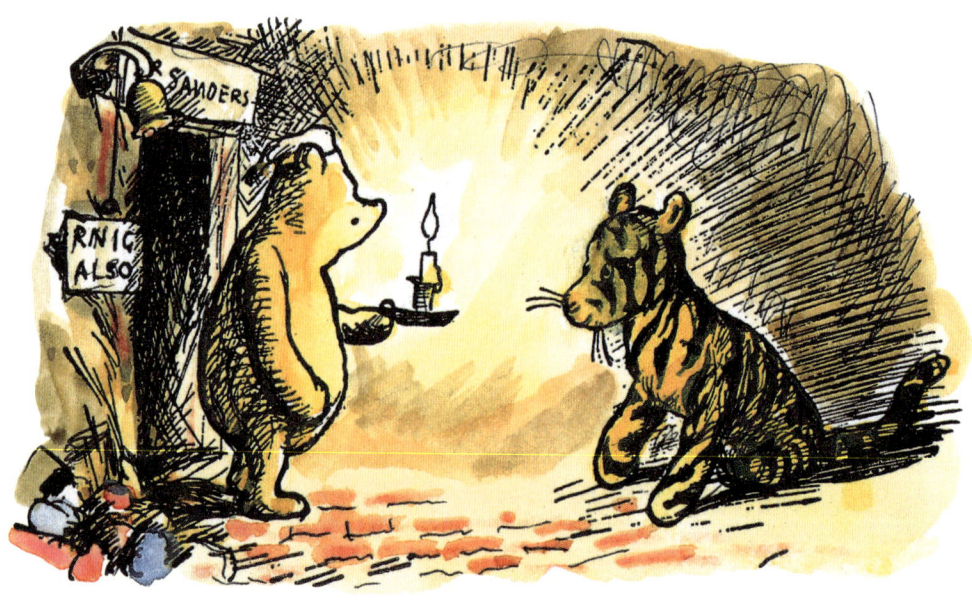

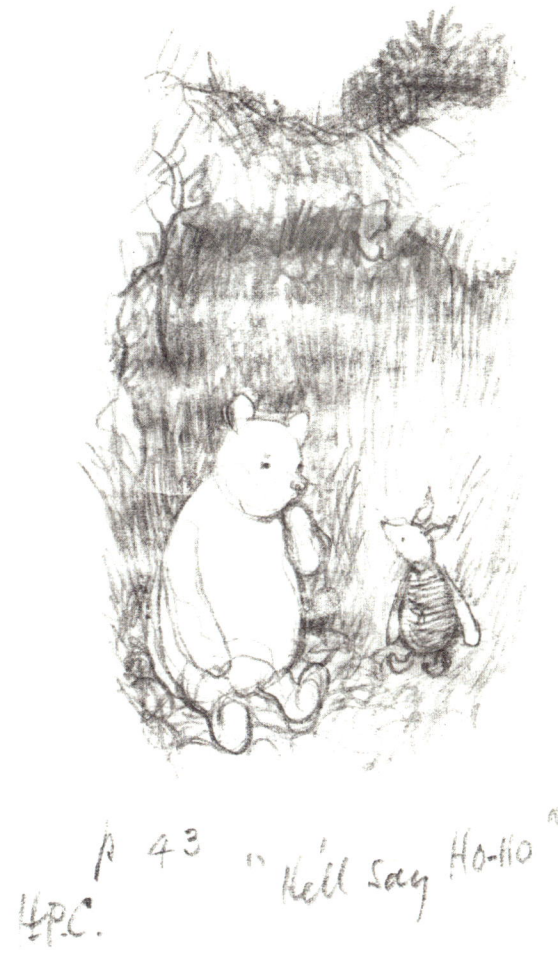

P 43 "He'll say Ho-Ho"

4 P.C.

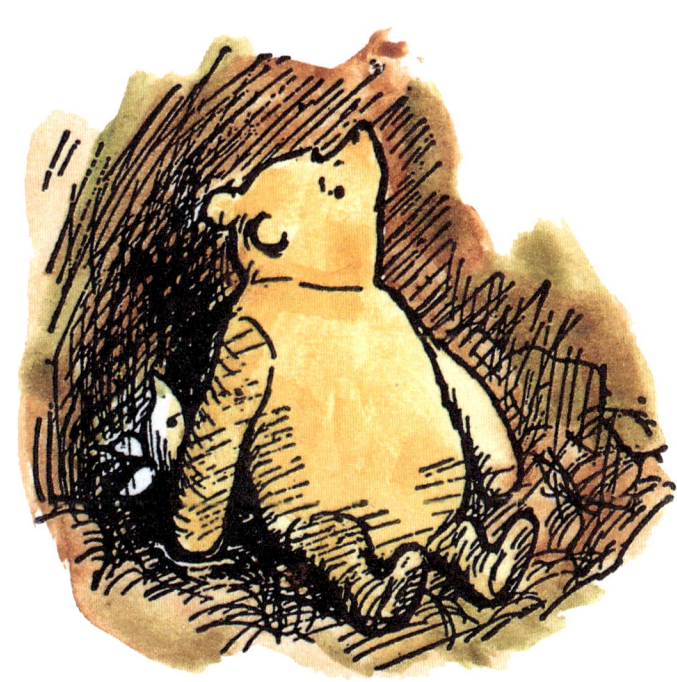

When Pooh and Piglet fell into Piglet's Heffalump Trap, Shepard initially drew a confused Pooh with his left paw up to his mouth and Piglet looking anxiously towards him for inspiration (above). However, in the final illustration (below) Pooh lands right on top of the hapless Piglet, leaving him unable to tell where Piglet's voice is coming from.

For Shepard, Pie had been his soulmate and companion since he had been a student; he had never loved anyone else and, certainly in the early years of their marriage, she had also been a maternal figure to him, to some extent replacing the much-loved mother he had lost at such a tender age.

The next few months went by in a blur. Shepard went through the motions, trying to comfort and support his grieving children, particularly Mary, who was only seventeen, with the support of his sister, Ethel, as well as attempting to maintain his work practice and deal with his own emotions, which he kept very much to himself. There was much to keep him busy and occupied, not least the completion of the new house. This was a heavy workload but, along with the support of family and friends, it helped carry him through that tragic time.

Now We Are Six was published simultaneously in London and New York on 13 October 1927, now following an established pattern. The timing allowed the initial flurry of reviews and publicity to drive sales over the Thanksgiving weekend in the United States, and to catch the lucrative Christmas market on both sides of the pond. And while the critical response was not quite so emphatic as for *When We Were Very Young*, this was generally acknowledged as being because Milne had set the bar so high that it was always going to be almost impossible to maintain the standard of his first Pooh book. So while reviews were generally positive, they actually made little difference to the public's reaction as the pre-publicity and promotion almost guaranteed huge sales. Methuen's initial print run was 50,000 copies, but this was again a significant under-estimate of demand, as sales roared away. The book sold 94,000 copies by the end of the year in Britain alone, while in New York, Dutton had pre-orders for 90,000 copies by publication day itself.

Milne and Shepard had created what seemed to be an unstoppable appetite for their works for children. There were queues at bookshops, many people bought multiple copies of the book, and there was a wave of popular enthusiasm for it. What is perhaps interesting to note is that *Now We Are Six* sold more copies in six weeks than all the sales of *Winnie-the-Pooh* over the previous year, and that the two volumes of poetry consistently outsold the Pooh stories until after the Second World War.

The personal publicity bandwagon was also rolling along. Daphne was in her element, being photographed by society photographers, with and without

Christopher Robin; breathlessly being interviewed by fashionable magazines on both sides of the Atlantic in the nursery at Mallord Street; taking Christopher Robin to a public 'Pooh' tea-party and arranging for him to record some of the Fraser-Simson songs onto a gramophone record. Milne reported that he tried to prevent this, leading to an argument between them, but whatever the true facts were, the recording was indeed made. Christopher Milne later recalled that he had been asked to sing in a 'Pooh' voice. His singing was only adequate for a child of his age, and so the recording itself, let alone the fact that the record was put on sale, was considered by many to be a step too far. Christopher's own cousins felt that this was inappropriate and smacked of exploitation. Not many years later, Christopher, who had a very tough experience being bullied at both his boarding schools, recalled his contemporaries in the adjacent study at Stowe School playing the record of him singing 'Vespers' over and over again, to his fury and mortification. He said it was 'intensely painful', and eventually he smashed the record and scattered the pieces across a field.

Daphne Milne joined in the whole make-believe experience around the Pooh stories, telling interviewers about her experiences of the Hundred Acre Wood and of the toys, as if she was trying to include herself in the world created by her husband about their son.

By this point Milne had had enough. What he considered to be just a temporary diversion from his main interests in writing books and plays for adults had gone on long enough. And while he had made a good deal of money from it, he felt it was time to move on. As a professional writer, and a man of the world in literary circles, he probably realized that it would be almost impossible to maintain the standard of the first books indefinitely and that by announcing that his next children's book would be his last, he would simultaneously guarantee further enormous sales as well as secure the reputation of his work for children. Doubtless Curtis Brown, Methuen and Dutton were disappointed when he made this decision, as the next book would obviously be the last egg that this particular golden goose would lay. But they realized and understood that Milne was definite in his decision, and that he would not change his mind. No one appears to have significantly pressed him on this point. And, by making the announcement in advance, and indeed in the introduction of the final book itself, it made a fine finale to a remarkable contribution to children's literature.

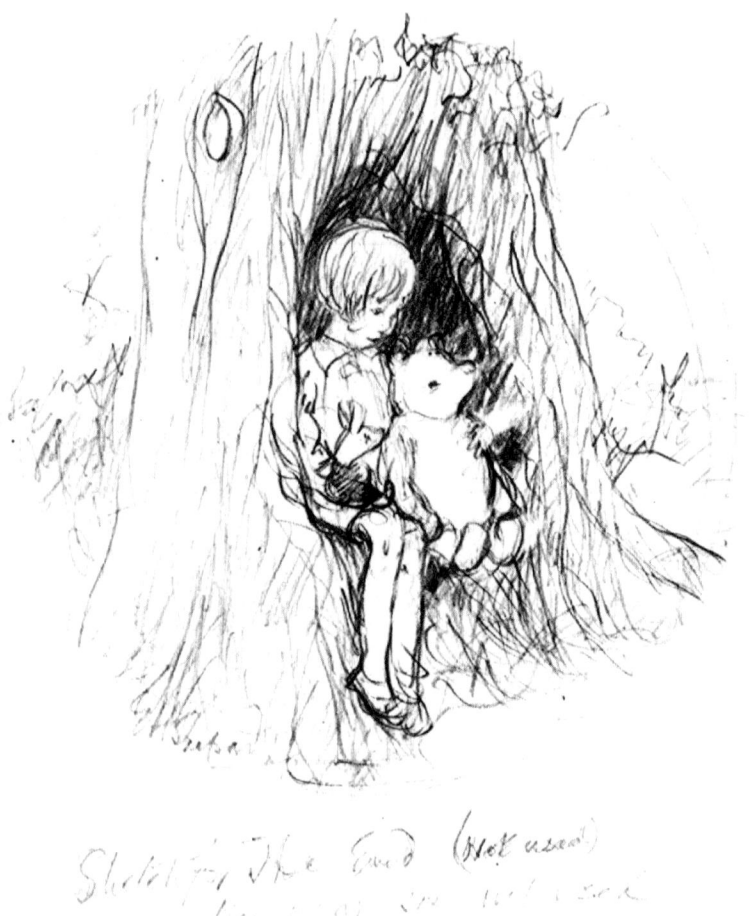

Sketch for the End (not used)

This sketch of Christopher Robin, Pooh and Piglet in the hollow of a tree was initially proposed as the closing illustration for *Now We Are Six* but was felt to be perhaps a little too static and restrained, so Shepard created the well-known image of them jumping in the air as a more fitting end to the penultimate book of the series.

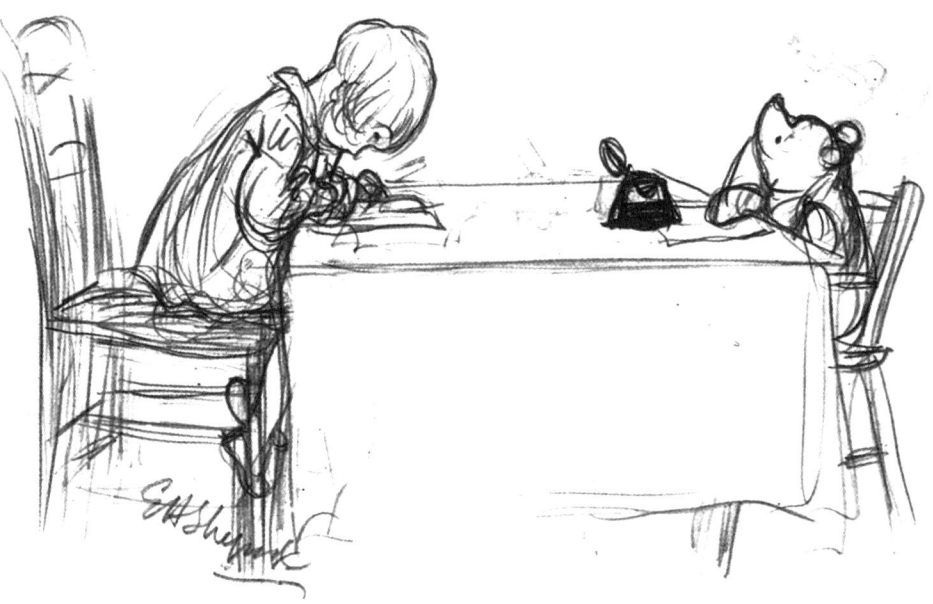

Shepard had a wonderful talent for giving animals human characteristics and for making them believable in a domestic setting, but he had to work hard at this. This pencil drawing shows him trying to create the impression of friendship when the two characters are separated by a table, and the lines around Pooh show how Shepard is experimenting to see how he can most effectively convey that sense of togetherness.

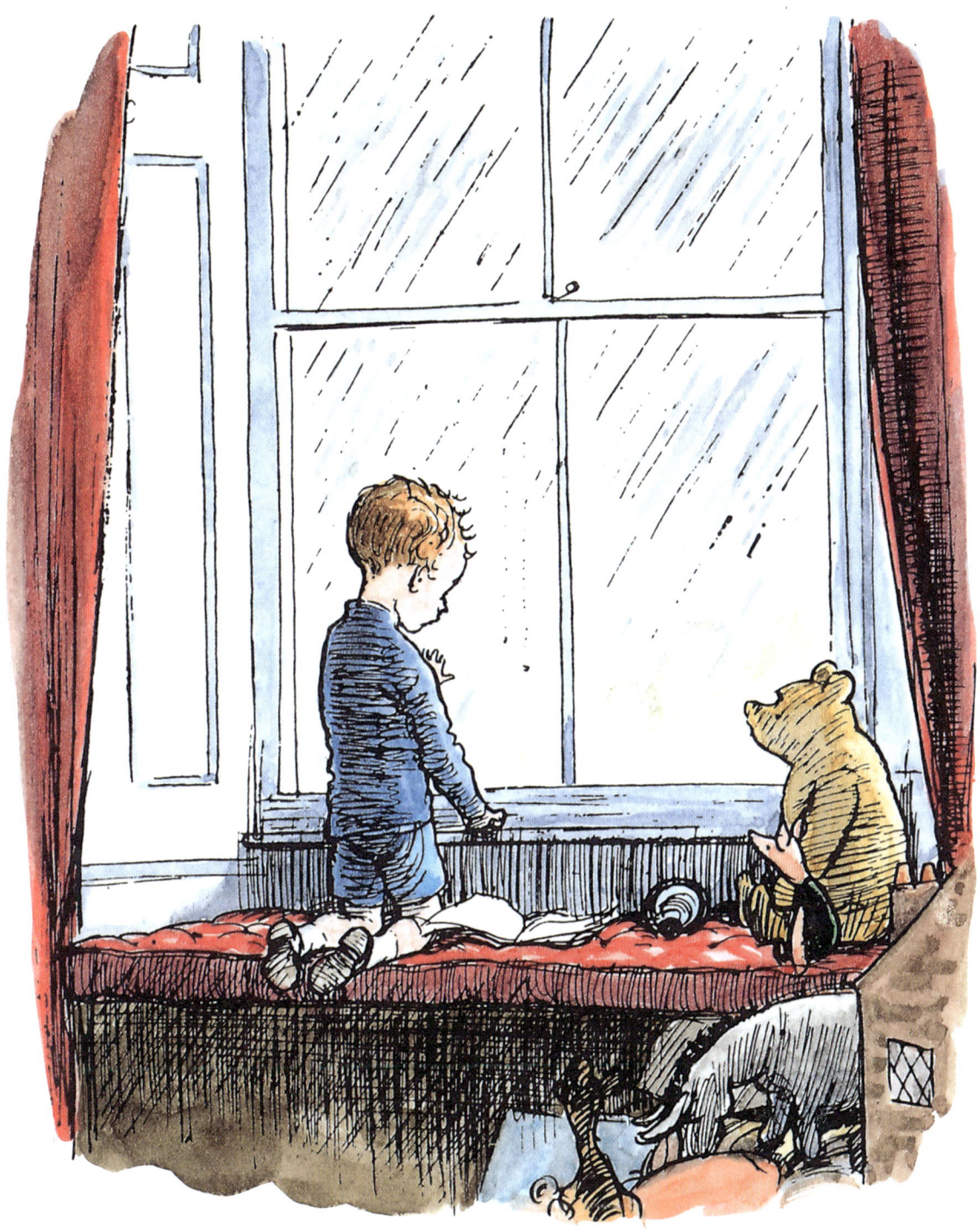

In contrast to the Winnie-the-Pooh stories, which are all set in the Hundred Acre Wood, many of Milne's poems in the two volumes of verse are set in London, and here 'Waiting at the Window', featured in *Now We Are Six*, shows Christopher Robin watching raindrops race to the bottom of the windowpane in the nursery of their London house in Chelsea, while Pooh, Piglet, Eeyore and others look on, as he wonders what to do on a rainy day.

Even before the publication of *Now We Are Six* both Milne and Shepard had started work on what would become *The House at Pooh Corner*. Milne was certainly not resting on any laurels. The introduction of new characters, and most particularly that of Tigger, was an inspiration, and Milne himself got quite excited about it, telling Shepard that he 'couldn't wait' to see the first sketches of

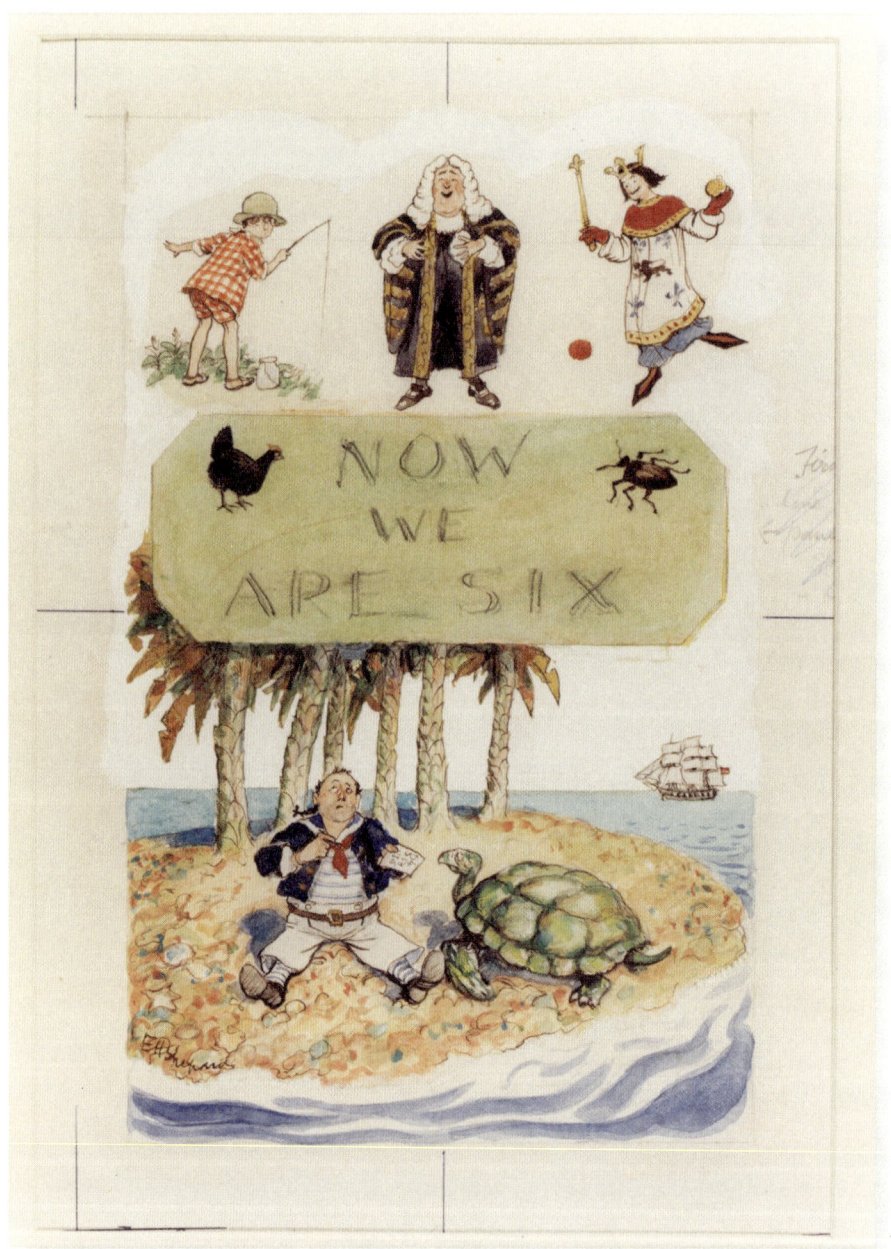

An early draft of a dust jacket from the 1950s or 1960s.

Tigger. Shepard also seems to have enjoyed this new addition and drew several preparatory sketches, experimenting with Tigger's limbs and movement. He developed a clever trick of drawing the front part of Tigger slightly higher than the back, and above the other animals, to give the effect of 'bounce', which it did very convincingly. Tigger made an immediate impact on the existing cast of characters, bringing a youthful energy and boundless enthusiasm to the Hundred Acre Wood.

The second, and perpetually enduring, addition to the stories was the new game of Poohsticks, now an established institution across the whole world. The original manuscript for *The House at Pooh Corner*, written in Milne's careful handwriting, shows that Poohsticks was not his first name for this pastime. Unfortunately, he heavily crossed out the original word on the manuscript, so it is difficult to see what it was, although the end would appear to be '… idge' – implying that it ended in 'bridge'. Shepard drew multiple versions of the bridge, based on the original wooden structure (since replaced several times owing to understandable wear and tear). Sometimes he included a stone base, sometimes a wooden one, until at last he came up with the one included in one of the most famous images of all, that of Christopher Robin and Pooh Bear leaning over the bridge playing Poohsticks. Seventy-five years later, London's *Evening Standard* newspaper recreated the image, with a photograph showing Shepard's great-great-grandson at the same age as Christopher Robin playing Poohsticks on the famous bridge with his own teddy bear.

The Winnie-the-Pooh publishing phenomenon was now a well-oiled machine and followed a successful pattern. Milne once again took a principal role in the production process, showing a keen interest in Shepard's initial sketches. Some of the scenes took place in the floods and in the snow, and Shepard experimented by putting some of the characters, notably Winnie-the-Pooh himself and Piglet, into clothes. But Milne did not feel this added to the appeal, perhaps feeling that it was straying too far across the line by making the animals seem too human. Whatever the case, the use of clothing was minimal, but in later years it was interesting that one of the most recognizable images of Disney's cartoon version of Pooh was the bear in a red T-shirt, and he has since been immortalized in Disney merchandise wearing this T-shirt. But this was all for the future. At the time, the publishing process continued as usual through 1928.

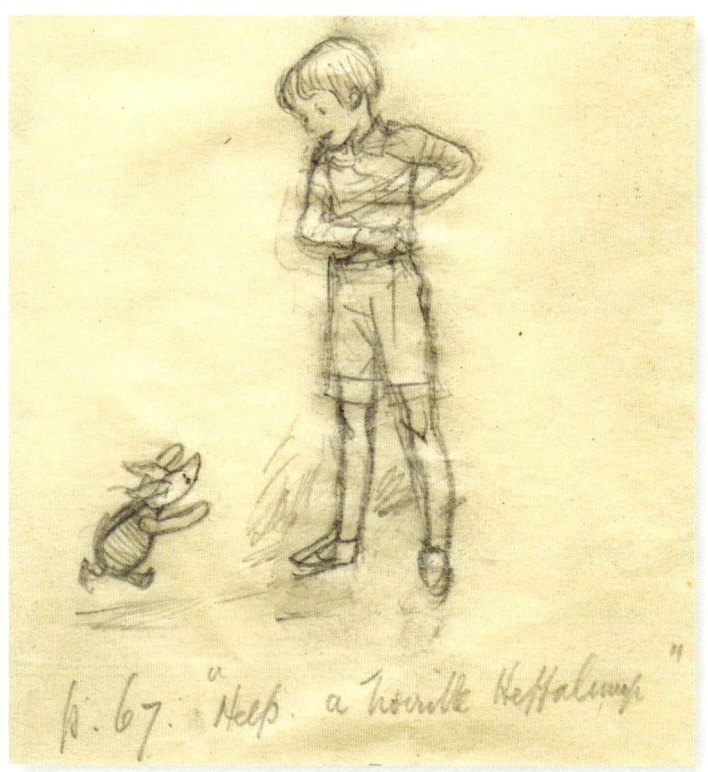

p. 67. "Help, a horrible Heffalump"

This pencil drawing from *c.* 1925 was a draft to share with A. A. Milne and shows the scene from *Winnie-the-Pooh* when Piglet is running, terrified, to get help from Christopher Robin as he is convinced that he has seen the 'horrible Heffalump', caught in the trap dug by him and Winnie-the-Pooh. See how Shepard is showing Christopher Robin as taller, and more of a boy than in the previous book, *When We Were Very Young*.

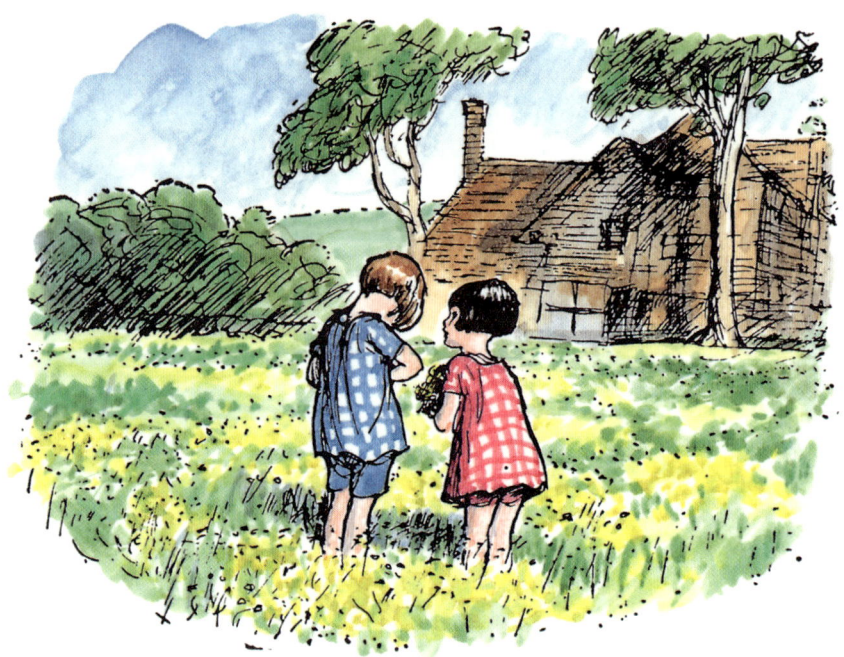

A charming coloured-in version of the illustration for 'Buttercup Days' from the second volume of poetry, *Now We Are Six*, which shows a boy and a girl in checked smocks in a field of buttercups. This picture is based on a series of photographs of Christopher Robin Milne and his friend Anne Darlington taken at Cotchford Farm, near Hartfield in Sussex, the Milnes' country home. Anne was the daughter of W. A. Darlington, a close neighbour in London and friend of A. A. Milne, who was the theatre critic of the London newspaper the *Daily Telegraph*. Cotchford Farm still looks very like this today.

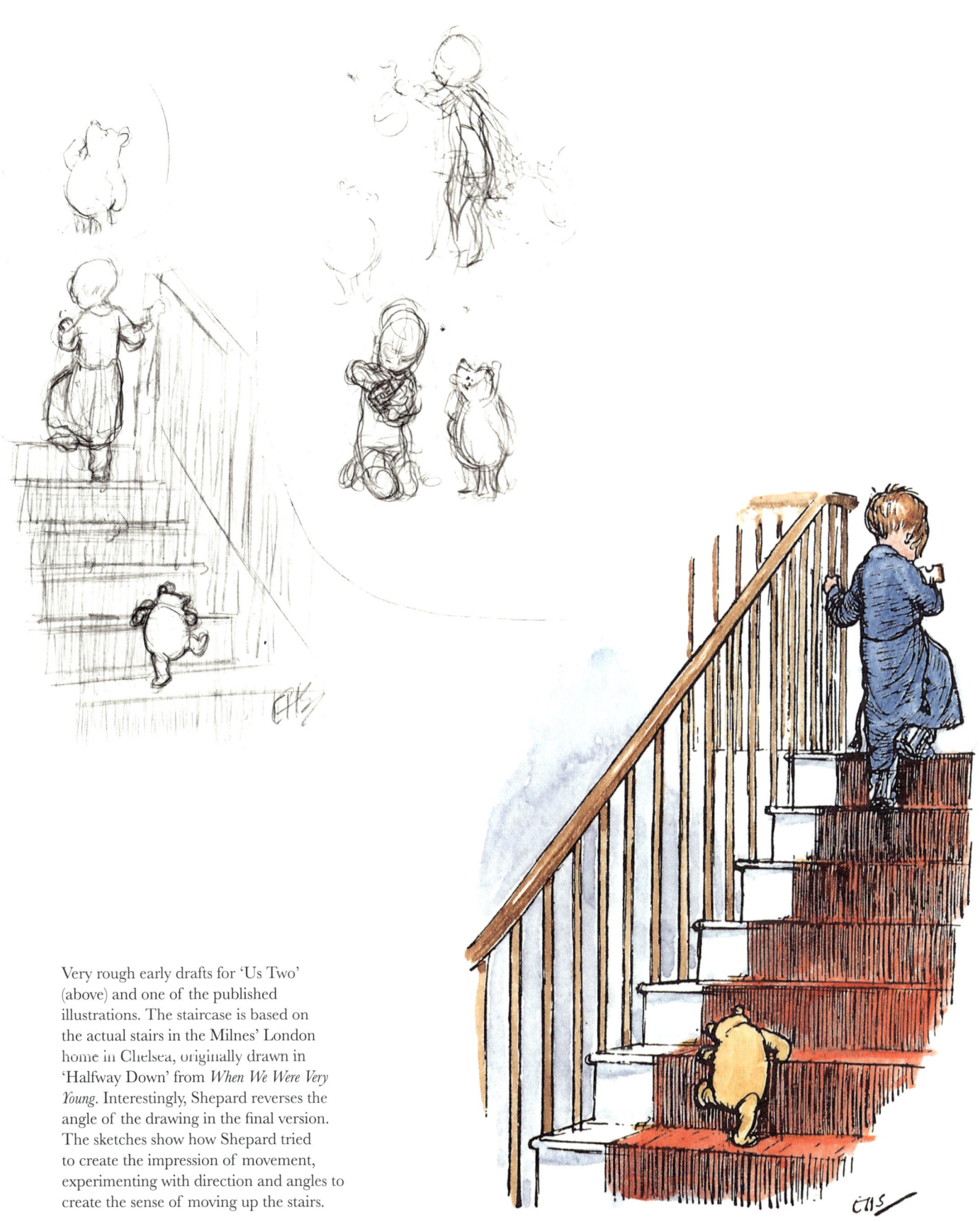

Very rough early drafts for 'Us Two' (above) and one of the published illustrations. The staircase is based on the actual stairs in the Milnes' London home in Chelsea, originally drawn in 'Halfway Down' from *When We Were Very Young*. Interestingly, Shepard reverses the angle of the drawing in the final version. The sketches show how Shepard tried to create the impression of movement, experimenting with direction and angles to create the sense of moving up the stairs.

Once again, *The House at Pooh Corner* was published simultaneously in London and in New York, on 11 October 1928. It was welcomed with renewed enthusiasm and acclaim, with widespread regret that this was to be the last outing for Christopher Robin, Winnie-the-Pooh and all the other characters from the Hundred Acre Wood. This time Methuen printed 75,000 copies for publication day and announced that *When We Were Very Young* had sold 179,000 copies, *Winnie-the-Pooh* 96,000, and *Now We Are Six* 109,000. Dutton's figures were significantly higher across the board. The realization that *The House at Pooh Corner* was the last in the series also drove up sales of the previous three books. Milne and Shepard both drew a sigh of relief. It had been an extraordinary experience, and it had changed both their lives.

For Alan Milne, his active involvement with the Winnie-the-Pooh books ended in 1928, and he wrote no more for children, delegating most of the inevitable administrative and management matters to Curtis Brown, then turning with relief to what he considered to be his 'real' work.

Shepard was in a different position. The huge success of the books meant that there were multiple new editions in different sizes, translations into different languages and constant demands from publishers, no longer simply Methuen and Dutton, for illustrations to be resized, amended or re-set for a different page layout. Later, as technology made colour printing possible, publishers initially wanted spot colour, and then in due course full-colour illustrations. These were sometimes achieved by colouring in the black-and-white originals, and sometimes by completely new colour drawings. Despite his reservations about Disney's 1960s reinterpretation of his original drawings, for the rest of his working life Shepard spent a proportion of his time working on Winnie-the-Pooh and, with some allowance for understandable frustration, professed himself to be fond of that silly bear.

Alan Milne was already wealthy before Winnie-the-Pooh, so to him the money from the books was relatively inconsequential. However, Shepard's twenty per cent of the royalties provided him with a welcome regular income. In addition, the prestige of having created the 'decorations' for the books, and the widespread awareness of his creative and artistic abilities, meant that he was in great demand as an artist, illustrator and cartoonist for the remainder of his life.

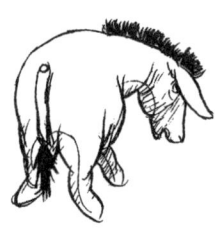

CHAPTER SIX

Poop! Poop! *The Wind in the Willows*

Kenneth Grahame, who was born in Edinburgh in 1859, had a successful and distinguished career at the Bank of England, culminating in the prestigious position of Secretary, before deciding to take early retirement, officially due to ill-health, but which allowed him to concentrate on his writing. In parallel with his day job at the Bank he had been writing short stories all his adult life, and from his mid-twenties onwards some of these were published in periodicals. In 1895 he published *The Golden Age* and in 1898 *Dream Days*, both volumes containing some new and some previously published short stories about the lives of children. The stories were unsentimental and realistic, unusual for the time, and both books were well reviewed and sold successfully.

There was then a pause, possibly due to his increased responsibilities and pressure of work at the Bank, but also connected to his change in personal circumstances. Having been a bachelor until his fortieth year, in 1899 he married, rather unexpectedly, Elspeth Thompson, and they had a son, Alastair, in 1900. Grahame told the boy bedtime stories about animals which inhabited the banks of the river Thames, an area where he had spent much of his own childhood when he lived with his grandmother at Cookham Dean in Berkshire. The fact that *The Wind in the Willows* was clearly inspired by his own experiences was later confirmed by Grahame when he said that, 'The part of my brain I used from four till seven can never have altered.' His return to live in the Thames Valley after many years in London re-awoke those memories.

Grahame wrote up these bedtime stories into a series of adventures as *The Wind in the Willows*, which was published in 1908, but only after some effort from Grahame, as initially a number of publishers turned it down. Even Methuen, which finally and somewhat reluctantly agreed to publish the book, only did so on the basis that they would not give Grahame an advance. This pessimism on the part of publishers seemed to be justified, as the reviews were unenthusiastic at best. Arthur Ransome, later to write another set of highly successful children's books of which the best known is *Swallows and Amazons*, wrote, 'If we judge the book by its aim, it is a failure.' Interestingly, there were to be a number of connections between Arthur Ransome and both Milne and Shepard. Reviewing *Swallows and Amazons* for the *Manchester Guardian* on the book's publication in 1930, at about the time Milne was recommending Shepard to Grahame as a possible illustrator, Malcolm Muggeridge wrote:

> *'Mr. Ransome has the same magical power that Lewis Carroll had of being the child in terms of himself. He never talks down; never finds it necessary to be patronising or sentimental. And sentimentality is the most terrible pitfall that besets those who venture into the world of play … Captain John and Mate Susan, and Able-seaman Titty, and Ship's Boy Roger are not at all like Christopher Robin. They are children. And the story of their adventures on a little island in the middle of an English lake is thrilling just because it is not fabulous … It is make-believe such as all children have indulged in: even children who have not been so fortunate as to have a lake and a boat and an island but only a backyard amongst the semis of Suburbia.'*

This implied criticism of Christopher Robin and the Winnie-the-Pooh stories for being sentimental was rare at a time when Pooh-mania was at its zenith, and indeed even at the time *Swallows and Amazons* itself was considered by some to be insufferably goody-goody.

These reviews were all incidental to the fact that the reading public hugely enjoyed *The Wind in the Willows*. Word of mouth led to gradually escalating sales, and over time the book became a great success, recognized as Grahame's finest work. Despite the initial critical mauling and slow start, Methuen was to publish a further eleven editions of *The Wind in the Willows* by 1921, and the book has never been out of print.

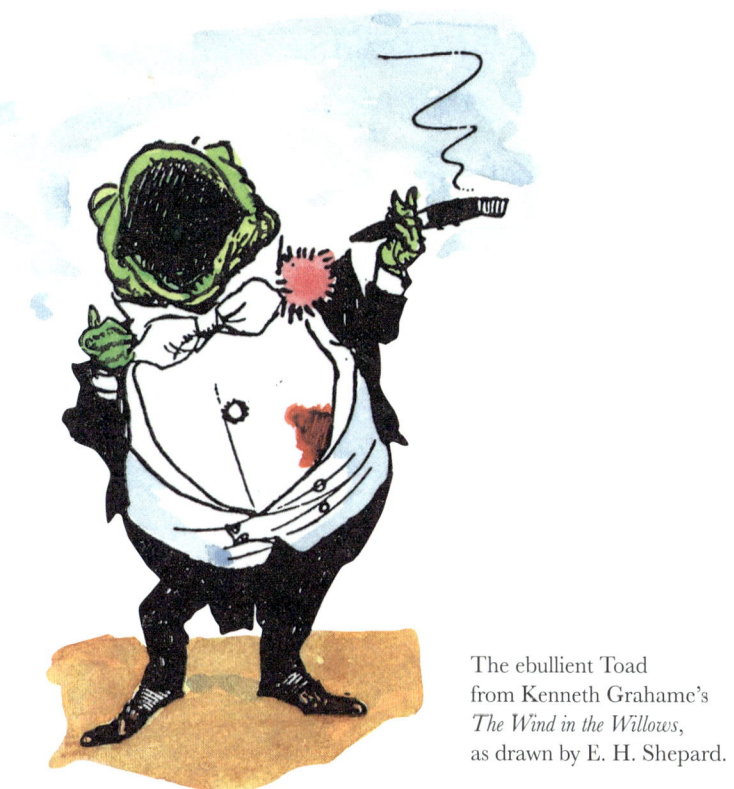

The ebullient Toad
from Kenneth Grahame's
The Wind in the Willows,
as drawn by E. H. Shepard.

Both A. A. Milne and E. H. Shepard were introduced to *The Wind in the Willows* early on, Milne because as assistant editor of *Punch* he was aware of Grahame's short stories, and Shepard because he read the book to his children. Milne was enchanted by the book, and always said that he felt it was the best children's book ever written. In due course, when he had a son of his own, *The Wind in the Willows* became a staple in the nursery at Mallord Street. In his autobiography, the occupant of that nursery, Christopher Robin Milne, wrote of *The Wind in the Willows*:

'A book that we all greatly loved and admired and read aloud or alone, over and over and over: The Wind in the Willows. *This book is, in a way, two separate books put into one. There are, on the one hand, those chapters concerned with the adventures of Toad; and on the other hand there are those chapters that explore human emotions – the emotions of fear, nostalgia, awe, wanderlust. My mother was drawn to the second group, of which "The Piper at the Gates of Dawn" was her favourite, read to me again and again with always, towards the end, the catch in the voice and the long pause to find her handkerchief and blow her nose. My father, on his side, was so captivated by the first group that he turned these chapters into the children's play,* Toad of Toad Hall. *In this play one emotion only is allowed to creep in: nostalgia.'*

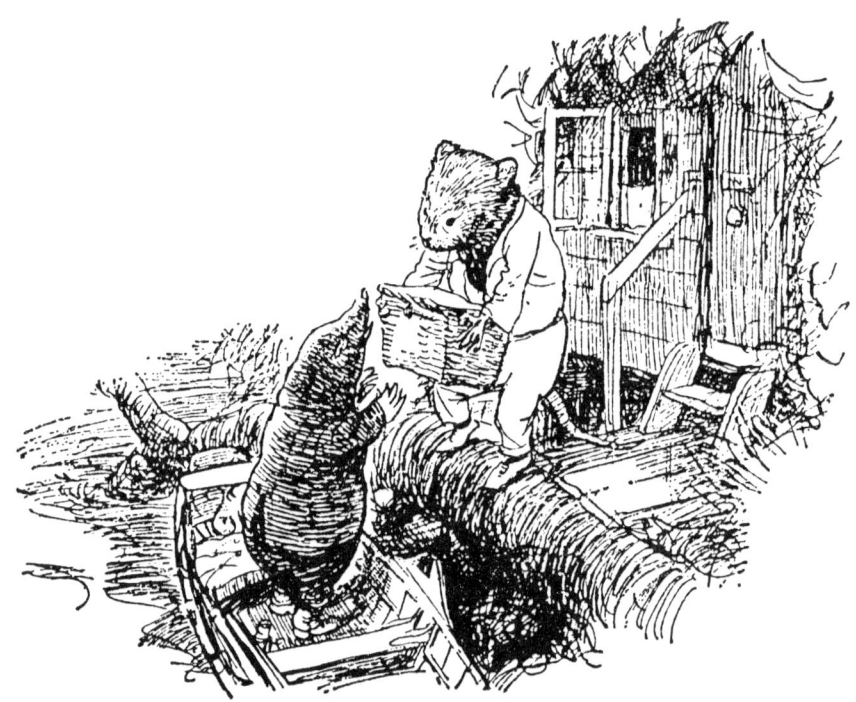

One of Shepard's original black-and-white illustrations for *The Wind in the Willows*.

The literary agency Curtis Brown acted for Grahame, as well as for both Milne and Shepard, and were keen to capitalize on the increasing success of *The Wind in the Willows* by arranging for a play based on the book. They tried to interest various theatrical producers but, perhaps somewhat surprisingly given the acknowledged success and popularity of the book, there was a marked reluctance to take it on, and certainly not without a script endorsed by Grahame. Curtis Brown therefore next suggested to Grahame that a play could be created from his original stories, hoping that he would be inspired to do this himself. Grahame, however, published no more in his lifetime. He suffered a deep tragedy in 1920 when Alastair died at the age of nineteen, and the overwhelming sadness which followed convinced Curtis Brown that Grahame would never write the play himself.

Consequently, Curtis Brown turned to another of its distinguished clients, one whom they knew had a high regard for Grahame and a boyish enthusiasm for *The Wind in the Willows*, which he constantly pressed on friends and acquaintances as being the finest children's book he had ever read. Alan Milne was only too delighted by the suggestion that he should adapt it into a play. In November 1921 he replied enthusiastically to Curtis Brown, saying that

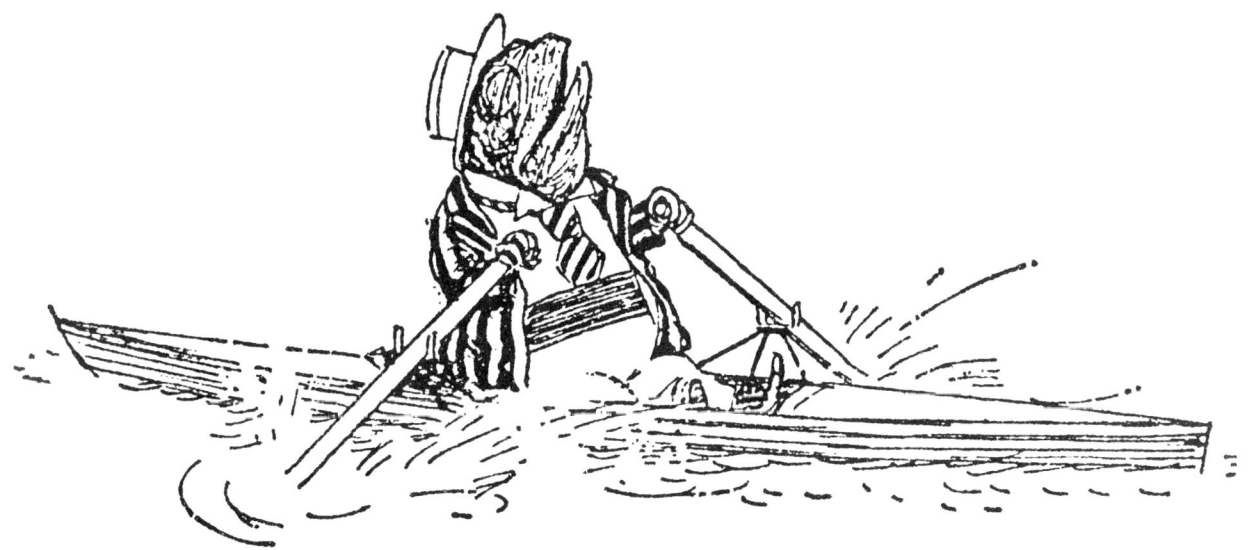

Shepard's ability to pick out the human traits in the animals he drew was remarkable.

he thought it should be a children's play and possibly with some music. His admiration of Grahame was so strong that he refused Curtis Brown's initial financial offer, settling for one to his own disadvantage and in favour of Grahame.

As for Grahame, Milne's very public support for his book and reputation at the time as one of the country's leading contemporary playwrights likely swayed him towards the idea. In January 1922, for example, Milne had no less than three plays running simultaneously in the West End of London alone. Nonetheless, although the idea was first mooted in 1921, it was to be 1929 before Milne's interpretation of *The Wind in the Willows* would be first performed as *Toad of Toad Hall*.

The problem was that no sooner had Milne sat down to approach the task than he realized that he might have, if not bitten off more than he could chew, certainly underestimated the difficulties of adapting a book with two very different themes. These were, essentially, the adventures of Toad and a series of morality tales with Ratty and Mole at their heart. The two strands were going to be extremely challenging to reconcile on stage. He also had to deal with the problem that Grahame had the characters moving from animal-like behaviour to human behaviour almost chapter by chapter, and it was going to be difficult to present these characters on stage in a believable way. After some experimentation, Milne sensibly decided simply to omit those sections of the original book which would be almost impossible to dramatize, and to focus instead on the adventures of Toad. Hence the title of his play was just *Toad of Toad Hall*. Milne tried to keep the dialogue as close to Grahame's original as he could, later noting that even he struggled at times to recall which were his words, and which were Grahame's.

There was a further long gap between Milne finishing the play and its first performance in Liverpool in 1929. However, in the end the critics generally liked it, some effusively, with comments such as 'extremely adept adaptation of a difficult original' and 'as funny as anything in *Alice's Adventures in Wonderland*', although as usual there were a few detractors. Reviewing the Liverpool premiere, *The Stage* magazine commented that Milne had succeeded brilliantly in putting Grahame's characters on the stage but thought the play might be over the heads of a children's audience, having 'so much in it to appeal to the adult mind'. Interestingly, the *Daily Telegraph*'s theatre critic, Milne's old friend W. A. Darlington, drew comparison between the Wild Wood and the Hundred Acre Wood, even though Milne had begun work on *Toad of Toad Hall* well before he had started on the Winnie-the-Pooh stories. In a perhaps acute observation, at least one critic pondered whether the dialogue was so well crafted that it appealed effectively to children at one level and to adults at another, giving equal if different pleasure to each.

The Liverpool production was sufficiently successful that *Toad of Toad Hall* was put on at the Lyric Theatre in London's West End from December 1930. Milne was understandably anxious when Kenneth, by then an old man, and Elspeth Grahame came to see the play for themselves and asked Milne to join them in their box. To his relief Grahame and his wife seemed to enjoy it. It was a much more relaxed occasion when the Milnes and a party of friends attended a performance on 2 January 1931, and the run was successful enough that there was a further revival at London's Savoy Theatre in December 1931, after which it became a fixture of the Christmas season until 1935. It was then revived in 1953 by the Royal Shakespeare Company at Stratford-upon-Avon, and this production went to London the following year. From the early 1960s onwards it has regularly returned to the stage at Christmas time, with the charismatic actor

Richard Goolden reprising his inimical Mole for many years. Other performers who have appeared on stage in this audience favourite include Paul Scofield, Judi Dench and Ian McKellen.

While Milne was obviously delighted at the critical and commercial success of *Toad of Toad Hall*, it coincided with a rare setback for one of his plays for adults, *The Ivory Door*. Although it was reasonably successful on its opening in New York in 1927, it received poor reviews for its London production in 1929 and closed after only three weeks. Milne again blamed the poor response from the critics for this failure, but after the success of *Toad of Toad Hall* he became concerned that he was being lauded for his writing for children, which he looked upon only as an amusing sideline. What he really wanted was critical approval for his 'real' work of writing novels, plays and articles for adults.

There was an issue with the illustrations for *The Wind in the Willows* when it was first published in 1908. Methuen was unwilling to spend money on a book that they thought likely to fail, and Grahame was not inclined, in the circumstances, to press the point. So the original edition was plain text, with a single black-and-white frontispiece by Graham Robertson. As the word-of-mouth popularity of *The Wind in the Willows* gradually grew, and Methuen began to realize that it had a potentially profitable asset on its hands, they only then began to consider illustrations for future editions.

The New York publisher, Scribner, stole a march on Methuen by commissioning the relatively young American artist Paul Bransom, still only in his twenties, to illustrate an American edition published in 1913. In line with usual publishing practice, Grahame had not been consulted about the choice of illustrator, nor had he any veto over the drawings. Perhaps predictably, he was disappointed with them. This was to be the case with all the other artists commissioned to illustrate *The Wind in the Willows* for the first twenty years.

The issue was that it was extremely difficult to convey human characteristics within believable representations of animals, and countless artists and illustrators had long struggled with this conundrum. Harry Rountree had faced this problem with his initial drawings for Milne's 'The Dormouse and the Doctor', for while he was a highly proficient illustrator of animals, he was unable to convey the necessary human emotions. On the other side of the coin were the pictures of another well-known bear, Rupert Bear, originally created for the *Daily Express* in 1920 by Mary Tourtel and later taken over by Alfred Bestall. The Rupert Bear stories showed the various characters as mainly human but with animal heads, for example Rupert and his parents walked upright on two legs, lived in a normal house and wore typical clothes of the period, but had the heads of bears.

Kenneth Grahame felt personally and emotionally close to the animals and their characters, which he had created in part from his imagination, but which linked back to his childhood by the river Thames. They also recalled his happy memories of telling the stories to Alastair, and these feelings were exacerbated after Alastair's tragic death. He understood why Methuen and Scribner wanted the book to be illustrated, but he could not bear to see the creatures, so clear in his own imagination, desecrated by drawings which bore no resemblance to what he could see in his mind's eye.

By the end of the 1920s, Shepard had been collaborating increasingly harmoniously with Milne on the illustrations for the Winnie-the-Pooh books. Milne appreciated Shepard's ability to solve the conundrum of how to give human characteristics to animals in visual form. He decided to see if he could develop a connection between Shepard and Grahame with the aim of persuading Grahame to allow Shepard to attempt some illustrations for *The Wind in the Willows*.

Methuen pre-empted Milne by commissioning Shepard to produce some drawings for a new edition of Grahame's *The Golden Age*. Shepard thoroughly enjoyed this project, as the setting of the original stories in the late Victorian period meant that he could summon up his memories of the costumes and surroundings of his own childhood. Grahame liked Shepard's new illustrations and, emboldened by this positive reaction, Methuen further commissioned Shepard to illustrate a new edition of *Dream Days*. This was equally successful. Encouraged by this, Milne took the bull by the horns and tackled Grahame directly, saying that there was a real opportunity that Shepard could catch the magic of *The Wind in the Willows* creatures. If Grahame did not take up this opportunity, Milne said, then future illustrations for the book were likely to continue to be unsatisfactory, particularly after Grahame was dead and would have no further control. The issue was really about Grahame's legacy for *The Wind in the Willows*.

Grahame finally agreed to consider it, and Shepard went down to Pangbourne

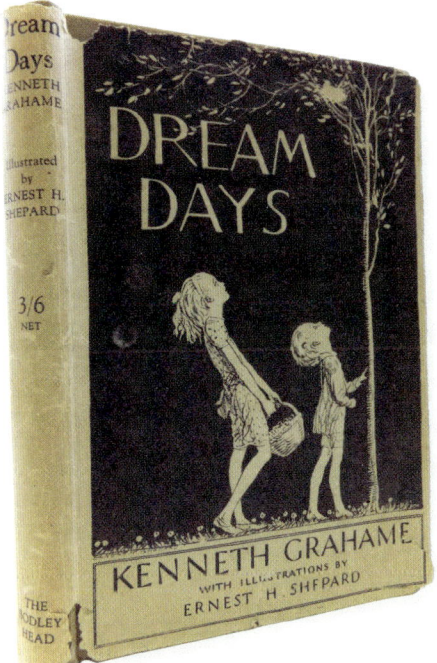
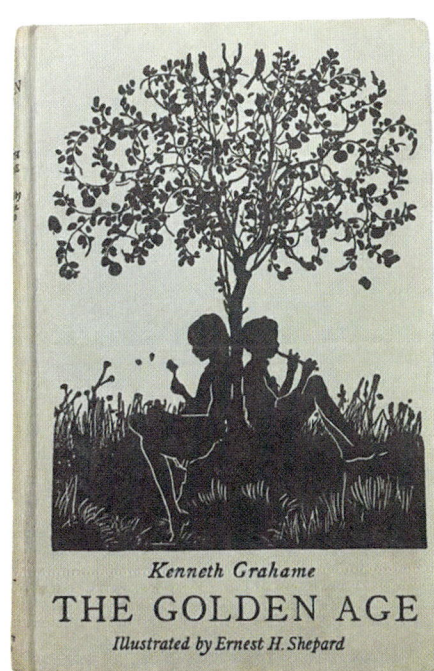

Shepard went on to illustrate several of Kenneth Grahame's earlier works.

in Berkshire, where Grahame was then living, to discuss the commission. The two men were equally nervous to start with, but Grahame settled Shepard down and explained to him how he felt about his creatures and the locations for the stories. Then he escorted Shepard to the front gate, said that due to his age he was unable to accompany Shepard personally, and then pointed him towards the riverbank, the water meadows and the path to the woods. For the next few hours Shepard simply walked about, taking in the atmosphere and trying to get a feel for the locality, much as he had done for Milne in the Ashdown Forest.

A few days later he returned with his drawing materials and began to sketch. Shepard thought long and hard about the drawings for *The Wind in the Willows* as he understood that to do them, and Kenneth Grahame, justice, he needed to try to capture the very different characteristics of the various animals. It would be a similar process to the way that he had captured the essence of Winnie-the-Pooh and the animals in the Hundred Acre Wood, but within a different context. Whereas the Winnie-the-Pooh stories are set in a contained environment with no external influences, *The Wind in the Willows* is set in a very human world, with houses, roads, inns, prisons, police stations, railway trains and interactions with real human beings. It was a much harder challenge in terms of scale and how readers would relate to the characters.

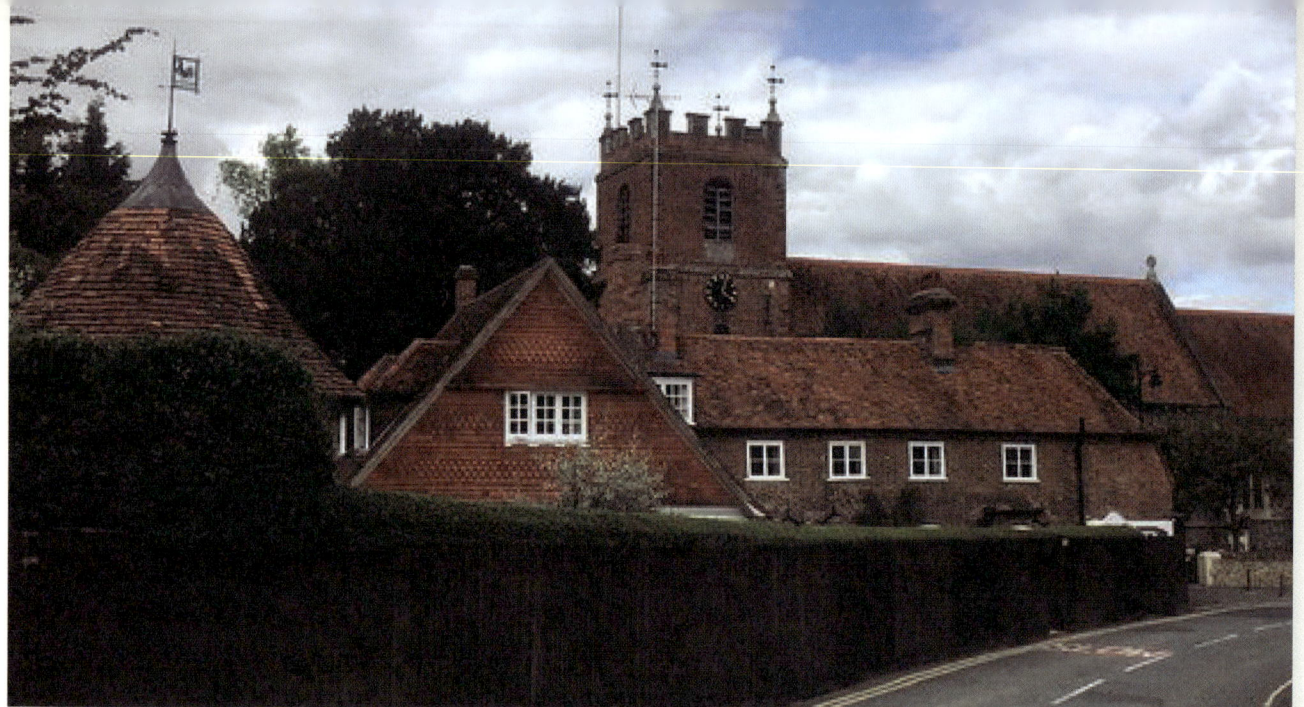

Church Cottage, Pangbourne, Kenneth Grahame's final home, from where Shepard walked down to the Thames Valley riverbank for inspiration for his drawings for *The Wind in the Willows*.

A particular difficulty was that so many different forms of transport are described in *The Wind in the Willows*. Depending on Toad's current predilection and situation, the story moves from a horse-drawn caravan, through a large motorcar ('poop-poop!'), to a police van, a train, a canal barge and a boat. Shepard had to include images of all of these while keeping a realistic sense of scale and proportion. And although we now see these vehicles in a historic context, they still convince us that they are an integral part of the story.

Shepard managed this complex scenario with confidence and ability. For example, his images of Toad, puffed up with self-assurance outside Toad Hall, and then later, swathed in shawls, diminutive and collapsed, in the dock at the Magistrate's Court, are both utterly convincing, but completely different. As in the Ashdown Forest, Shepard drew the very different landscape of the Thames Valley riverbank from life. He sat in those water meadows, conjuring up both the images he could see in real life – the meadows, the trees and Toad Hall (an amalgam of a number of those Edwardian mansions which line the banks of the Thames to this day) – and those he could not: the interiors of Badger's and Ratty's homes and of Toad Hall. He drew the characters as their human counterparts might have been: Mole as perhaps a shy, diminutive schoolteacher, slightly bowed down and self-deprecating; Ratty as a brusque gamekeeper, knowledgeable about country lore but with a simplistic view of human emotions; Badger as a retired man of the world, bookish, clever and thoughtful; and Toad as bombastic, over-confident and full of bluster and bluff, like those men who had built the Toad

Hall-like mansions along the Thames. Shepard's ability to see this in his mind's eye and reproduce it all in his illustrations was remarkable.

When he felt that he had created a representative portfolio of sketches, he returned to Pangbourne and very tentatively showed them to Grahame. There was a long silence, broken by Grahame, clearly moved, turning to Shepard and saying, 'You've made them real.' This was a great relief to Shepard, a source of real pleasure to Grahame, and a quiet satisfaction for Milne. Grahame was able to see and to approve the final versions of those original sketches for his beloved stories. However, he sadly died in 1931, before the next edition of *The Wind in the Willows* was published with the new Shepard illustrations in 1932. This new edition was received with much acclaim from critics and readers alike.

Since then, although many artists have tried to illustrate *The Wind in the Willows* in new and often contemporary ways, most observers agree that none has come near the magic of Shepard's pen, which is why editions with his illustrations for *The Wind in the Willows* have never been out of print.

Nowadays, while *The Wind in the Willows* is considered to be a classic of children's literature, it has been further enhanced by Milne's script for *Toad of Toad Hall* and by Shepard's iconic illustrations. It has become a quintessential story of Englishness, and yet has an ongoing and universal appeal to audiences

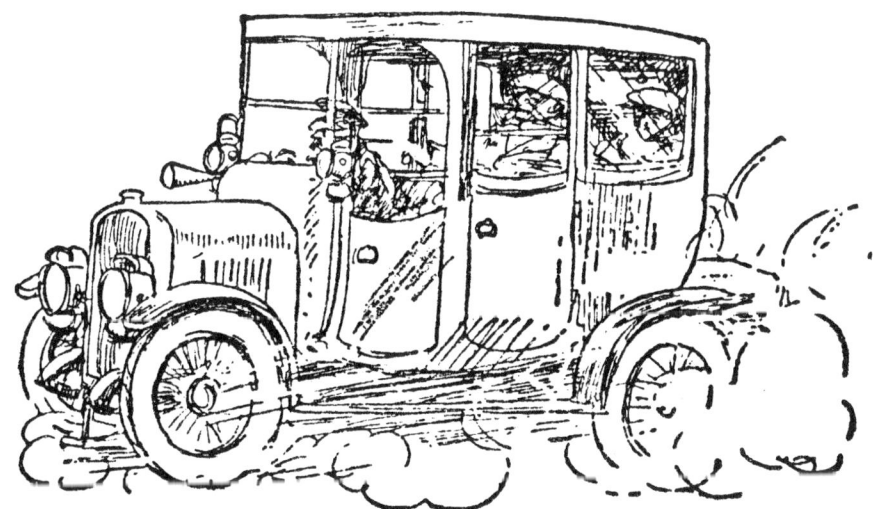

'Poop-poop!' The 'shiny new motor-car of great size' so beloved of Mr Toad.

across the globe, most of whom have never experienced that pastoral riverbank on the river Thames in southern England. It is fair to say that Milne and Shepard have taken a classic of English literature – not just children's literature – and elevated it to a higher plane, making it one of the few internationally recognizable stories still as fresh and relevant today as it was at the start of the twentieth century. This is perhaps just one of the many reasons why *The Wind in the Willows* is consistently included in any list of the top ten children's books and was included in the opening ceremony of the 2012 Olympic Games in London as a representation of what it means to be British.

Milne's play, *Toad of Toad Hall*, continues to delight audiences through provincial and amateur dramatic productions. In 1990 London's National Theatre produced an exciting production of *The Wind in the Willows*, written

Shepard's illustrations for Kenneth Grahame's classic book have never been out of print since publication.

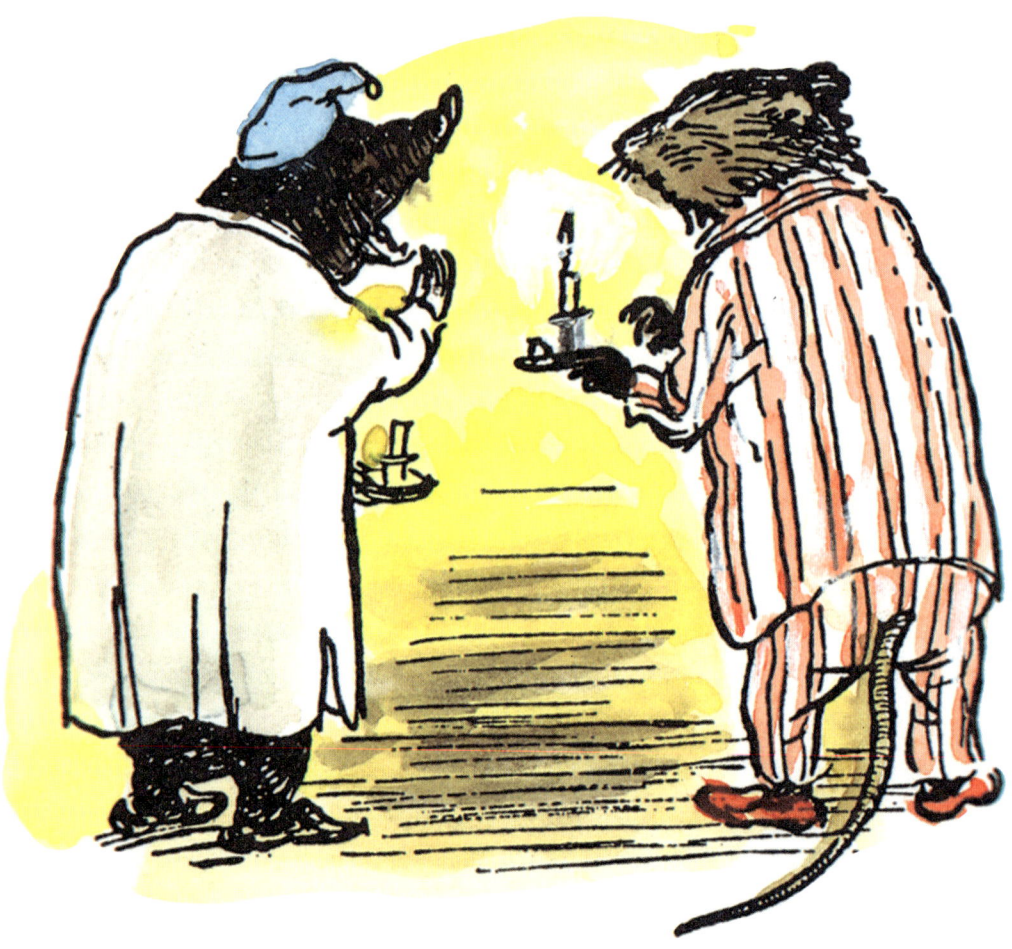

by the acclaimed writer Alan Bennett, which brought to the stage, and to life, the very characteristics of the animals as written by Grahame and enhanced by Milne and Shepard. At a performance of this production in the 1990s a small boy in the front row was so engaged and excited by the performance that he shouted out an answer to a rhetorical question put by the actor playing Toad, who stopped, came down to the front of the stage and said in a kindly way to the small boy, 'I do the funnies here!' The audience laughed and the play moved on. Little did anyone there know that the small boy was E. H. Shepard's eldest great-great-grandchild, at the theatre for the first time in his life.

Shepard himself felt that his drawings for *The Wind in the Willows* were some of his best ever. While his wonderful 'decorations' for Winnie-the-Pooh were timeless and iconic, they had, after the first book, been essentially a collaborative process. Milne as the author was more closely involved in the illustrations' creation than any other writer, before or since. But here, on the riverbank, Shepard had a free hand to interpret *The Wind in the Willows* in his own way, without intervention, without someone breathing down his neck. He was able to create his images from his own mind's eye and imagination.

Much, much later, in the 1960s, and when he was older than Kenneth Grahame had been when the two had met, Shepard wrote and illustrated two small and modest children's books of his own. There he could do exactly what he wanted, and what he chose to do was to tell and illustrate stories that had much more in common with *The Wind in the Willows* than with anything else. *The Wind in the Willows* remains, and probably will for ever remain, an enduring classic by Kenneth Grahame, but one enhanced and elevated by Alan Milne and Ernest Shepard.

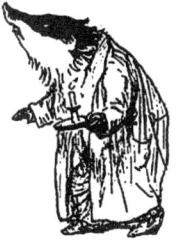

CHAPTER SEVEN

The Approaching Storm

Milne's last play, *Michael and Mary*, a tale of marriage and inadvertent bigamy, was produced in 1929. Like so many of his plays, it was centred on relationships – how these had come together and grown apart, developed or changed direction – as well as the interactions between people in and out of marriages. In the play, in the interval between the death of a man in the home of a happily married couple and the arrival of the police, the husband and wife desperately discuss what to do, as the dead man is the long-lost husband of the wife. She had failed to divorce him before bigamously marrying her second husband, whose child is therefore illegitimate. It is a clever play, was successful at the box office, and was a satisfactory swansong for Milne as a playwright.

It was also in 1929 that Milne's most important emotional relationship was brought to an early close by the death, after many years of ill-health, of his beloved elder brother Ken. Milne was bereft by the loss, but continued to maintain a close and warm relationship with Ken's widow Maud, and he supported her and their children for the rest of his life.

The following year, 1930, was a watershed for the Milne family. Christopher Robin left the nurseries at Mallord Street and Cotchford Farm for the last time and, in his tenth year, went to boarding school, Boxgrove in Sussex, somewhat late for a boy at that time. As a result, his beloved nanny, Olive Rand, left at long last to marry her fiancé, who had been patiently waiting for her to be free. Her departure removed any rival for Christopher's affections, and from then on, Alan and Christopher developed a close bond which lasted until the outbreak of the Second World War.

Christopher Milne tells his own story well in his two books of autobiography, *The Enchanted Places* (1974) and *The Path Through the Trees* (1979). Basically, his miserable experiences at boarding school, both at Boxgrove and later, from 1934, at Stowe School, affected him for the remainder of his life. He was routinely teased, humiliated and bullied mercilessly by his peers for being the small boy of the popular poems and stories, immortalized as wearing a childish smock or kneeling to say his prayers.

Alan visited Christopher at school regularly, Daphne rather less so, possibly because many of the visits revolved around sport, which bored her. For Christopher,

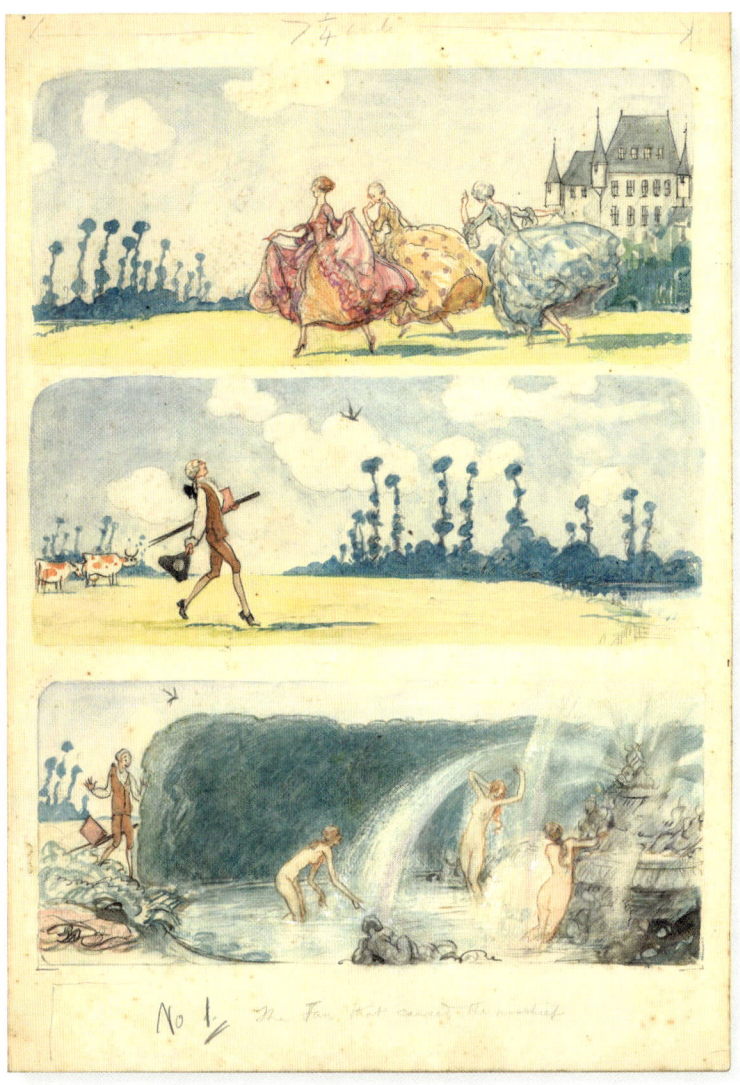

A typically whimsical Shepard illustration from the 1930s.

the holidays were a welcome relief from the horrors of school and were spent mostly at Cotchford in the company of his father, developing their close bond over games, particularly cricket, reading and crossword puzzles. Even at that young age Christopher was aware of his father's detachment, that Alan remained buttoned up and closed in on himself, and it still seemed at times as if it was just the two of them against the world.

In 1931 the Milnes visited America and were feted guests, greeted with widespread publicity and an avalanche of invitations. Milne found the unrelenting attention tiring and had little privacy. Daphne loved it and was in her element, enjoying every moment of the publicized arrivals at social events, the flashguns of photographers, the adulation and the popularity. Alan Milne never went back to the USA, whereas Daphne returned every autumn for seven successive years until the outbreak of the Second World War. She referred to these trips as her annual holidays from her husband, when for weeks on end she could enjoy society, romance, being spoiled and a sense of importance as the elegant wife of the author of the Winnie-the-Pooh books.

It was an opportunity for them both to have a breather from a marriage which was no longer enough for either of them. As Milne's star faded through the thirties, he became frustrated and difficult to live with, and she came to realize that her ambitions for him were unlikely to be fulfilled. They both turned to increasingly separate lives, with romantic interests for both of them. Whether or not there were physical relationships is unclear, but it is certainly the case that they both developed close emotional friendships outside their marriage.

Daphne became particularly attached to Elmer Rice, an American writer and playwright, while Alan grew close to Leonora Corbett, a British actress who appeared in his plays on the London stage. The Milnes' marriage was never seriously threatened, as neither wanted the upheaval or scandal of a divorce. But regular time apart each year when Daphne spent the autumn months in New York gave them both a release from the tensions between them.

In 1934 Milne submitted his last prose article to *Punch*. It was about cricket, and unwisely he chose to send this in under Daphne's old pseudonym C. Brice, to see how it would fare. Unsurprisingly, he was very disappointed when it was returned by the editor, then Evoe Knox. He then, even more unwisely, re-submitted it in his own name, and this time *Punch* published it. However, Milne's light style no longer suited the times. Knox had to tell him that, although his writing was still as excellent as ever, *Punch* would not be able to publish his prose pieces any longer. It was a sad and undistinguished finale to a prose-writing and publishing relationship which had started with such promise back in 1906.

In the autumn of 1934, just as Christopher was starting his first term at Stowe School, Milne published *Peace with Honour*. He had been working on this book for at least five years, but in fact it had been gestating since his decision to become a pacifist before the First World War. It was an extraordinarily well-written book on the pointlessness of war, and the failure of politicians, statesmen and leaders to focus on peace, rather than on circumstances which would inevitably lead to war. The book was well-received, with an unexpectedly positive review from *The Times* newspaper, which normally followed the establishment line, as the

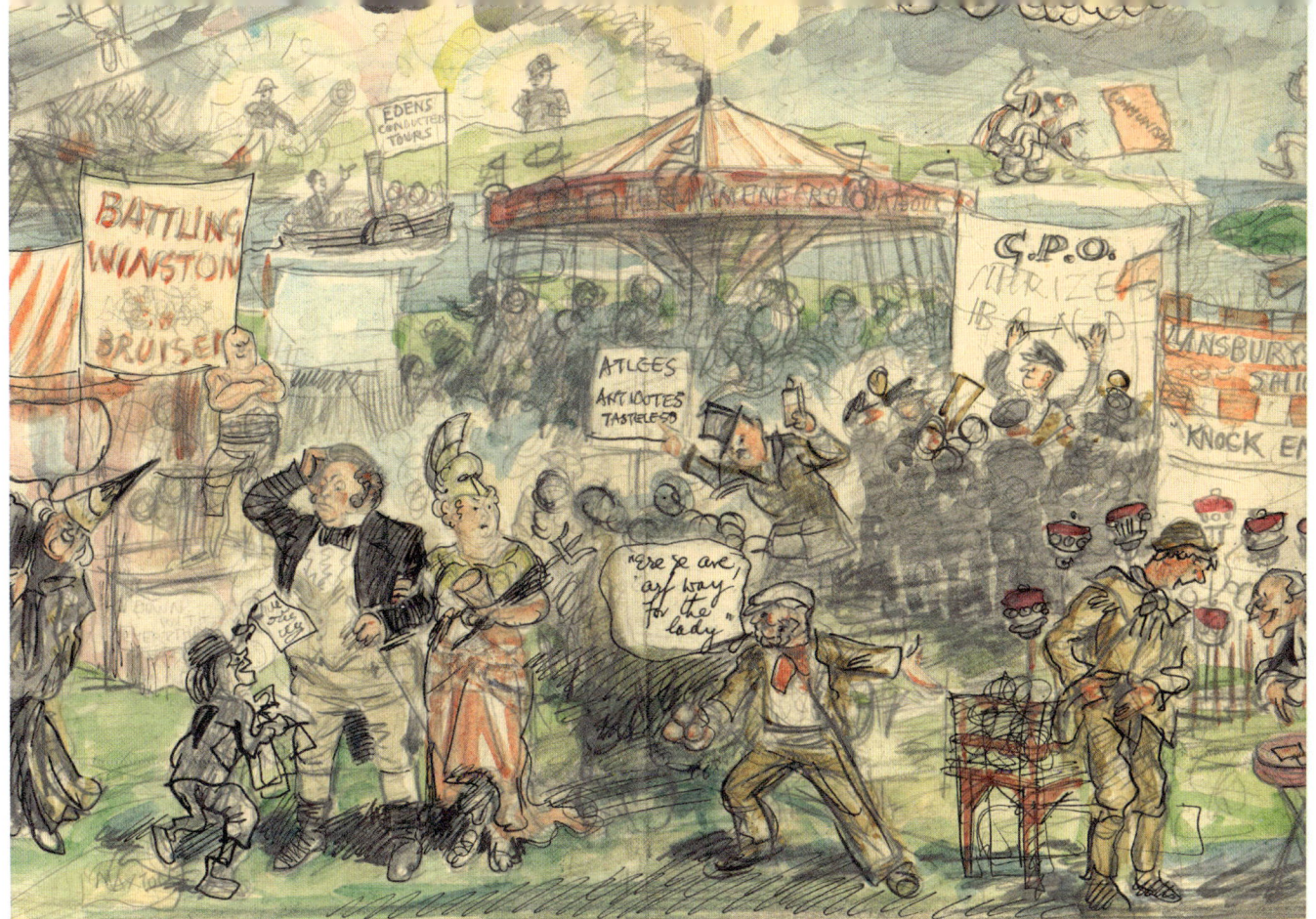

A cartoon reflecting the political challenges of the period leading up to the Second World War.

editor, Geoffrey Dawson, was a strong supporter of appeasement. The book sold over 12,000 copies and Milne received a huge postbag from enthusiastic correspondents. It reinforced his view that a pacifist approach to international relations could make a very significant difference to resolving issues of dispute between nations. He had the book sent to politicians he thought would benefit from it. Few replied.

As for Shepard, after *Everybody's Pepys* he received further commissions to follow this popular formula with *Everybody's Boswell*, the abridged and illustrated version of Boswell's life of Dr Johnson, which was published in 1930, followed by *Everybody's Lamb*, a similar abridgement of Charles Lamb's writings, published in 1933. Shepard was further acclaimed for his drawings in a new edition of *Bevis: The Story of a Boy* by Richard Jeffries, which had previously been illustrated by Harry Rountree. Shepard greatly enjoyed this commission, spending time in Wiltshire drawing from life as he so liked to do, and when the book was published in 1932 there were great plaudits for his new illustrations. He then embarked on another enjoyable project, the trilogy of 'Palace Plays' by Laurence Housman. Based on the life of Queen Victoria, these were *Victoria Regina* in 1934, *Golden Sovereign* in 1937 and *Glorious Majesty* in 1941. Shepard had great fun with them, as he hired models and dressed them up in Victorian costumes and spent some happy days researching the locations at Osborne on the Isle of Wight, and at Windsor, as well as at Buckingham Palace.

In 1930 Shepard's son Graham met a Canadian girl, Ann Gibbon, and they were married from Long Meadow in 1931, with the cartoonist and writer Osbert Lancaster as the best man. There was a muddle over the arrangements for the post-wedding accommodation, and Lancaster ended up sharing a bed with the happy couple, probably not the wedding night they had anticipated.

A sociable man, Shepard kept up with old friends as well as he could given his heavy workload, and he made some new ones. In the 1930s he became friends with the well-known pioneer of family planning, Marie Stopes. Her views on birth control and eugenics were at the time extremely controversial, although they were endorsed by many liberal and open-minded supporters, including a number of people known by Shepard from the literary and cultural establishment. They lived close by each other in Surrey, and while the extent of their relationship is unclear, they saw a good deal of each other in the years leading up to the Second World War.

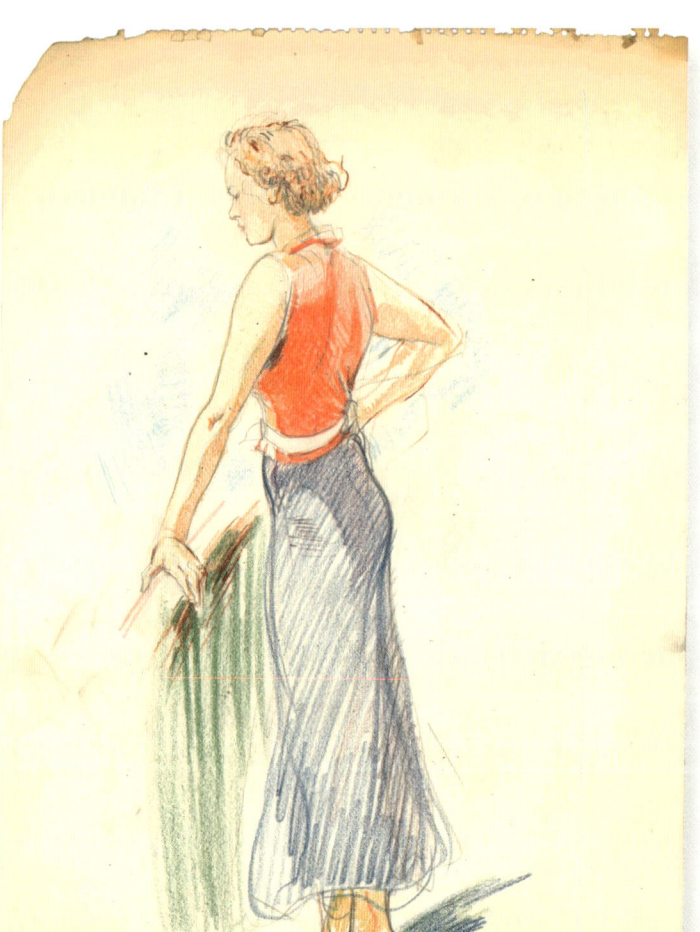

This colour sketch is thought to have been Shepard's daughter-in-law, Ann Gibbon.

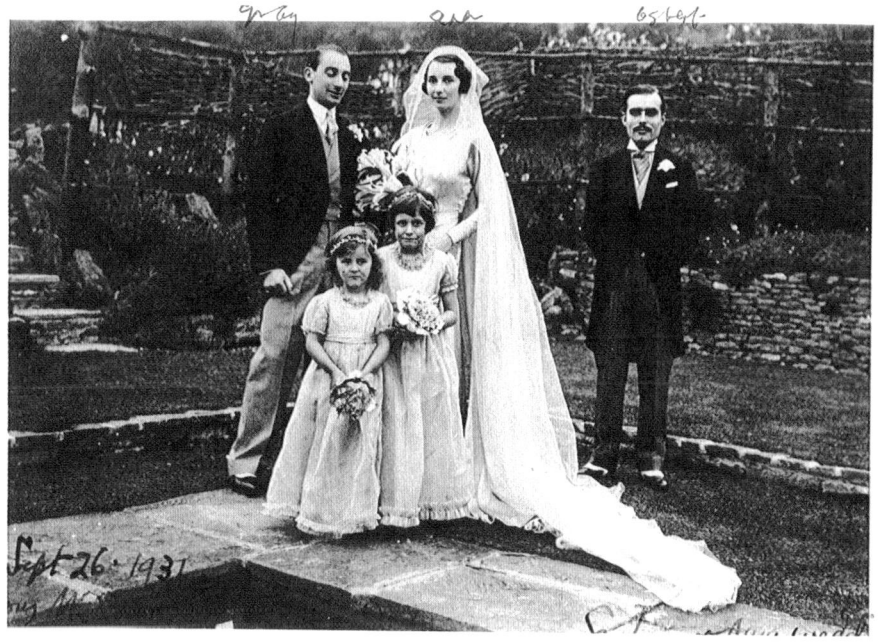

Graham Shepard and Ann Gibbon's wedding day – the best man was Osbert Lancaster.

Shepard also became friendly with Jan Struther, the writer best known for *Mrs Miniver* and her hymn 'Lord of all Hopefulness', when he illustrated her book *Sycamore Square*. He found her high spirits and amusing company very refreshing, and he introduced her to Graham and Ann, with whom she became good friends. Another of his art projects had been *The Little One's Log* by Eva Erleigh, an illustrated journal to record a baby's progress. Both this and *Sycamore Square* appealed to parents of young children, and Shepard's pictures expressed a sentimentality which bore more than a passing reference to *When We Were Very Young*.

In 1935 he and Mary enjoyed a visit to the South of France where he was drawing from life the illustrations for *Perfume from Provence*, a hugely popular book of memoirs by Winifred Fortescue. Her late husband, Sir John Fortescue, had written *A History of the British Army*, so Shepard was delighted to be able to spend time in his excellent military library while Mary explored the French Riviera.

The ongoing success of the four Winnie-the-Pooh books had catapulted Shepard, as well as Milne, into a new league. In addition to his continuing work on Winnie-the-Pooh which now included spin-offs, new editions, merchandising requirements, and so on, he was deluged with offers of work, many from people simply hopeful that the Shepard name would increase sales. He was pleased that his agents, Curtis Brown, were a buffer between himself and these offers,

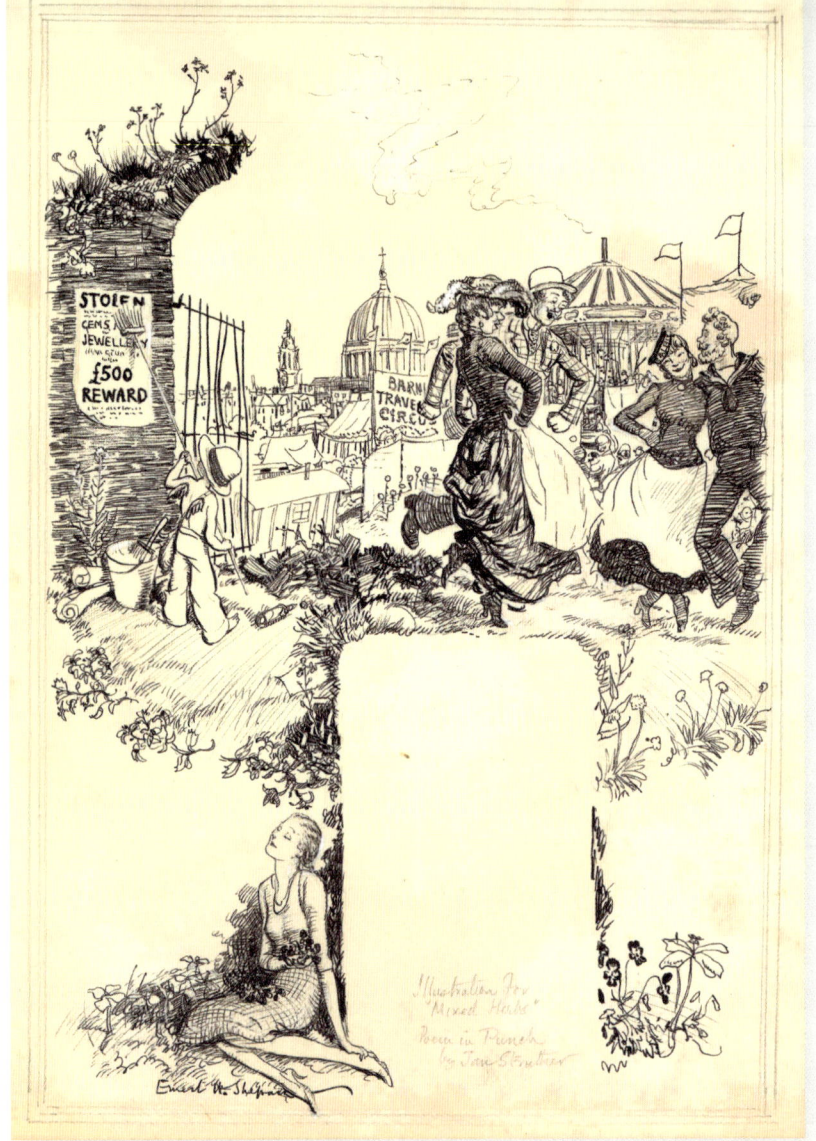

A typical draft magazine layout, with an empty text box for the
accompanying words.

as he was trying to juggle a wide range of responsibilities and commissions.
Among the work he rejected was an approach from the then unknown writer
P. L. Travers, who asked him to illustrate her new book, *Mary Poppins*. Shepard
had to turn her down due to pressure of work, but in an interesting twist,
P. L. Travers, disappointed, then saw and liked an illustrated Christmas card
and approached the artist. By one of those extraordinary coincidences, the artist
was Mary Shepard. She accepted Travers' proposal and illustrated all the *Mary
Poppins* books from 1934 to 1988.

Evoe Knox's wife, Christina, died in 1935 from cancer. Having undergone a
similar bereavement just a few years earlier, Shepard was very sympathetic to his
old friend, now editor of *Punch*. Shepard and his children, Graham and Mary,
and Graham's wife Ann, who were all living in the same house in Melina Place,

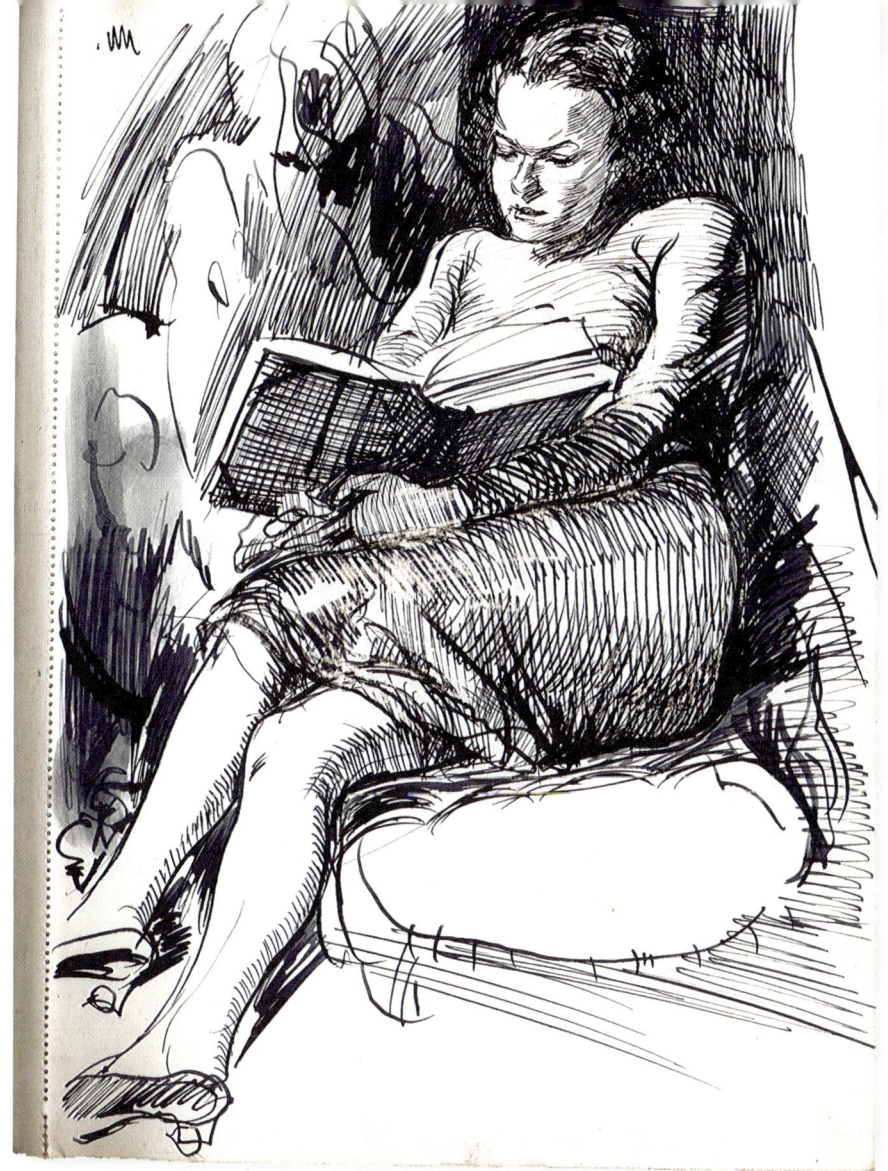

A swift pen-and-ink sketch of Mary Shepard.

in St John's Wood, made sure to include Evoe and his two children, Rawle and Penelope, as much as possible, and to help them through this difficult time.

There was an unexpected consequence to this kindness: in 1937 Mary Shepard and Evoe Knox became engaged to be married. Mary had been her father's companion and support since her mother's death ten years earlier, and they were very close. Evoe was Shepard's contemporary and friend, and a generation older than Mary. The relationship and engagement seems to have taken both families and their friends by surprise. Shepard had decidedly mixed feelings. While he was happy that Mary had found love and happiness, he could not help feeling that his old friend had taken advantage of the Shepard family's generosity to Evoe in his bereavement, and that Evoe had essentially used this situation to gain Mary's affections. While outwardly the usual courtesies were observed,

Ernest, Graham and Ann felt considerable disquiet at the match. Nonetheless, Evoe and Mary were married in the autumn of 1937 and it was, by all accounts, a happy and fulfilled marriage. But Shepard's relationship with Mary and Evoe was never quite the same. There was now an unspoken distance between them, and the previous intimacy between Shepard and his only daughter would never be fully rekindled.

In addition to the regular flow of work connected to Winnie-the-Pooh, Shepard's principal focus remained *Punch* magazine. He was now deeply involved in management, not only as a member of the *Punch* Table but also through acting as the deputy art editor, as well as providing weekly cartoons and drawings. In 1935 he became deputy to Bernard Partridge, the chief cartoonist. This was a significant promotion, meaning that Shepard was now the acknowledged second cartoonist for the most widely read English language publication in the world. As Partridge was by this time seventy-four years old, Shepard inevitably had to shoulder much of the burden and regularly produced the lead political cartoon.

During the decade up to the Second World War, Shepard began to draw meaningful and influential cartoons reflecting not just politics, but also wider changes in society. From 1935 onwards he recorded the issues of the day and in 1936 produced one of the most memorable and moving drawings of the abdication crisis. He pictured a harrowed-looking King Edward VIII in Westminster Abbey, turning his back on the Coronation Chair and the Stone of Scone. It is still a poignant and moving image reflecting a tipping point in the historic relationship between monarch and people, and demonstrates yet another of Shepard's remarkable abilities as an artist. This drawing is neither cartoon nor illustration; it is a magnificent set-piece, almost photographic in its representation, conveying the quiet personal reflection of the subject and drawing an emotional response from the audience.

A wonderful contrast, produced just months later, was Shepard's watercolour painting of a river pageant marking the coronation of King George VI and Queen Elizabeth. In a vivid colour palette we see an image of royalty that refers back to Queen Elizabeth I and to Queen Victoria – the golden royal barge coming down the royal river Thames, with the stunning backdrop of the royal Windsor Castle towering above and over the river scene. Their Majesties are shown in formal robes, and with them are the enchanting images of their two daughters, the

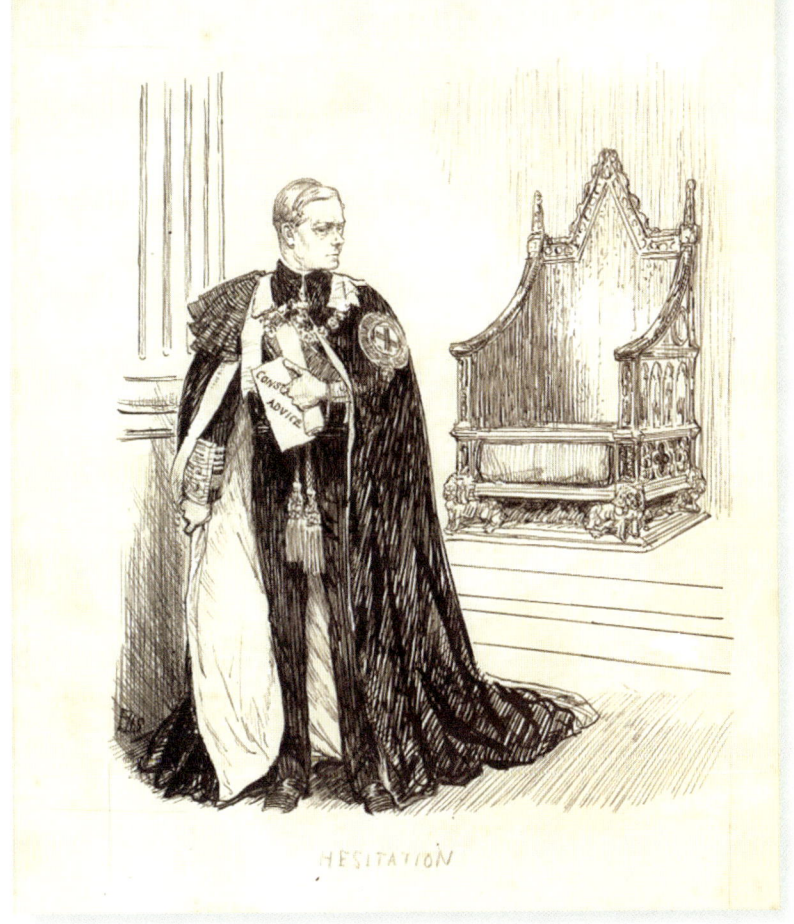

King Edward VIII at the time of the abdication crisis in 1936, shown
turning away from the Coronation Chair with the caption 'Hesitation'.

Princesses Elizabeth (later, of course, to be Her Majesty Queen Elizabeth II) and
Margaret Rose. It was the very embodiment of a happy family (in contrast to the
childless former king, the now exiled Duke of Windsor, who had just married
his brittle, tough, twice-divorced American wife, Wallis Simpson). Rounding
out Shepard's illustration was the parade along the towpath demonstrating the
diversity represented by the British Empire.

Here we see Shepard's extraordinary flexibility, from knockabout humour to
moving formality, which was so well expressed by his range of work through the
1930s. And at *Punch* not only was he dealing with the abdication, the ensuing
constitutional crisis and the upheaval which that brought about, but also with
the alarming affairs in Europe. He had to find ways to illustrate the rise of
fascism, the widespread desire among the British establishment for a policy of
appeasement towards Nazi Germany, the ill-fated Munich Agreement between
British Prime Minister Neville Chamberlain and German Führer Adolf Hitler
that let Germany take over Czechoslovakia, and the inexorable build-up to war
in 1939. Appeasement was in many ways an understandable policy for anyone
who was anxious to avoid any repeat of the terrible events of the First World War.

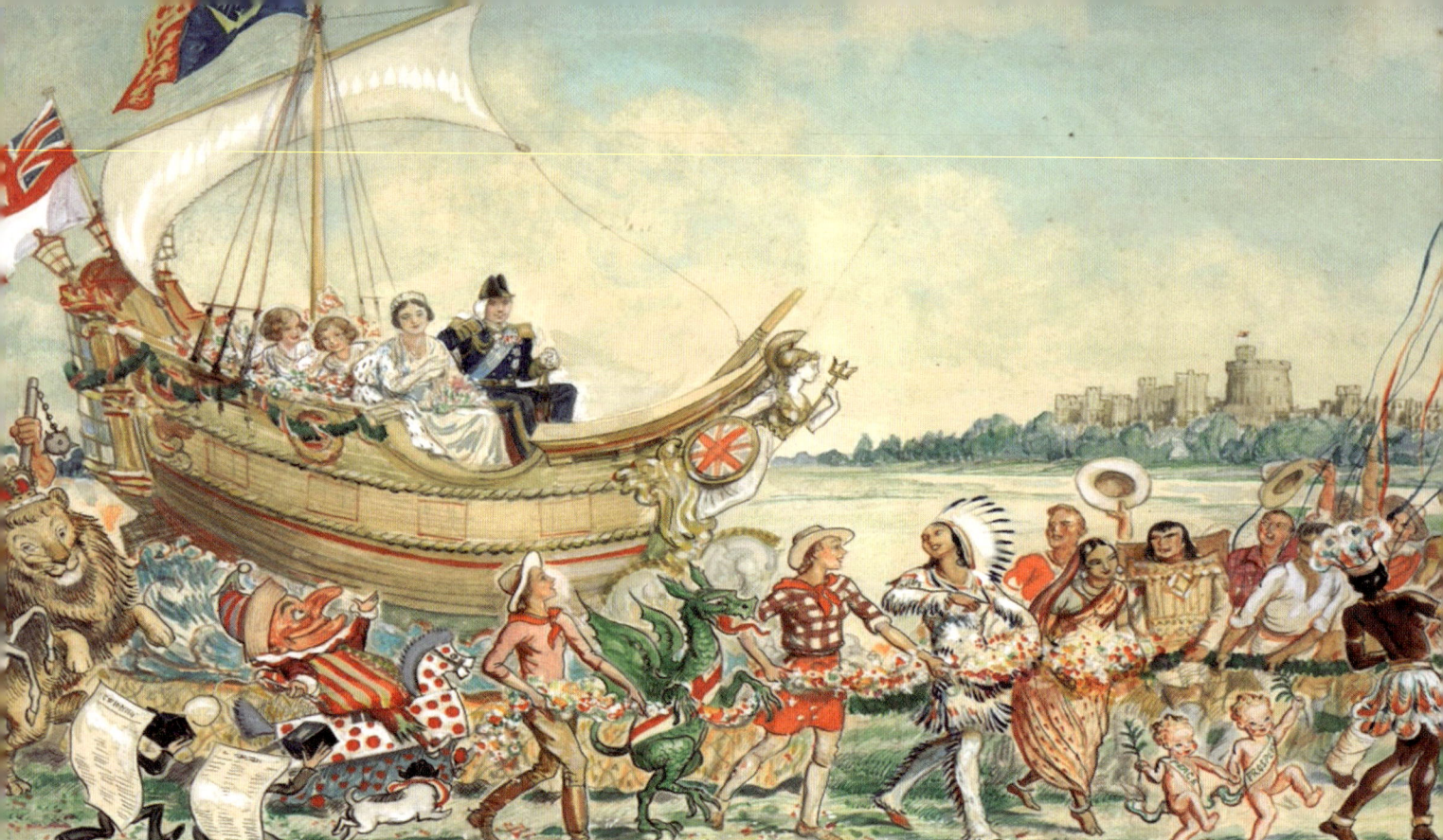

A royal river pageant colour drawing created by Shepard in 1937 to mark the Coronation of King George VI and Queen Elizabeth.

Those horrors had been experienced by many people in positions of authority in Britain, and of course by Milne and Shepard as well.

The outbreak of the Second World War was deeply disappointing to Shepard, even though he understood the reasons behind the decision to go to war. He felt, as he had in 1914, that Britain had no choice other than to stand up to the threat of fascism. From his position at *Punch* he had a ringside seat at the unsuccessful attempts to broker an acceptable compromise between Hitler and other democratic nations under threat in Europe, and he genuinely believed that there was no alternative to conflict.

For Milne, this new war was a catastrophe, a complete rejection of his ideals and beliefs, and a return to the horrors of conflict. He railed against the inability of politicians and statesmen to find a way in which to resolve political and territorial issues, and was infuriated by the resumption of the jingoism and anti-German rhetoric which seemed to him to have been so misplaced at the start of the First World War in 1914.

Christopher did not have the usual teenage rebellious phase but, rather like his father, was quiet, introspective and eager to please. In an external sign of his inner tension, however, he was often anxious and had a stammer. He was

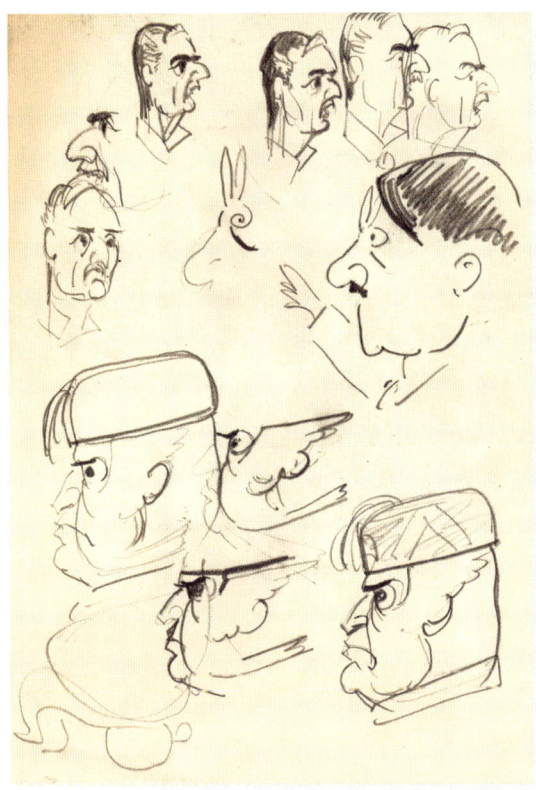

A page from Shepard's sketchbook showing caricatures of Chamberlain, Hitler and Mussolini.

nineteen in August 1939, about to go up to Trinity, and his father optimistically hoped that the war would be over before he might become involved. For Christopher, the war would finally allow him to cut the umbilical cord between himself and his father and let him develop into an adult without constant oversight and scrutiny. It would give Christopher the time and space to work out his own views and opinions, and to live his own life as he wished to do. This time of reflection would be the catalyst for his increasing anger and the sense that his childhood had been betrayed. It began his gradual but inevitable distance, later to become estrangement, from his parents.

The Phoney War – the months of inaction after war was declared in September 1939 – allowed life to go on much as usual at Mallord Street and Cotchford Farm. Slowly, however, wartime restrictions and the introduction of rationing began to impact on the Milnes' lifestyle. There was no longer sufficient petrol to spend every weekend at Cotchford, and jaunts to play golf were increasingly limited. As a pacifist, Milne had to decide what his public response to the war was going to be. He knew that, as a public figure, how he reacted would be widely noted. Just one day after the declaration of war, on 4 September 1939, he wrote one of a regular series of letters to *The Times* (which would publish some fifteen of his letters through the war years), making the important distinction between the Nazis and the German people. He recalled the anti-German jingoistic furore in 1914, and argued that the objective of the war was the defeat of the Nazis, and that there should then be a negotiated peace with the German people.

At the end of September 1939 Milne's long-awaited autobiography, *It's too Late Now: The Autobiography of a Writer*, was published in Britain and in America. It was a well-written account of his life but was carefully edited so that it revealed little of his inner self. It nonetheless received good reviews on both sides of the Atlantic, and sold well, particularly in the uncertain period during the first weeks of the war. It was fortuitous timing, since restrictions on paper and printing would have a significant impact on publishing later on in the war. At times Methuen struggled to keep even the Winnie-the-Pooh books in print, and they were seen as important for public morale.

In October 1939 he returned to print in *Punch*, but with poems, not prose. The magazine published thirty-six poems between then and June 1940, when the war really started. This marked a turning point, not only in the conflict, but also in the lives of the Milnes. They decided to give up the house in Mallord Street, and to move permanently to Cotchford Farm. This put them out of the immediate danger zone, allowed them to consolidate into a single household and to secure the necessary staff to support them. This was no mean feat, and Daphne, imperious and grand though she might be, ran a very effective domestic ship, managing to retain both indoor and outdoor staff right through the war and beyond. At the time, many households went down to a bare minimum of staff, or even none, as domestic employees sought more patriotic and usually better paid war work.

In a pattern which would be set for the following ten years, Alan and Daphne tended to spend a separate day in London each week, travelling by train. She dealt with her personal appearance and women's lunches, and he engaged with publishers, business and lunch at the Garrick.

Milne offered his services where he felt he could make the best contribution to the war effort, and so in June 1940, now permanently at Cotchford, he enrolled in the Local Defence Volunteers, better known now as the Home Guard. He was appointed a lieutenant and served the Hartfield community in that capacity. Christopher decided to leave Trinity to enlist in the army, and joined his father in the LDV until the regular army was ready for him. This proved to be more difficult than he had expected, so Milne pulled some strings to get Christopher into the Royal Engineers as a private soldier. Alas, Christopher was so nervous during his medical that the doctor decided that he was likely to be mentally unsuitable, and so he was rejected. This was a disaster for Christopher. He tried and failed to have the decision reversed, so eventually Alan again intervened at a higher level, and a second medical exam passed Christopher as fit to serve. In February 1941 he joined the Royal Engineers at last, but it was not until July

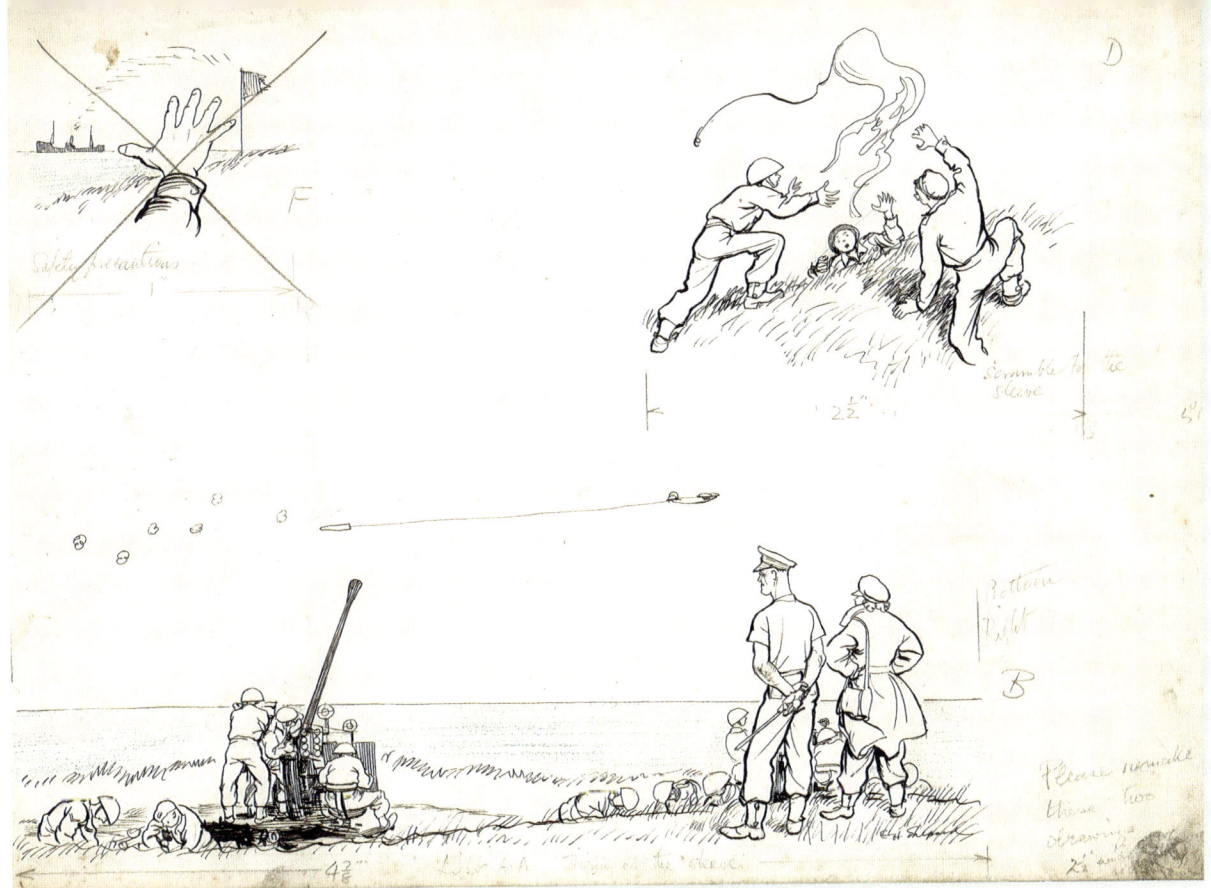

A group of sketches depicting scenes from the Second World War.

1942, some eighteen months later, that he was commissioned as an officer.

As well as his Home Guard duties, Alan Milne's own Second World War service saw him also back working for the Ministry of Information. He produced two leaflets which were specifically addressed to pacificists. The first, *War Aims Unlimited*, discussed the reasons why pacificists should join the war effort and focused on the defeat of Hitler and the Nazis as being the best way to ensure a lasting global peace. The second, deliberately titled *War With Honour*, was a nod to his earlier book, *Peace With Honour*, and further refined some of the arguments made in that first publication. Originally, Milne had not taken account of the possibility of a deranged dictator taking power and acting in a completely irrational manner. In his new title, Milne reiterated the difference between the Nazis, with whom there could be no negotiation, and the German people in general, with whom there might be diplomatic compromises. He continued to write articles for a variety of periodicals and magazines through the war years, mostly on a similar theme: the pointlessness of war and the need to end it by any means possible.

In 1941 he became embroiled in an unfortunate spat with fellow author and contemporary P. G. Wodehouse. At the start of the war Wodehouse and his wife had failed to appreciate the danger of remaining at their home in Le Touquet in France and were interned by the Germans as enemy aliens. In due course, the Nazis realized that they had an opportunity for propaganda by exploiting this extremely well-known and popular writer. Wodehouse was moved to the comfortable surroundings of Berlin's Adlon Hotel, and he was persuaded to make a series of seemingly innocuous broadcasts about his experiences of being interned for radio audiences in the USA, or so he was led to believe. Wodehouse acted foolishly, failing to grasp the true intentions of his German hosts, and his talks were broadcast from Germany to Britain. At the time, the British people were suffering in many ways: from the effects of the Blitz on many towns and cities, with significant loss of life and property; from the impact of the Battle of Britain and the Battle of the Atlantic; from rationing and low public morale. There was outrage from a furious public at what they saw as 'treachery' by Wodehouse. Public figures queued up to denounce him for supporting the Nazis, and one of the most prominent was Milne.

The two men had much in common: they were contemporaries in age, background and life experience, and both had substantial literary success from the 1920s, Milne as playwright and Wodehouse as novelist. Though not friends, they were acquainted with one another in literary London circles. But now Milne issued a series of blistering attacks on Wodehouse, choleric in tone and which added to a feeling among the public that Wodehouse should be charged as a traitor. It was an unedifying episode which did no one much credit and ended in destroying any respect Wodehouse may have had for Milne, the former pointing out to a mutual acquaintance that Milne had 'a jealous streak'. In the next decade it must have been galling for Milne to see Wodehouse regain his phenomenal success with his light novels of Jeeves and Blandings fame, while his own literary canon was sinking faster than a U-boat's target.

Christopher remained the focus of Alan and Daphne's lives, and they followed his war travels with both interest and anxiety as he moved around the Middle East and North Africa, eventually ending up in Italy in 1944. However, in October of that year they received the telegram that every parent dreaded: Christopher had been wounded in action, in the head, and was seriously ill.

Beside themselves with worry, the Milnes waited desperately for more news, until at last they received a letter from Christopher himself. The injury had been exaggerated, it had been relatively minor and required only a local anaesthetic, and he had been unaware of the terrible anxiety his parents had suffered.

In Trieste for the final phase of the war, Christopher fell in love for the first time, with a local girl. The experience taught him a lot about himself, about growing up, about independence and also about building a future life for himself, separate from his parents. It was a late awakening for Christopher, but it meant that by the time he returned from the war he had a very different attitude to his life. He was now determined to find his own path and independence.

As for Alan Milne, the war ended as it had started, with a letter to *The Times* on the subject of the atomic bomb and the futility of war.

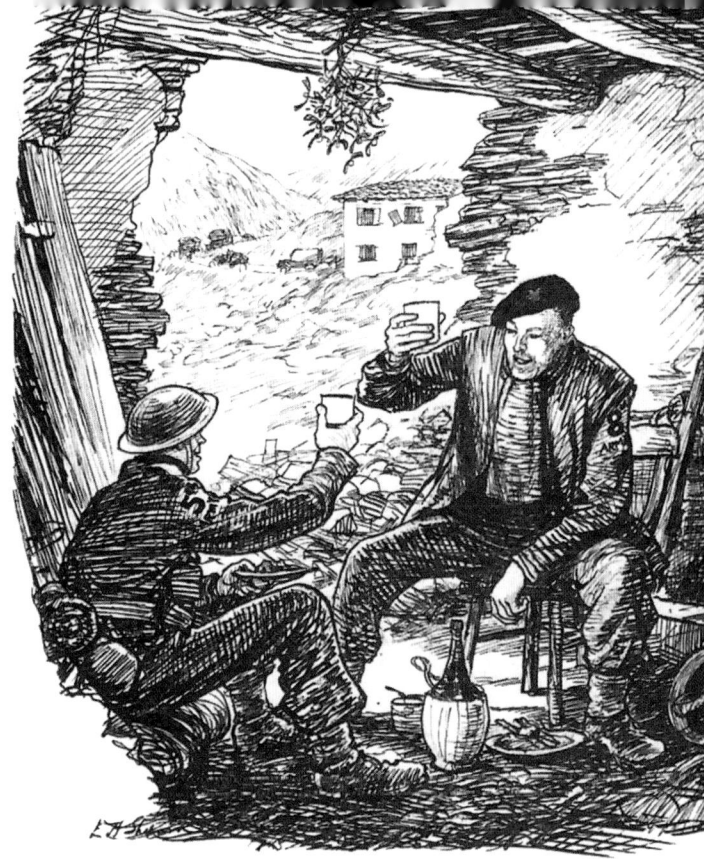

This drawing shows two soldiers toasting each other at Christmas (see the mistletoe hanging in the doorway) in a derelict building in Italy. Although this was in the middle of the Second World War, it looks back to Shepard's own experience fighting in northern Italy at the end of the First World War, and Christmases 'celebrated' while on the front line.

In 1939 Shepard had returned early from his sailing holiday, and joined Graham, Ann and their daughter Minette at Long Meadow. There, they heard on the wireless the announcement that war had been declared. He wrote in his diary that, 'I went to help fill sandbags at the hospital at Seaford.' He started as he meant to go on, making service to his country his priority. The Phoney War seemed very similar to the early months after the outbreak of war in 1914 when initially everything was much as usual. And so until the spring of 1940 he continued to spend the weekdays in London, producing a weekly *Punch* cartoon and completing his usual busy schedule of work, returning to Long Meadow at weekends. *Punch* remained operational in London throughout the war, and although Bouverie Street was bombed during the Blitz, the *Punch* office survived. However, the archives and the *Punch* Table were moved to safe storage, and the weekly dinner was moved to a Wednesday morning meeting for the duration of the war.

In May 1940 the war started in earnest, and Shepard volunteered for the Local Defence Volunteers in Guildford. He was appointed to C Company,

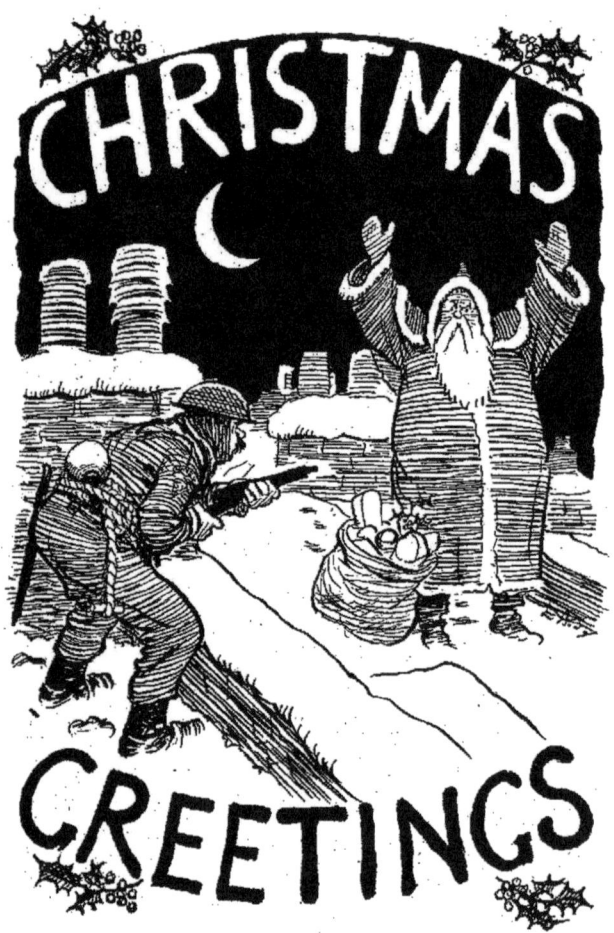

Shepard's gloomy Christmas card for 1943, reflecting a low point in his life.

4th (Guildford) Battalion, Surrey Home Guard, and was immediately engaged in training and patrolling, particularly after dark. In some ways it was reminiscent of his previous army service, but to begin with it was not very efficient. The rifles supplied to his unit were American, and did not match the ammunition provided, which was British. In addition, at first there were no uniforms, and when they did arrive, they did not fit.

The Home Guard was still an important part of local defence, however, looking out for enemy aircraft on bombing missions, and fire watching. Even while all this was going on, in quiet moments Shepard would still get out his pocket sketchbook and start to draw. One of his comrades recalled a night when they were on patrol and saw the fires from the London Blitz lighting up the night sky, at which point Shepard tried to draw a night-time scene where you could see the images but at the same time realize that it was dark.

It is worth recalling that during this period Shepard was in his sixties and was still holding down a full-time job which involved frequent commuting to and from London on often unreliable and frequently overcrowded trains. He would then stay out all night several times a week. By this time he was on his own at Long Meadow. Graham had decided to volunteer for the Royal Naval Volunteer Reserve, which meant that he was away for extended periods. The lease on the Melina Place house had been surrendered, and as Ann did not want to stay at Long Meadow for the duration of the war, she and Minette left in June 1940 for Canada to spend the war with her parents in Montreal, just as Graham was commissioned in the Royal Navy and began training.

By 1943, Graham's ship, the corvette HMS *Polyanthus*, was operating out of

St John's, Newfoundland, and as Ann was now in Canada, she and Minette could see Graham on his leaves when *Polyanthus* was in St John's, and when he was at sea on active service they returned to her parents in Montreal. In September 1943 HMS *Polyanthus* was torpedoed by a German U-boat while on convoy duty in the North Atlantic, and was lost with all hands.

This was shattering news for Ann, Ernest and Mary. For Ernest, having lost his only brother on the battlefield of the Somme in 1916, now to lose his only son in the battleground of the North Atlantic seemed a particularly cruel irony. His sister, the only survivor of his own immediate family, had died just the year before, so he inevitably felt isolated, alone and despondent. After Graham's death, Ann and Minette left immediately for England, desperate to see Shepard and the familiarity of their home environment. They arrived in November 1943.

However, no sooner had they reached Britain than Shepard dropped a bombshell of his own. Out of the blue, he announced his engagement to Norah Carroll, a nurse working at St Mary's Hospital in Paddington, London. The pair had met at a concert in London and, for about a year, he had been conducting a discreet relationship with her, which neither his children nor close friends had known about. No one had anticipated an engagement so shortly after Graham's tragic death, so everyone was surprised by what seemed to be a hasty wartime arrangement. It seems possible that, overwhelmed with grief and sorrow, feeling lonely and isolated, he decided that formalizing his relationship to Norah, who was

A wartime pencil sketch of soldiers in battle.

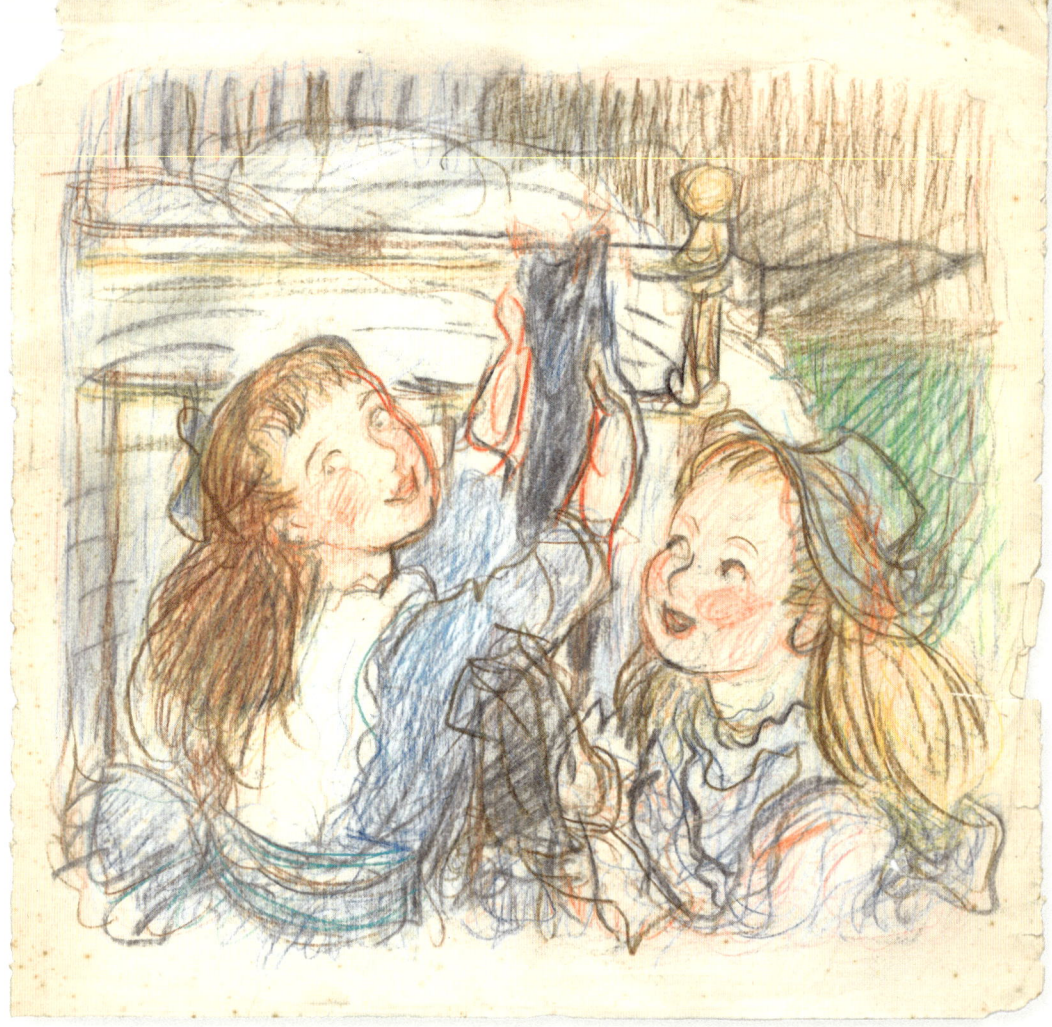

A charming colour pastel portrait.

clearly keen to marry him, would give him the love, support and security which he so desperately needed. Ernest Shepard and Norah Carroll were married in St Marylebone Parish Church in London the following year.

This was not only a great surprise to Mary Knox (neé Shepard) and to Evoe, but was devastating news for Ann. She had assumed that she could live at Long Meadow, perhaps keeping house for Shepard until the end of the war, and meanwhile plan a future for herself and Minette. But now the rug was completely pulled from under her. She did not know Norah at all and understandably was reluctant to play second fiddle to her father-in-law's new wife. This feeling was probably mutual. So, with no other alternative, she returned once more to Canada with Minette and went back to her parents in Montreal, as she had insufficient means to afford a separate establishment of her own.

Ann got on well enough with her father, but had a strained relationship with her mother, and although her parents offered her accommodation and support, she was wary of being pushed by them into a way of life that was conservative and conventional. After the relaxed and unconventional life she had led in London with Graham, she found Canada stifling and restrictive – the very reason she had left in the first place.

In England, she and Graham had lived a bohemian existence, often very hard-up and dependent on financial support from his father, sometimes sharing accommodation with him at his expense. Graham had been a freelance journalist, author and artist, and they moved in artistic and cultural circles, his close friends included Osbert Lancaster, John Betjeman and the Irish poet Louis MacNeice. However, dependent on freelance earnings, often from publications which paid little and late, Graham lurched from financial insecurity to insecurity, and had had little time to establish himself and to generate a reasonable income stream, nor to amass any nest-egg for a rainy day. At that time, pensions for war widows were modest, and neither he nor Ann had had any capital or other resources. Ann and Minette, then eight years old, moved from family to friends in turn as Ann tried to decide what to do for the future.

In the end, concerned about Ann's indecisiveness and worried about the effect on Minette of such an unsettled way of life, Shepard proposed that if Ann made her home in England, near Long Meadow, he would cover the expenses of their accommodation and Minette's education. Ann decided that this would give her some degree of independence and was preferable to either remaining within the confines of her parents' home in Montreal or an uncertain nomadic existence. She accepted Shepard's offer gratefully, and soon after she and Minette returned to England in 1945, they found a cottage in the village of Puttenham, near Guildford, just a short drive from Long Meadow.

By 1944, it was becoming clear that the tide was turning in favour of Britain and her allies, and Shepard's responsibilities in the Home Guard were reduced. His company was finally disbanded on 31 December 1944. He and Norah were settled at Long Meadow, with a new London base in Park Road, St John's Wood (just a stone's throw from his childhood home at Kent Terrace) for use as a working studio and for occasional overnight stays.

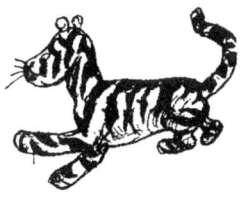

CHAPTER EIGHT

Now They
Were Sixty …

Understandably, the Milnes were relieved and delighted that the war had ended with Christopher safe and fully recovered from his head wound and looked forward keenly to his return. In fact he was not demobilized until August of 1946, returning to Cotchford Farm in time for his twenty-sixth birthday.

In some ways, the war was Christopher's delayed adolescence. During it he moved away emotionally as well as physically from his parents and returned to England as his own man. His first serious romantic relationship in Trieste had further opened his eyes to adult life, and he was determined not to surrender the independence he had achieved during the war years. The war had forced a dislocation that Alan Milne forlornly hoped might be temporary, but which Christopher knew would not. Inevitably, Alan Milne was being unrealistic when he expected that his connection with his son would return to its pre-war closeness. Instead, it became obvious that Christopher now wanted to loosen the ties that had previously bound them together. It was a significant change for the older man: he would no longer have any relationship as emotionally intimate as that which he had had first with Ken, and then with Christopher.

The weeks that Christopher spent at Cotchford before returning to Cambridge University to complete his degree were strained. There seemed to be little in common between the three of them, and Alan and Daphne struggled to understand that it was perfectly normal – and only to be expected – that Christopher was growing away from them. It was an awkward time for all of them, as of course it was for so many post-war family relationships, and there was a collective sigh of relief when he went back up to Cambridge.

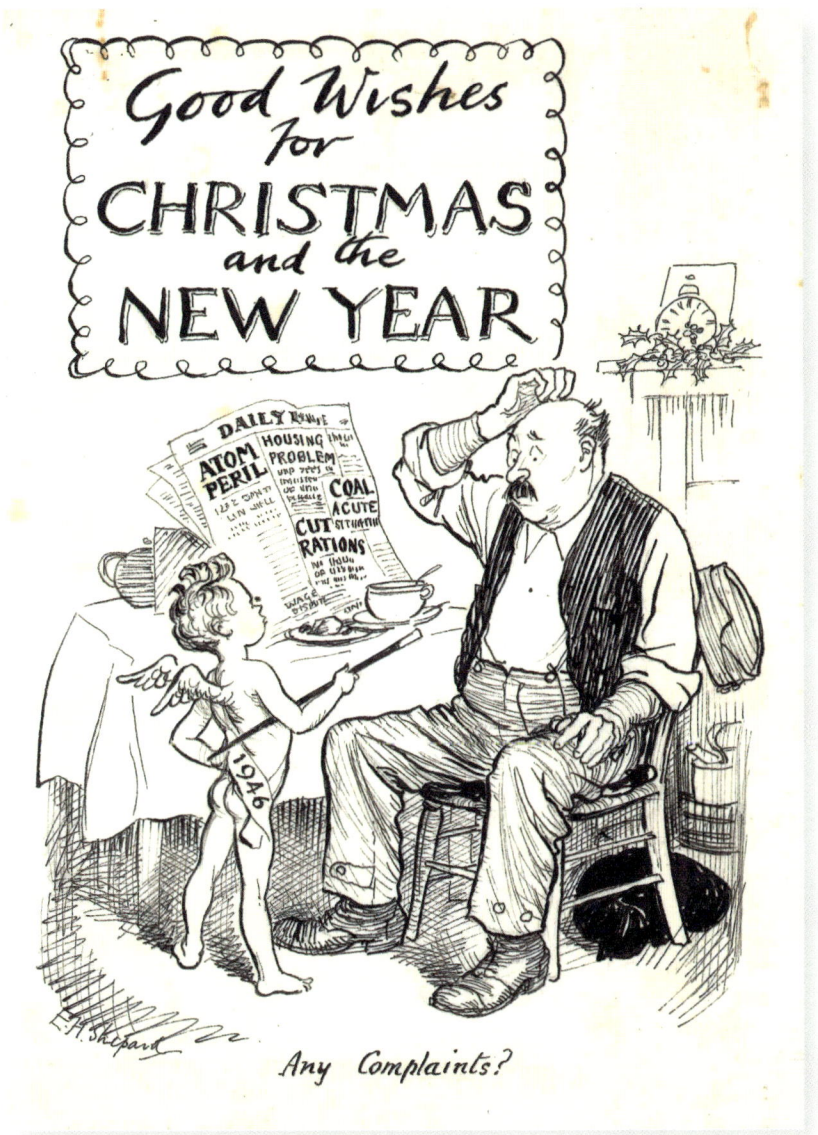

Shepard's Christmas card for 1946 all too clearly demonstrates the economic
hardships of the post-war era.

After completing his interrupted studies at Trinity College with an
undistinguished third-class honours degree in English Literature, and coming
down from Cambridge, Christopher embarked upon a fruitless search for a
job. He tried writing short stories, but only received rejection slips; he applied
to work at the Central Office of Information, the successor to the wartime
Ministry of Information, with no success; even a traineeship with the John
Lewis Partnership failed. Christopher was living on his own in a flat in London,
lonely, frustrated and angry at how life had failed him, and bitter that his father,
after his own return from the First World War, had used his son as a springboard
to success, fame and riches. Christopher felt that this process had left him
equipped for nothing other than being the Christopher Robin of the Winnie-

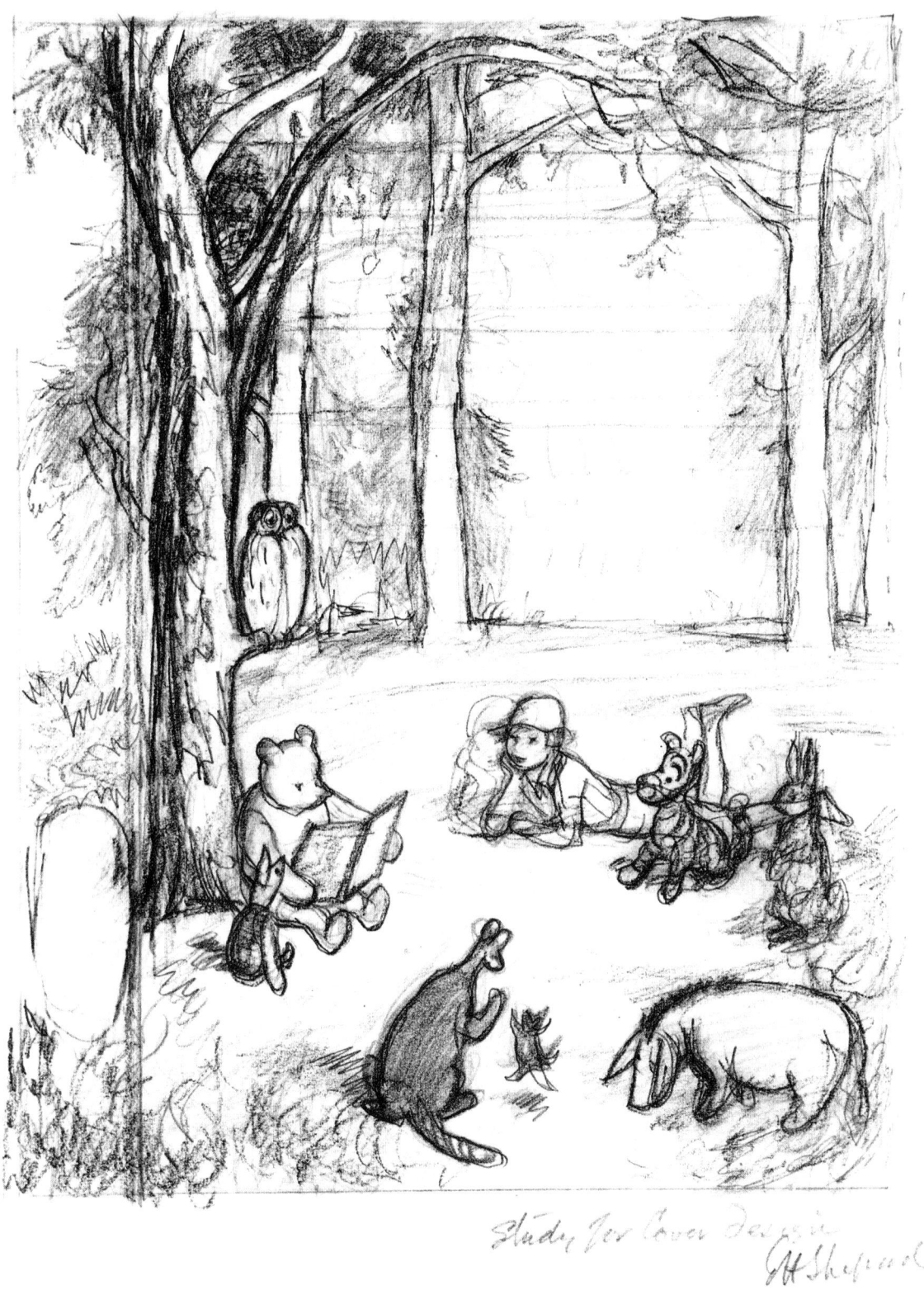

Study for cover design

E.H. Shepard

The introduction of affordable colour printing and the increase in demand for the Winnie-the-Pooh books led to new editions with coloured illustrations. For some, Shepard simply coloured in the original black-and-white drawings but increasingly he had to create completely new coloured illustrations, as for this book, *The World of Christopher Robin*, an edition containing both *Winnie-the-Pooh* and *The House at Pooh Corner*, published by Methuen in the early 1960s.

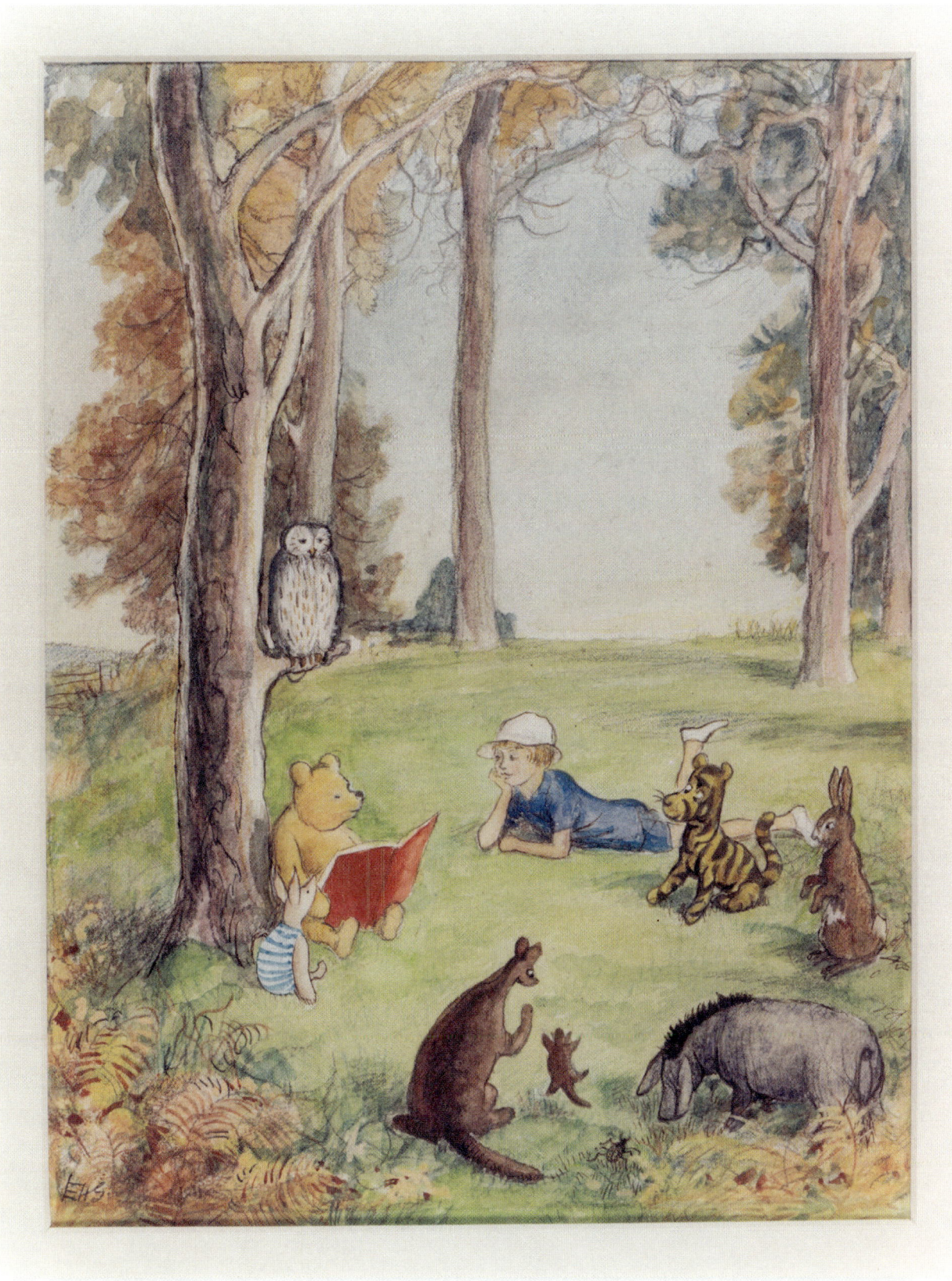

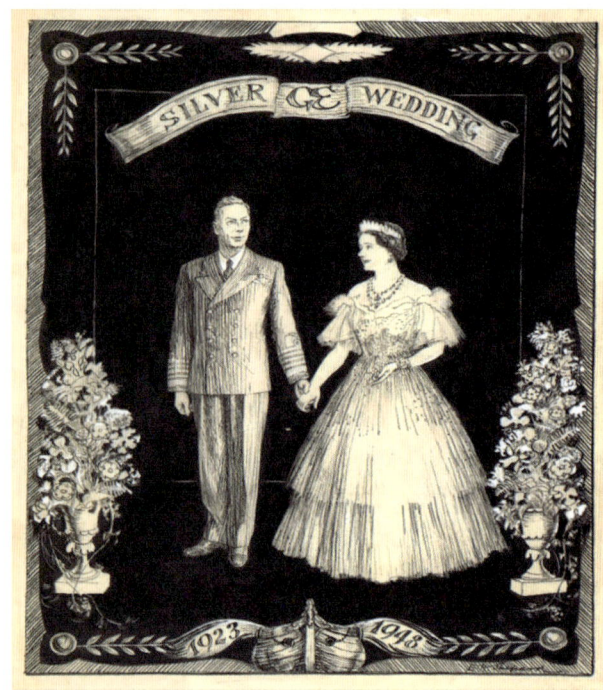

A formal image to mark the Silver Wedding of King George VI and Queen Elizabeth in 1948.

the-Pooh stories. This attitude was plainly unfair and did not represent the whole story, for many other demobbed soldiers were in a similar unemployed and miserable situation in post-war austerity Britain. However, there were sufficient grains of truth in this narrative that Christopher felt justified in his feelings of resentment.

It was in the depths of the gloomy post-war winter of 1947–8, with rationing in full force and the bankrupt state of the nation all too obvious, that Christopher's step-grandmother Nancy, the second wife of Daphne's father, decided that it was ludicrous that he and his first cousin Lesley, who was also living and working in London, did not know each other (Lesley being the daughter of Daphne's estranged brother Aubrey). Nancy therefore introduced the cousins to each other on 5 February 1948. There seems to have been an almost instant attraction between them.

At the end of March Christopher spent a fraught week at Cotchford, according to his father almost monosyllabic except when he was correcting his parents, and they all seem to have been counting the days until his return to London. When Alan and Daphne discovered that Christopher was seeing Lesley, and worse, that the two first cousins intended to marry, they were beside themselves with disappointment and distress. They simply could not comprehend how Nancy could have introduced the two while knowing of the breach between their respective parents. They also could not fathom how Christopher, aware of the family schism, had allowed himself to be bewitched by the enemy camp. They still considered Lesley's parents Aubrey and Irene, with whom they had fallen out so many years before over money, as the enemy. Worse still, Lesley did not worship at the altar of Pooh. She seemed indifferent to the charms of the books, and firmly adopted Christopher's narrative of their toxic impact on his childhood.

Christopher and Lesley married on 24 July 1948 at Holy Trinity, Brompton, a fashionable church in London's South Kensington, with both families present at what was an inevitably fraught occasion. After his marriage, the relationship between Christopher and his parents was sporadic and difficult. He was simply unable to be what his father wanted, and his mother was so devastated that he had joined forces with her estranged brother's family that it seemed as if no meaningful reconciliation could be possible.

One perhaps unexpected consequence of Christopher's decision to break away from his parents was that Alan and Daphne became closer again. After the semi-detached years, in their joint misery and disappointment at their failure to build a lasting post-war rapprochement with their son, they turned back towards each other. More tolerance and understanding, more give and take, a greater commitment by Alan and a more relaxed attitude from Daphne, helped both of them through their sense of grief and loss to build a much more harmonious twilight for their lives together. They found activities to share, Alan showing much more of an interest in Daphne's garden and, more to the point, helping in it, and they would together tackle *The Times* crossword puzzle. And so their relationship became more companionable, calm and loving than at any time since the heady days of Winnie-the-Pooh and their joy in Alan's success, Daphne's popularity and the fun they had together with the young Christopher Robin.

Alan Milne was also adjusting to a changed working life. He had moved his working space from the rather dark ground-floor room at Cotchford Farm, which he had previously used as a study, into his bedroom on the floor above, a much better-lit room. Here he resumed work on his last novel, *Chloe Marr*, which had been in gestation since the middle of the war. It was different, a breath of fresh air in the post-war gloom, as he created a character entirely seen from others' viewpoints, not from within, and which challenged conventions. Published in 1946, the critics were surprisingly positive, and *Chloe Marr* sold well: over 15,000 copies in Britain and double that in America. Could it be that after ten years in the doldrums, Milne had found a refreshed voice which resonated with the reading and buying public again?

It was not to be. With increasingly rare exceptions, his work was simply out of fashion. While he had come to loathe the word 'whimsical', this did sum up, reasonably accurately, the tone of so much of his literary output. And while the whimsicality of Winnie-the-Pooh was part of its integral charm and DNA, the same could not be said for his work for adult audiences in the changing times after the Second World War. His writing continued to be light, mildly entertaining and frothy. During the inter-war years, when audiences and readers were seeking escapism from the horrors of war and the challenging realities of peace, his plays, books and articles were considered delightful. They chimed perfectly with the Roaring Twenties, the Bright Young Things and the anticipation of a new order. But, by the mid-thirties, so much had changed. There was a new reality, issues of the day were more challenging, darker clouds were looming on the horizon, and there was a gradual change in what audiences and readers wanted. Milne seemed unable to respond to this shift in mood and to change his style of writing to reflect this.

This inevitable mismatch between his writing and the expectations of readers accelerated after 1945. There were massive changes in society, first demonstrated by the election of the Labour government in 1945 by an unexpected landslide. And, as the forties gave way to the fifties, the social changes spread out to encompass all areas of life. Milne was rooted in an earlier period and was simply unable to adapt. He realized this himself perfectly well, not least because of declining book sales, royalty income and receipts from plays. Apart, of course, for the income from the Winnie-the-Pooh books, whose ongoing success nonetheless hung over him like a dark cloud.

One of the few visitors actively welcomed to Cotchford after the war was Elliot Macrae of Dutton, probably because he came over from New York especially to see Milne with an encouraging proposal, and it would have been churlish to have insisted on a formal meeting in London. Dutton also seemed to Milne to be treating him more respectfully than Methuen, with a willingness to take risks based on his reputation, which Methuen seemed unwilling to do.

Macrae proposed a substantial reboot by re-issuing all Milne's adult novels, promoting them widely, and anticipated substantial sales. It must have been a ray of light in the gloom of the news from publishers and editors in London, who remained outwardly respectful but did not anticipate any resurgence in enthusiasm from the buying public for his adult work. It turned out that

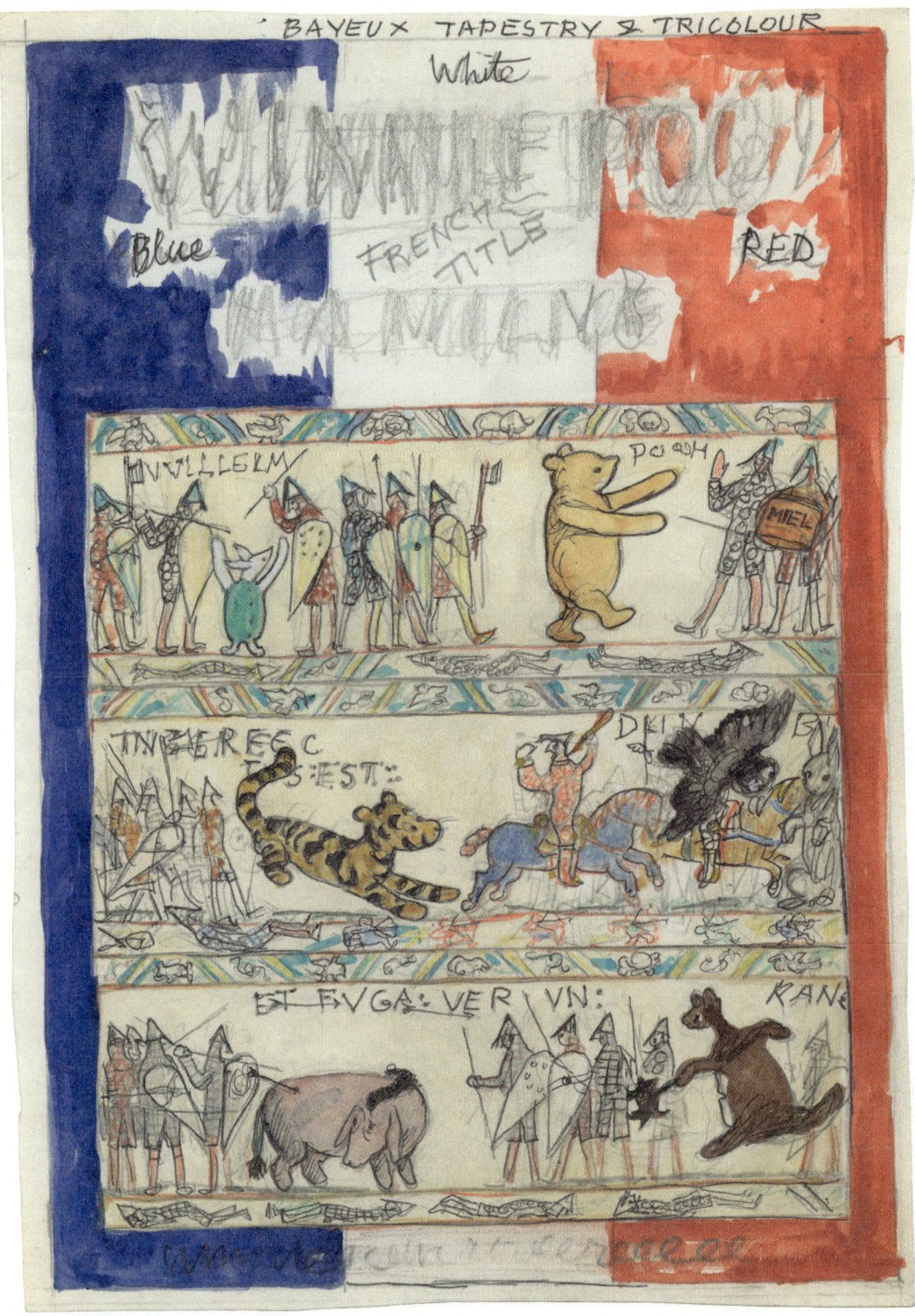

In a design intended for the cover of the French edition of *Winnie-the-Pooh*, Shepard depicted the characters of the Hundred Acre Wood in a version of the Bayeux Tapestry and the colours of the Tricolore.

Methuen was right and Dutton was wrong. Dutton did indeed reprint a substantial number of Milne's adult books in America, but it was a humiliating failure. Having initially and over-optimistically intended to order more than half a million copies, at the last minute wiser counsel prevailed and this was cut approximately in half. But despite a targeted sales campaign and the added support of a states-wide tour of the Winnie-the-Pooh animals (which was a huge success), fewer than 20,000 copies were sold in total, less than ten per cent of the reduced print run. It was a disaster for Dutton, an unhappy vindication for Methuen, and a humiliation for Milne.

When Elliot Macrae had visited Cotchford in 1947, he had been shown the original Winnie-the-Pooh toy animals. They were still in Christopher's old room, looking rather sad and uncared for. On the spur of the moment, he asked if he could borrow them for the purposes of publicity in America, and greatly to his surprise the Milnes agreed. They do not appear to have consulted Christopher. And so the remaining soft toys, with a replacement Piglet (the original had been chewed to destruction by a dog in the thirties, the same fate which befell Growler in the forties), were despatched to New York with a certificate of authentication handwritten by Milne. Dutton made the most of this unexpected bonus, and the Pooh animals set off on an extensive tour around America.

This touring exhibition was wildly popular and was enthusiastically received throughout the States. Dutton had the clever idea of having a visitors' book at each location for people to sign and write comments in, and these provided glowing contributions which Dutton used for further promotions. A selection of these visitors' books was sent to Milne, who much appreciated both the gesture and the enthusiastic comments made by so many fans. This initiative was so successful that Dutton asked for an extension to the animals' visit, so that the tours could be extended and repeated. The animals criss-crossed North America, resting in the pauses between tours at Dutton's New York office, where they were also much admired. Milne was quietly delighted by this commitment from Dutton and reception in America, and decided that Dutton could keep the toy animals in America.

Christopher does not appear to have been unduly upset by this decision. He felt that these soft toys of his childhood were in the past, a past which he still found difficult and challenging, and that he now enjoyed having around him things relevant to him as an adult, not harking back to his childhood. Neither Methuen nor Curtis Brown appear to have been consulted, and there was no agreement that the arrangement would be reviewed, or any commitment for the toy animals to return to Britain, even for visits. It was a spectacular coup for Dutton and America. There was one condition, however, and that was that the toy animals should never be cleaned but remain just as they were, as if they were just out of the nursery cupboard, ready for play, and not for display. In due course, and after Milne's death, Dutton came to the sensible conclusion that it was no longer appropriate for the toys to continue touring since they were inevitably deteriorating. There were also security and insurance issues, which also applied when the toys were at Dutton's New York office. Eventually they were transferred to the New York Public Library, somewhere where they would be secure and yet accessible. They have remained there ever since, although they have recently been cleaned and restored.

As for Shepard, as well as being the lead cartoonist from 1945, his position as a senior member of the *Punch* Table was critical in setting the agenda for *Punch*'s approach to current affairs. The post-war period was one of significant social, economic and political change in the United Kingdom, and his weekly cartoons still throw light on the issues of the day. After the retirement of Evoe Knox as editor of *Punch* in 1949, Ernest Shepard might have felt that at the age of sixty-nine it would be time for a change himself. In fact, the new editor, Kenneth Bird, stepping up from the position of art editor (he was himself a *Punch* staff cartoonist of considerable talent, known as Fougasse), was keen to retain continuity and talent. Shepard, who had a strong work ethic and a loyalty to *Punch*, was happy to oblige. This was his final period of producing weekly contemporary cartoons and covered another fascinating period in British political and social history. The era included the end of the first full-term Labour administration, the inconclusive general election of 1950, the return of a Conservative government led by wartime leader Winston Churchill in 1951, and the unexpected death of King George VI and the accession of Queen Elizabeth II in 1952. One of Shepard's most poignant drawings from this period was of the coffin of King George VI lying in state in Westminster Hall, with shafts of sunlight falling across it, overlooked by Britannia holding a wreath on behalf of the nation.

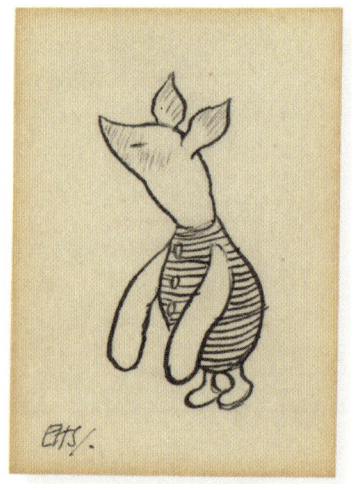

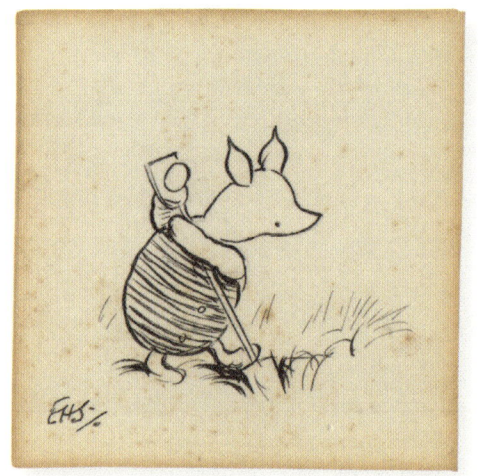

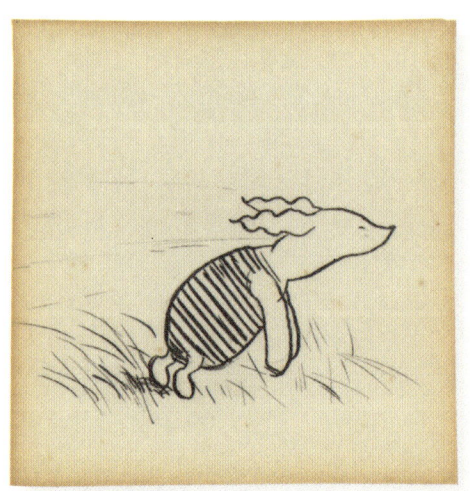

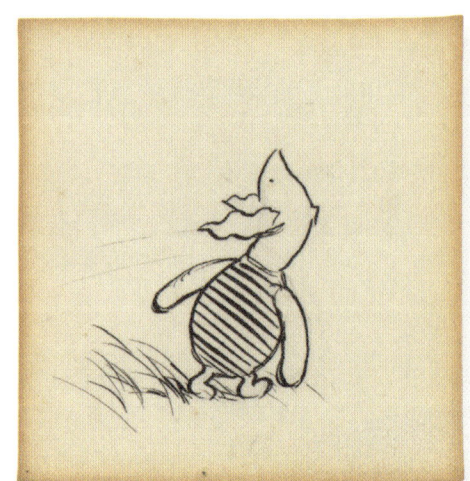

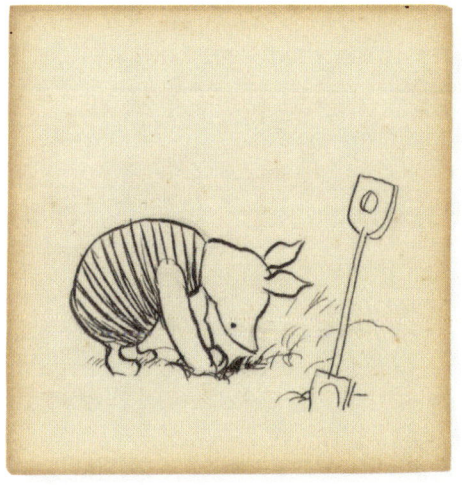
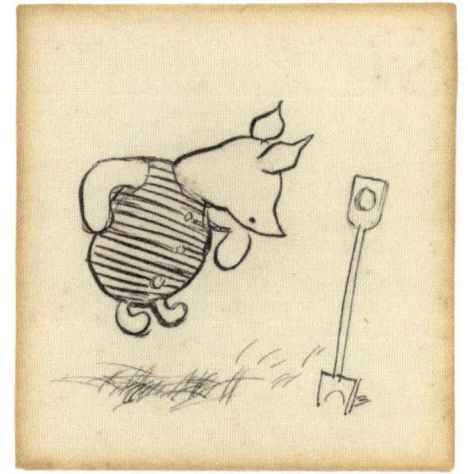
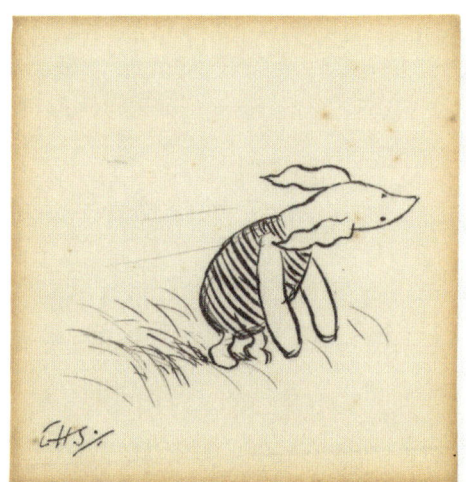
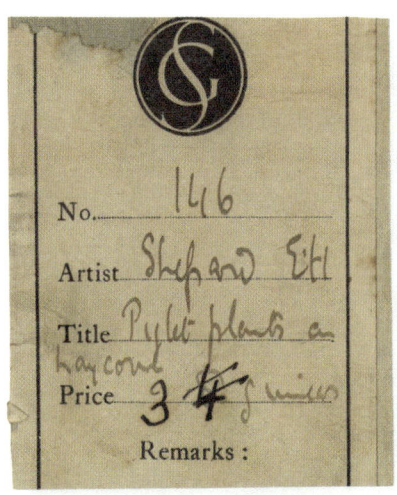

No. 146

Artist Shepard Eti

Title Piglet plants an haycorn

Price 3 4 guineas

Remarks:

Shepard never revealed which of the Winnie-the-Pooh characters, if any, was his favourite, but he seems to have had a soft spot for Piglet, as he retained this set of original drawings of Piglet in his studio until the end of his life. Most of us know someone with the character of the plucky yet anxious Piglet, always a follower and Pooh's loyal friend.

The image referenced back to his earlier drawing at the time of the abdication in 1936 which showed a sombre King Edward VIII at the end of his short reign.

In 1953 Bird was replaced as *Punch* editor by Malcolm Muggeridge. It was an external appointment that appeared to have surprised even Muggeridge himself, as he reputedly claimed that, 'There is no occupation more wretched than trying to make the English laugh.' He had no compunction in sacking Shepard as one of his first editorial decisions. Shepard was hardly surprised by this, as he was seventy-three years old and had worked for *Punch* in various roles for nearly fifty years, but he was unsurprisingly disappointed by the peremptory manner of his dismissal. His lengthy service to the magazine and valuable contributions over the years were barely acknowledged. Shepard was not one to bear a grudge, however, and despite what he may have felt at the manner of his dismissal, he bore it with his usual stoicism in difficult situations. This allowed him, in due course, to continue to submit freelance drawings and illustrations to *Punch* and to extend his connection for the following decade. It was also the case that, freed from the constraints of a weekly deadline, he had more freedom to accept a range of different work.

In 1951 Christopher and Lesley Milne moved to Dartmouth in Devon, putting a further physical distance between them and his parents, and there was little further contact with the older Milnes. Christopher and Lesley decided to open a bookshop, Daphne helpfully pointing out how illogical this was as it would involve Christopher having to deal with so many of the things he had long railed against. He acknowledged this wryly, but it made no difference to their plans.

Alan celebrated his seventieth birthday in January 1952 quietly, but it was marked by a total absence of any acknowledgement from Methuen, and by the gift of a case of whisky from Dutton, a drink which Milne did not like, as his publishers should have known. His last book, *Year In, Year Out*, was published in the summer in Britain and in the autumn in America of that year, and fittingly contained an E. H. Shepard illustration specially drawn for it. This was a charming frontispiece which showed the Winnie-the-Pooh animals with other characters, including Alice from *Alice's Adventures in Wonderland*, drawn in the style of Alice's original illustrator, John Tenniel. *Year In, Year Out* was a satisfying finale to Milne's professional career. It was a collection of individual

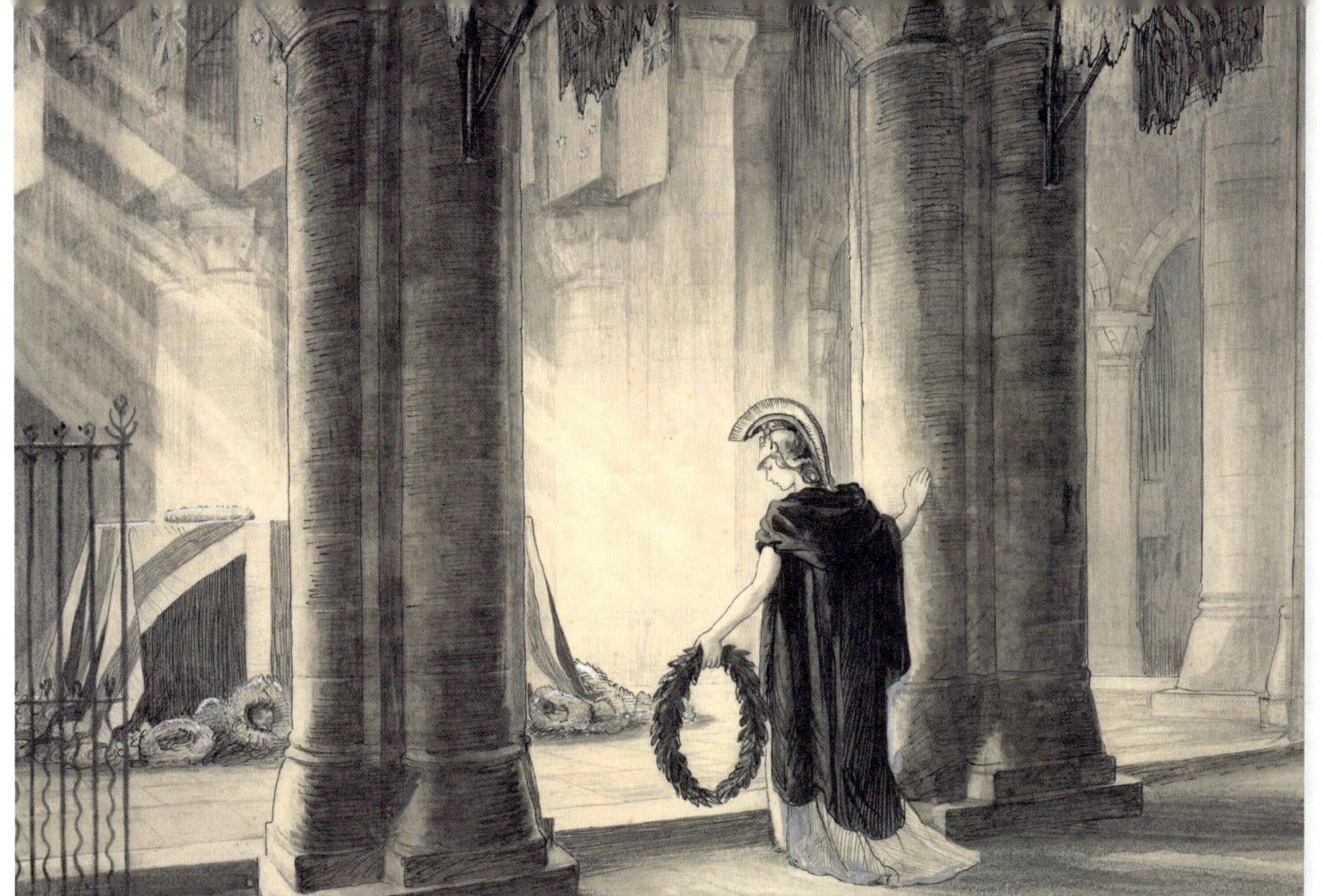

Britannia, representing the nation, holds a wreath before the coffin of King George VI lying in state in Westminster Hall.

articles on a range of topics, and was thoughtful, well written and apposite. It was well reviewed and sold satisfactorily. It was Milne and Shepard's last professional collaboration, almost thirty years after the first. Much water had since flowed under their respective bridges, both professionally and personally, and both had lost their only sons, albeit in different circumstances. Milne's last piece of published writing was a short verse in the *New York Herald Tribune* newspaper to promote the book.

In mid-October 1952 Alan Milne suffered a catastrophic stroke. He was taken to the local hospital near Cotchford and was not expected to survive more than a few days. However, he rallied sufficiently to be transferred to London's Middlesex Hospital, which had better facilities. And there he was visited by his old collaborator, professional colleague and ally in the most successful partnership in children's literature of all time, Ernest Shepard, for the last time.

Towards the end of 1952, as Alan lay seriously ill in hospital, Christopher Milne naïvely and ill-advisedly gave an interview to a London newspaper in which he was highly critical of his father. Christopher shared his belief that he

157

had been exploited for the commercial success of Winnie-the-Pooh, and how bitter he was about the impact this had had on him. Inevitably Milne was made aware of the article and was deeply wounded, but the damage had long been done. Later he said to a medical attendant that, 'We have *all* given our only sons.' Christopher had already been irrevocably lost to him.

By December, his condition had stabilized sufficiently for Milne to undergo a risky surgical procedure which would essentially be 'kill or cure'. The procedure, which went badly wrong, did neither. It was a disaster, as he remained alive and aware of his situation, but was left partially paralyzed and in a wheelchair. But much, much worse, it changed his character. The self-effacing, polite, calm and reflective man disappeared overnight, and was replaced by an angry, belligerent, rude and selfish caricature of his previous self. His remaining years were a misery. He was moved back to a hospital nearer to Cotchford and in due course returned home, where he was looked after by a series of nurses and medical professionals managed and overseen by Daphne, who stepped up to the plate and ensured that his care was the best it could be. Milne could read a little and write a little, but it was an inexorable decline, and it was nothing other than a relief when he finally died in January 1956.

The obituaries were predictably respectful and fair, but inevitably focused on the enormous success of his children's books. His writings for adults – the highly successful plays of the 1920s and 1930s, the thrillers, novels, short stories, journalism, anthologies and pacifist polemics – were relegated to also-rans.

Daphne arranged a memorial service at the church of All Hallows by the Tower in London, where the usual mixture of family, friends and London's literary establishment gathered to pay tribute. Christopher attended his father's memorial service alone, as Lesley was pregnant, which was an excellent excuse for her to be absent. The service was devised by Daphne and she thought that it was perfect, although others it found overly sentimental. As part of the service, the mourners sang Pooh's song 'How Sweet to be a Cloud'. That was bad enough, but then came 'Vespers'. This spectacularly ill-judged inclusion was the final straw for Christopher. He never saw his mother again.

By 1956, no longer needing to be regularly in London, the Shepards moved to the village of Lodsworth in Sussex, where they found a comfortable home which they renovated to include a working studio. It was to be Shepard's final

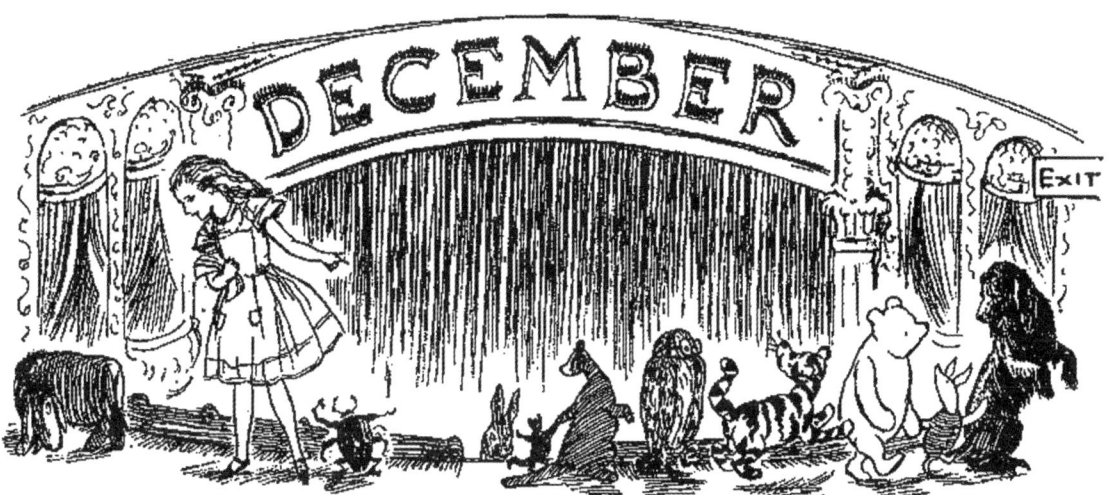

Shepard's frontispiece for Milne's *Year In, Year Out* in 1952.

home and became a happy and contented environment for the last twenty years of his long life. Meanwhile, what continued to be extraordinary was the sheer volume and quality of work which he undertook in the period after his retirement from *Punch* and at a time when most men of his age were fully retired and relaxing on a comfortable pension. As well as his usual work, he also regularly undertook artwork for advertising agencies, including for the writing-paper firm Basildon Bond and for Horlicks, 'The Malted Milk Drink'. In addition, he continued illustrating children's books, working on Malcolm Saville's *Susan, Bill* series and a new edition of *Hans Christian Andersen's Fairy Tales*, among other publications.

Once he had settled into life in Lodsworth, Shepard had more time on his hands, so he started work on his memoirs. When his children were young he had delighted in telling them stories of his own childhood, and Graham had regularly encouraged him to write these memories down. He decided initially to take a single year of his childhood as a starting point and, understanding the universal attraction of stories about a nostalgic and happy childhood, he painted a portrait of a comfortable middle-class Victorian upbringing. He described this through a series of episodes recalled from his childhood, in no particular chronological order, with accompanying illustrations. Unusually, he approached this project by doing the drawings first, and then writing down the accompanying stories afterwards. The resulting book, *Drawn from Memory*, was published by Methuen in 1957 to almost universally positive reviews and strong sales. Shepard seemed to have struck a seam of charm and nostalgia in his prose as well as his illustrations, which together summoned up images of a golden

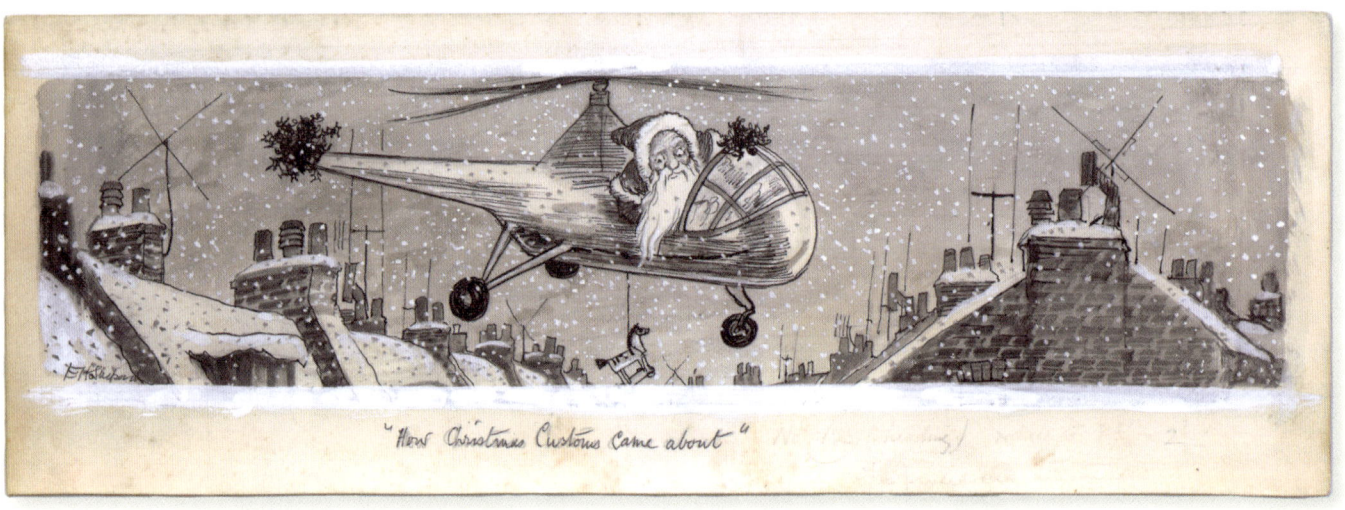

"How Christmas Customs came about"

One of a series of cartoons for the *Illustrated London News* – bringing Father Christmas into the 1950s.

autumn of the Victorian age. It was similar to the way that his 'decorations' for Winnie-the-Pooh had invoked memories of golden Edwardian summers before the First World War.

A little surprised, gratified and certainly emboldened by the success of *Drawn from Memory*, and strongly encouraged by his long-term agents Curtis Brown and publisher Methuen, he started work on a sequel, *Drawn from Life*, which covered the period from his schooldays until his marriage at the age of twenty-four. This, across a longer time span, roughly 1890 to 1904, and covering the death of his mother and the challenging times of his adolescence, was more of a narrative account of his early life. Inevitably, it lacked some of the spontaneity and charm of the first book. By all accounts, Shepard found it harder to write, possibly because it was in many ways more personal and related to his own feelings and emotions, which he found difficult to express.

Following the enormous success of the Winnie-the-Pooh books when they were first published, all four had consequently settled down to enjoy regular and substantial annual sales, with the two volumes of poetry initially outselling the two books of stories about Winnie-the-Pooh and his friends in the Hundred Acre Wood. They continued to bring in substantial royalties, but after Alan Milne's death, Daphne began to worry that, in an era of high taxation for the wealthy, her financial situation might become precarious and that she might

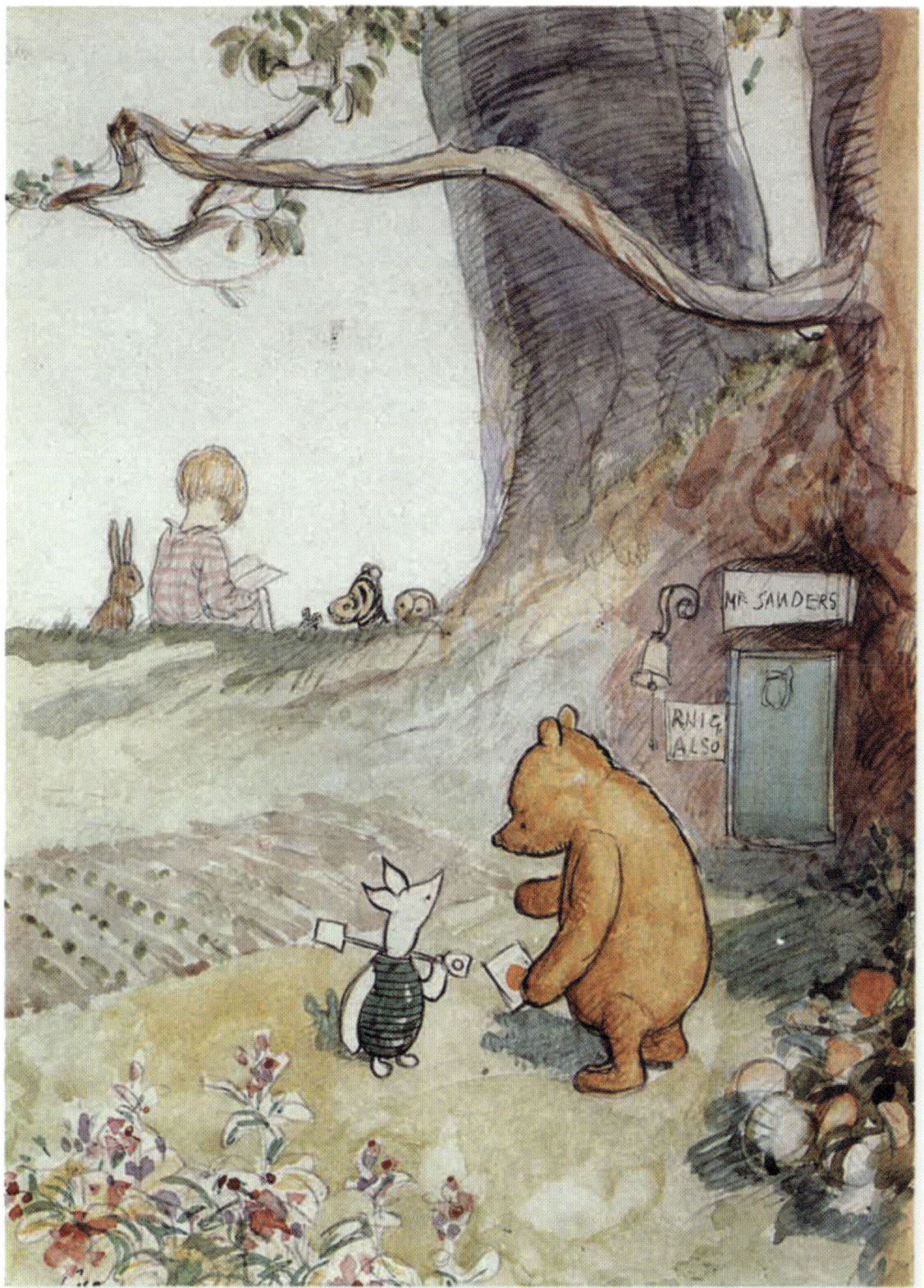

A coloured drawing for a new edition of the Winnie-the-Pooh stories.

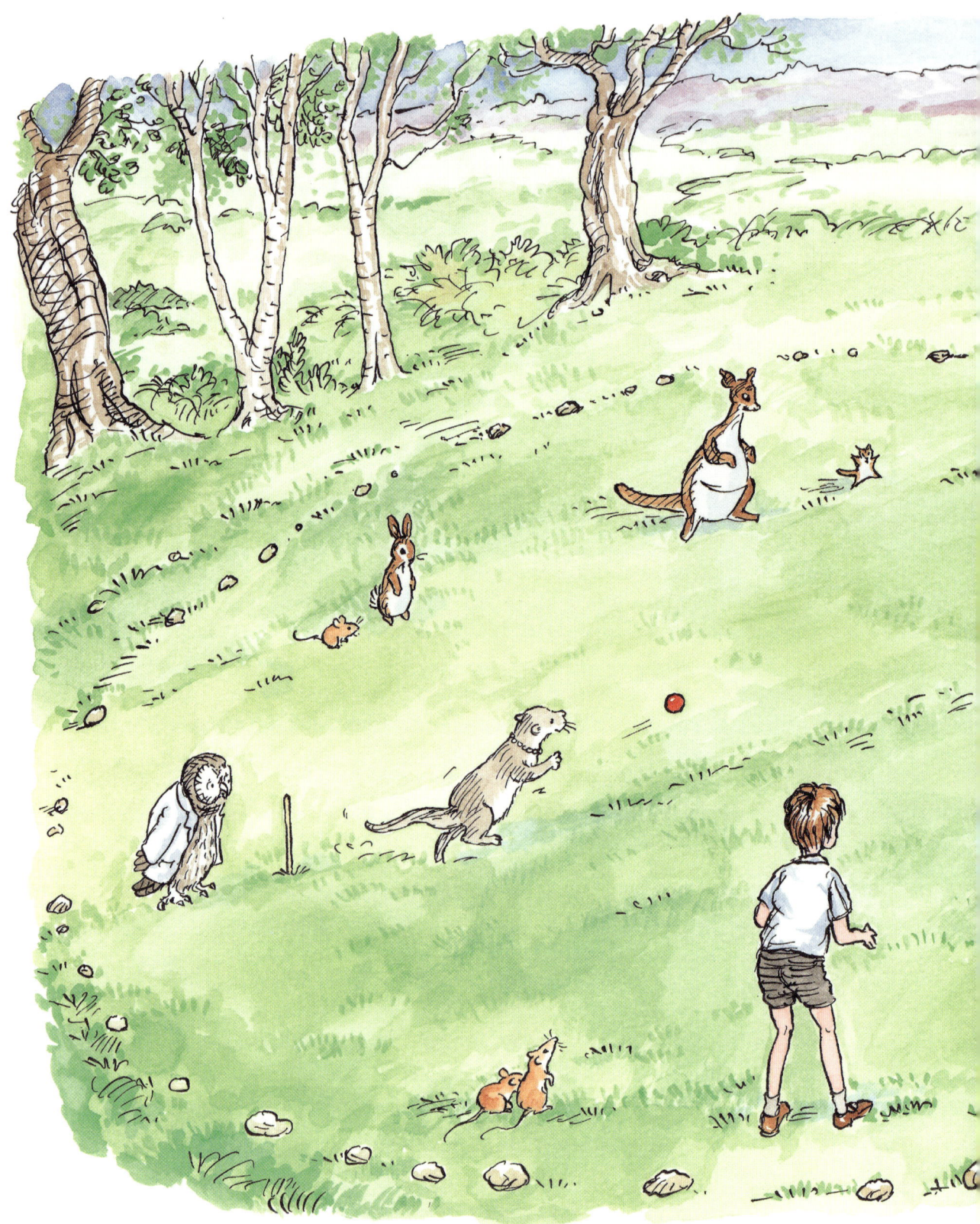

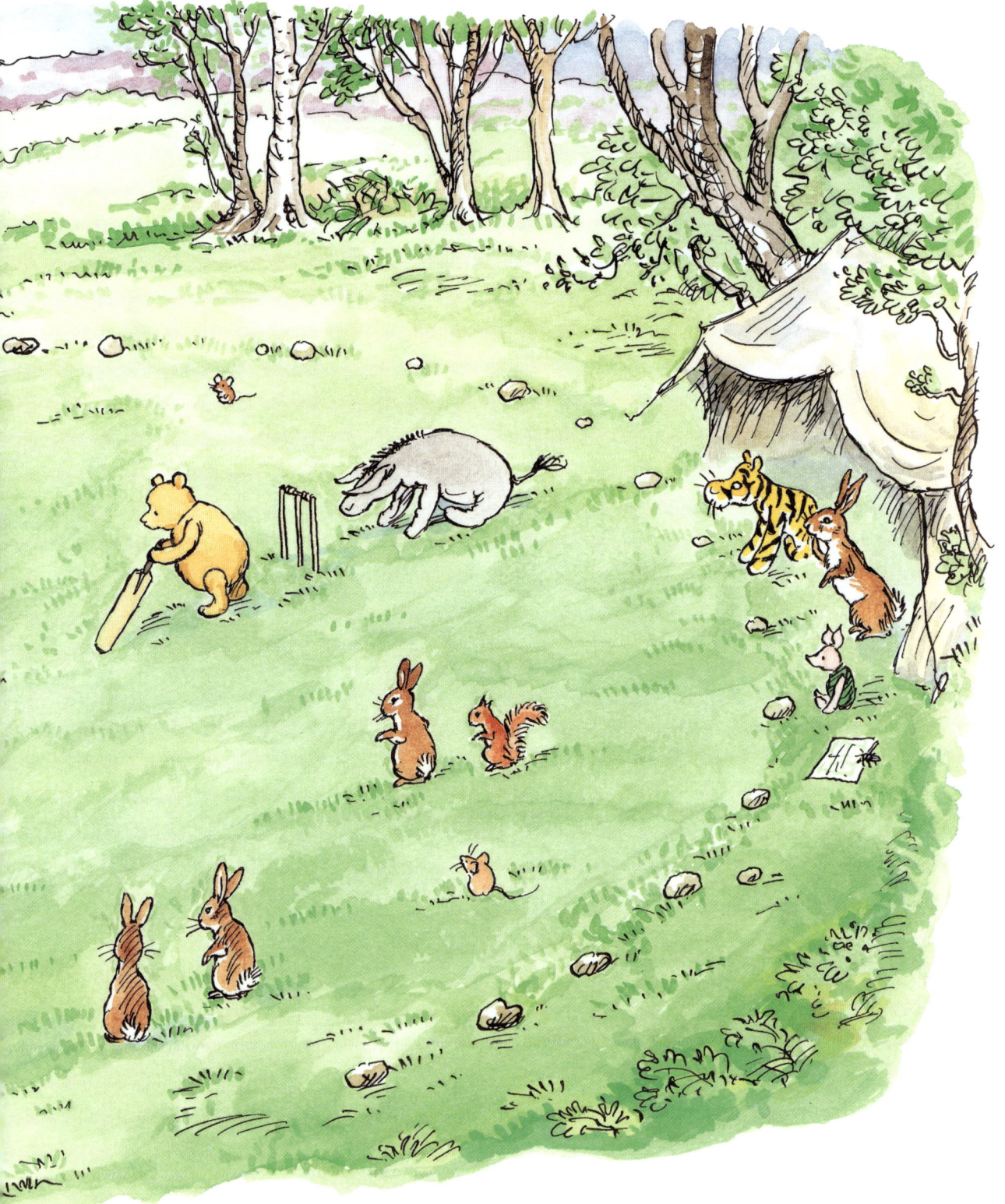

As Disney built a global audience for the cartoon and animated versions of Pooh, demand for more stories of the adventures of Winnie-the-Pooh and his friends in the Hundred Acre Wood grew steadily, and in 2009 the first in a series of prequels, sequels and new stories was published with the approval of both the Milne and Shepard estates. Here, in an illustration from *Return to the Hundred Acre Wood* by David Benedictus, Mark Burgess draws in the style of E. H. Shepard, still conveying the magic of the original.

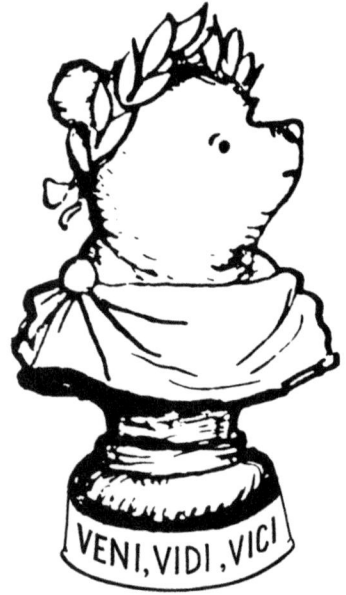

Winnie ille Pu, drawn by Shepard as a Roman bust complete with laurel wreaths for the Latin translation by Alexander Lenard, which originally appeared in an American edition. *Winnie ille Pu* was a surprising success, selling strongly despite most readers being unable to read Latin!

not be able to continue living in the style to which she had become accustomed. Daphne decided to discuss the possible assignment of the Winnie-the-Pooh rights to Disney without consulting Shepard nor, apparently until a late stage, with Curtis Brown, the agents still acting for both the Milne estate and Shepard. As what Walt Disney really wanted was the rights to the Winnie-the-Pooh images, not the text, so that that these could be converted into cartoon animations, it was an extraordinary decision not to involve Shepard. When the deal to transfer the Winnie-the-Pooh image rights to Disney was announced, it came as a profound shock to Shepard, the more so when he discovered that the deal left him with minimal rights and no veto to any changes to his original drawings.

When Disney subsequently began to convert Shepard's original work into cartoons it seems that the studio had very little, if any, direct consultation with him. Unsurprisingly, the first Disney animations of Winnie-the-Pooh were viewed by the majority of those who knew and loved the originals as a travesty, although Shepard himself prudently made no public comment.

However, it was undoubtedly the case that, from the 1960s onwards, the Disney cartoons, supported by the Disney marketing muscle, raised awareness of Winnie-the-Pooh around the world. The bear and his friends were introduced to a global population, many of whom, particularly in non-English-speaking territories, had been previously unaware of the books. This drove a significant expansion of sales of the original books, which increasingly became known as the 'classic' Winnie-the-Pooh, as people who were delighted by the Disney animated films became enchanted in turn with the original books from which these were derived.

In the late 1950s the first foreign language translations of the Winnie-the-Pooh books were published, including in Latin as *Winnie ille Pu* (which was surprisingly successful), and within twenty years the books were being translated into over thirty languages. By the year 2000, they were published in

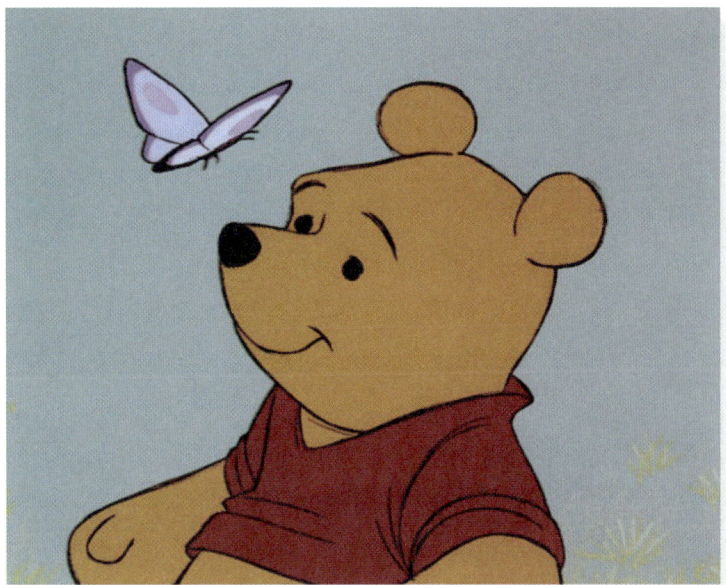

After Alan Milne's death in 1956, Daphne worried that her financial situation might become precarious, and so began discussions of the assignment of animation rights to Walt Disney Productions.

over fifty languages, such was the global reach of a bear who had truly become an international icon.

Apart from translations, the second impact of the Disney animations was an explosion in new editions of the original four books, both hardbacks and paperbacks in differing sizes. Many of these needed the existing illustrations to be resized and redrawn, with new dust jackets and cover illustrations. Then came the anthologies. For example, the two books of poems, *When We Were Very Young* and *Now We Are Six*, were repackaged in a single volume under the new title *The World of Christopher Robin*, and needed a new dust jacket and frontispiece.

His new drawings included a wonderful image for a French edition, involving the French Tricolore flag, Winnie-the-Pooh characters, and parts of the Bayeux Tapestry. Sadly, this edition seems never to have been published. In addition, he worked on other completely new books, such as Dutton's *The Pooh Cook Book*, published in 1966.

As the profile of the Winnie-the-Pooh characters and original books with their timeless Shepard 'decorations' grew and grew through the 1960s and 1970s, Shepard's postbag also grew and grew. He was punctilious in responding personally to letters and, particularly to children who had written to him, he would often respond with a small sketch of one of the animals in a handwritten letter. The number of visitors to his house also increased. They included professionals beating a path to his door in search of an interview, comment, or contribution to a book or media programme, as well as those simply wanting to meet the great man, though Shepard himself was always modest about his achievements. And there were higher profile visits. Lynda Johnson, the daughter of US President Lyndon Johnson, visited Shepard at his home in 1966. She was a great fan of Winnie-the-Pooh and was so taken by the experience that she not only returned again with her mother, Lady Bird Johnson, the First Lady of the USA, but also invited the Shepards to her White House wedding in December 1967. They seriously considered accepting this invitation and declined it only due to concerns about Shepard's health.

But perhaps one of the tributes which he found most moving came at the very twilight of his life in 1974, with the publication of Christopher Milne's first volume of reminiscences, *The Enchanted Places*. In this, Christopher paid a fulsome tribute to Shepard's unique contribution to the Winnie-the-Pooh legend. Despite Christopher's very public estrangement from his parents following his marriage, he had kept in regular touch with Shepard. It is perhaps surprising that Christopher maintained this connection, given Shepard's close links with the books which Christopher felt had caused him so much pain and anguish. Nonetheless, Christopher sent annual Christmas cards to Shepard, and they exchanged stories or information about Pooh from time to time. Shepard was even more touched when Christopher sent him a personally inscribed first edition of *The Enchanted Places*, with an accompanying handwritten letter reiterating his gratitude and thanks to Shepard for his part in capturing those carefree days of his youth in the Ashdown Forest. Shepard kept the letter inside the front cover of that first edition, where it remains today.

Shepard was ninety in 1969, at a time when life expectancy was seventy-one, and he had been working consistently since his teens with no formal retirement. He still drew and painted almost every day, filling numerous sketchbooks with drawings, sketches and notes. His health also remained remarkably sound, with few significant medical issues or concerns as he entered his tenth decade. In March 1969, for example, he was commissioned by Methuen to produce the full-colour edition of *The Wind in the Willows*; in June Methuen further commissioned a full-colour edition of *Winnie-the-Pooh*; and in December Methuen gave him a ninetieth-birthday lunch at the Garrick Club, the home-from-home where Alan Milne had so frequently lunched. Quite a year for a ninety-year-old.

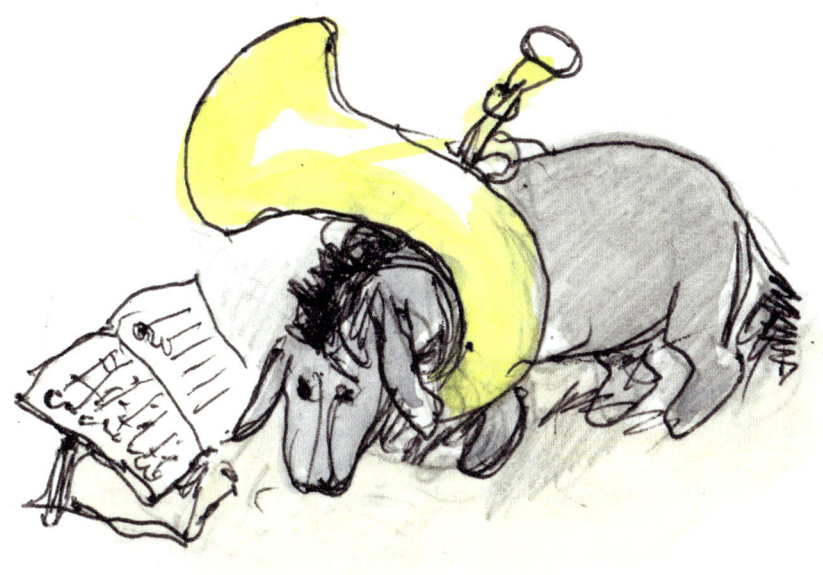

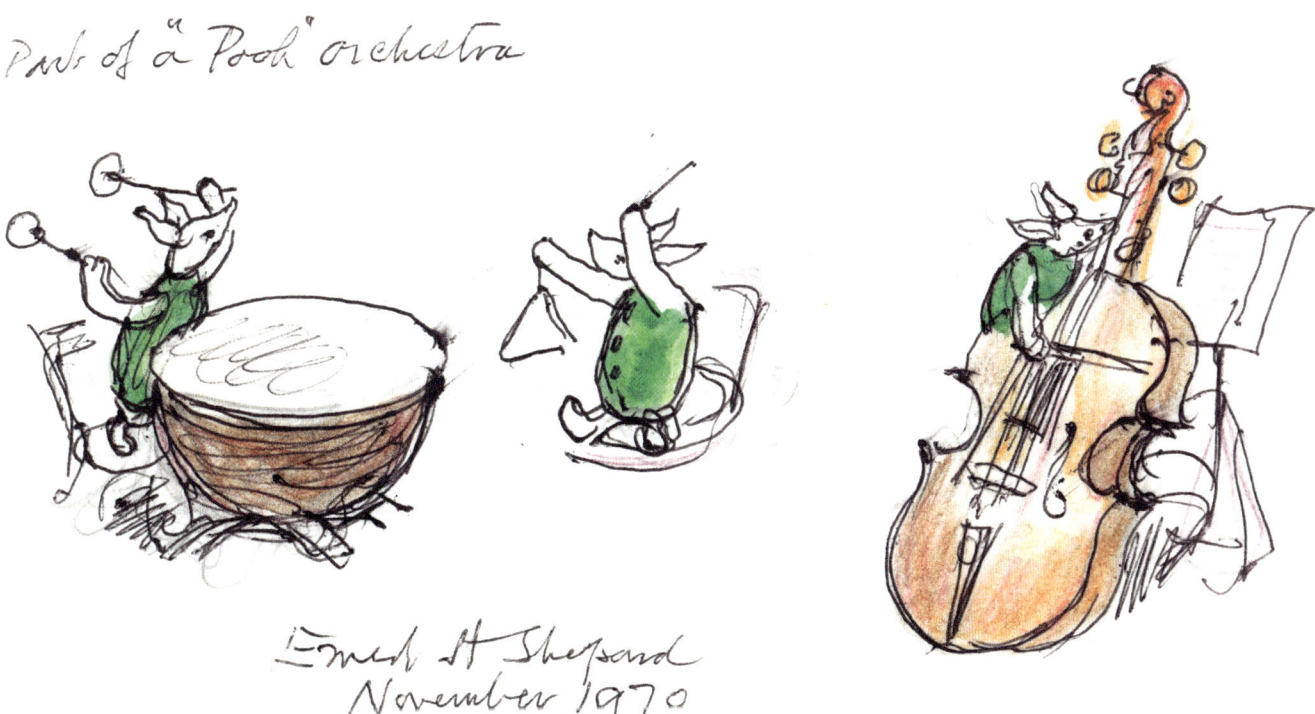

'Part of a "Pooh" orchestra, Ernest H. Shepard, November 1970'. In perfect tune with their characters, Eeyore tries his hand – somewhat forlornly – at the tuba, while Piglet attacks his instruments with gusto.

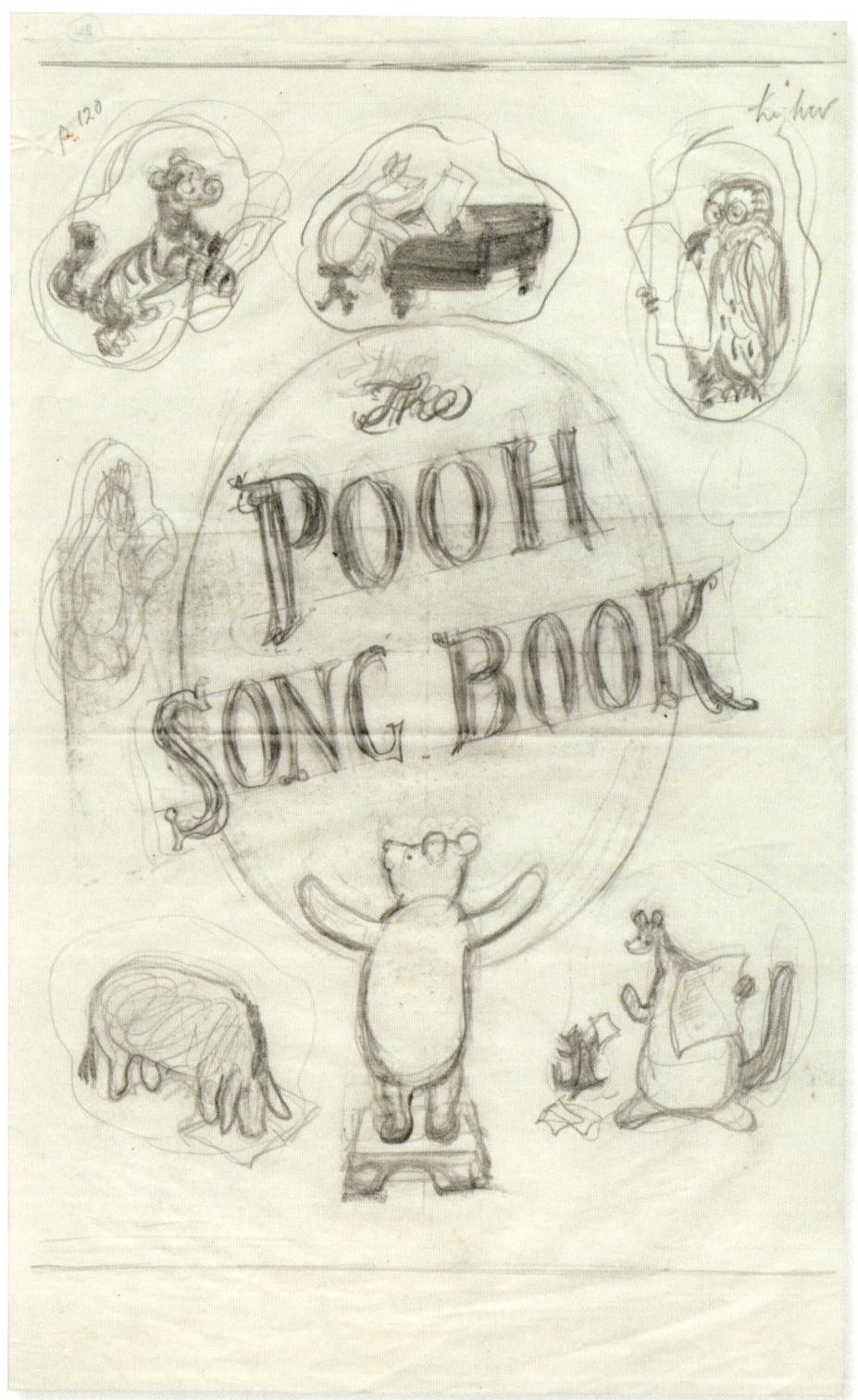

Shepard's early sketch for the cover of *The Pooh Song Book*, published by Dutton in 1961.

Gradually, however, as the 1970s drew on, Shepard inevitably became frailer, with his hearing loss probably the most obvious sign of his advanced age, although he used the rather basic hearing aids available at that time. He was a fixture of the local community, a committed member of the local church and a regular at village events. Towards the end of his life, increasingly deaf, villagers would watch him with bated breath as he would set out across the busy road, oblivious to the traffic around him. But he remained living independently at home, continuing to go to his studio most days to put pen to paper, and keeping up regular correspondence with family, friends, and the many people who wrote to him. Some of his correspondents had re-discovered his classic 'decorations' for Winnie-the-Pooh through the Disney cartoons. In 1972, perhaps rather belatedly, he was awarded the OBE in the Queen's Birthday Honours list, fifty-five years after his award of the Military Cross was presented to him by Queen Elizabeth II's grandfather, King George V.

Ernest Shepard died peacefully in Sussex on 24 March 1976, at the age of ninety-six.

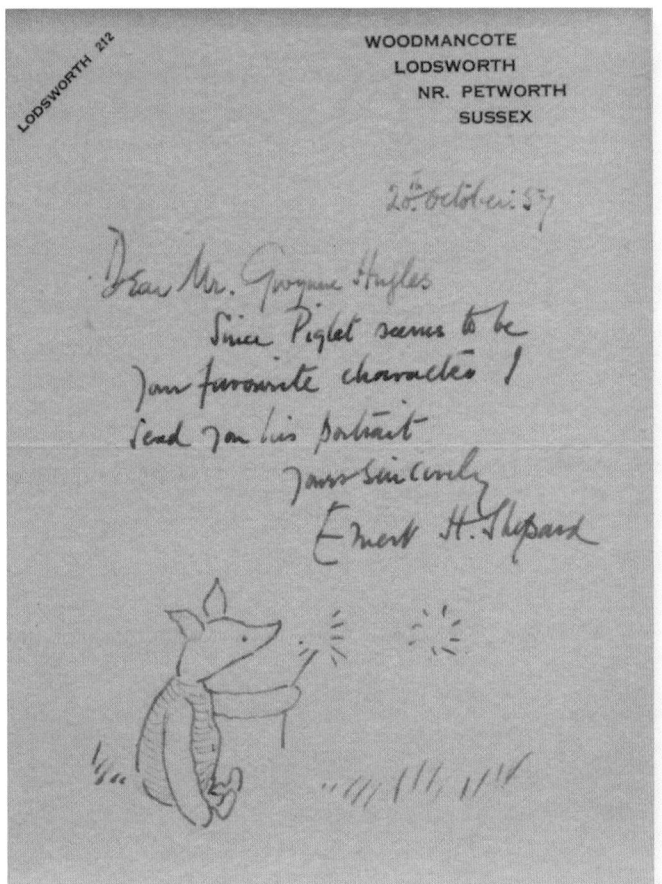

Piglet blowing a dandelion 'clock' in a letter to a correspondent.

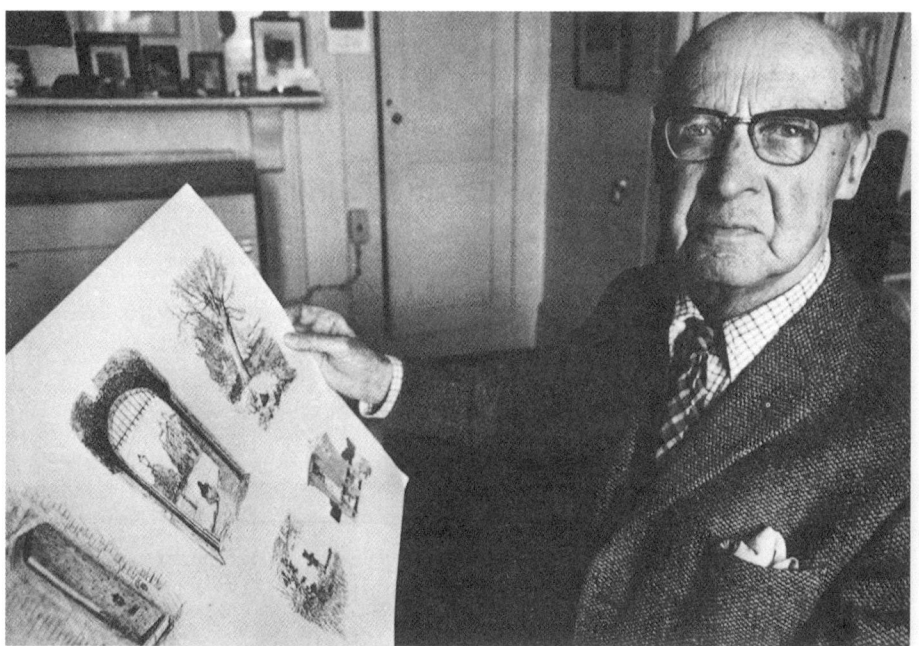

Shepard was still refining, redrawing and colouring illustrations for the ever-changing editions of Winnie-the-Pooh and *The Wind in the Willows* up to his very last days.

Many years before, Alan Milne had written:

When I am gone,
Let Shepard decorate my tomb,
And put (if there is room)
Two pictures on the stone:
Piglet from page a hundred and eleven,
And Pooh and Piglet walking (157) ...
And Peter, thinking that they are my own,
Will welcome me to Heaven.

And in the end, surely that was their joint epitaph.

Afterword

After Alan Milne's death Daphne Milne sold Cotchford Farm and moved back to London, where she died in 1971. Christopher and Lesley Milne's only child, a daughter, Clare, was born a few months after her grandfather's death and lived her life with cerebral palsy. Christopher died in 1996, Clare in 2012 and Lesley in 2014. Apart from the four Winnie-the-Pooh books and the play *Toad of Toad Hall*, all of A. A. Milne's other work is out of print.

After Ernest Shepard's death, his widow Norah barely survived him a few months. They had no children, but his daughter from his first marriage, Mary Shepard, continued to illustrate the *Mary Poppins* books until 1988. She died, childless, in 2000. Shepard's granddaughter Minette, daughter of his son Graham, who had been killed in action in 1943, still lives in Sussex, close to Lodsworth, the last home of her grandfather. She, and her children and grandchildren, are the only descendants of A. A. Milne and E. H. Shepard.

Apart from the four Winnie-the-Pooh books, *The Wind in the Willows* with the Shepard illustrations has never been out of print, and neither have Shepard's charming books about his early life, *Drawn from Memory* and *Drawn from Life*. In 2015, an exhibition in London showcased his work from 1914 to 1918, as part of the commemorations for the centenary of the First World War. An exhibition in 2017 to mark the ninetieth birthday of Winnie-the-Pooh, curated by London's Victoria and Albert Museum, was very successful, and then toured across the Americas and Asia to great acclaim and enormous visitor numbers, reinforcing the magic that is Pooh.

2026 – the centenary of the publication of *Winnie-the-Pooh* – also marks the seventieth anniversary of the death of Alan Milne, and the fiftieth anniversary of the death of Ernest Shepard. Back in the 1920s, when they were brought together by the publisher E. V. Lucas, neither of them could have had any idea that they were embarking on what would become initially a publishing sensation, and later a global phenomenon.

The completely unexpected worldwide success of Winnie-the-Pooh brought fame, fortune and a revolution in book publishing, innovative marketing and brand management. It fixed the names of A. A. Milne and E. H. Shepard forever with the four Winnie-the-Pooh books and defined them in perpetuity as co-creators of these iconic characters, charming stories and delightful 'decorations'.

It cannot be anything other than the case that Milne and Shepard together created a cultural phenomenon which is likely to be as long lived and sustained as any in history. Few have managed to create a language, an image and a brand which resonates so strongly across a global audience of children of all ages, generation after generation.

They changed the world, and it changed them.

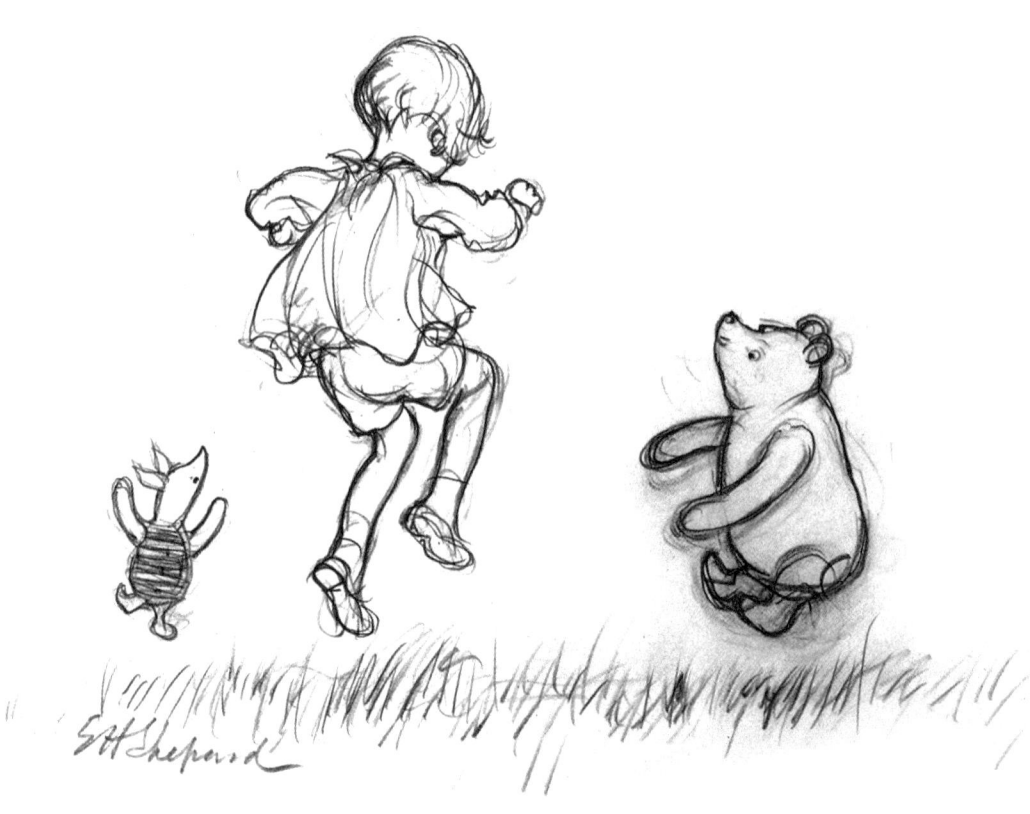

Acknowledgements

One sadness in bringing together this joint biography was that there are no living descendants of Alan Milne, and therefore no personal reminiscences, no anecdotes and no retained family papers. Ernest Shepard, however, is survived by a granddaughter and great-grandchildren who remember him well, and were able to give me first-hand stories and recollections and allowed me to see his private papers and remaining artwork still in their hands. Therefore, much of my research was in institutions where the relevant material has been deposited. I am particularly grateful to the British Library and its efficient staff for access to papers, books and radio recordings, and to the E. H. Shepard Archive at the University of Surrey, so efficiently managed by Helen Roberts and her team. The librarian and his staff at the Wren Library at Trinity College, Cambridge, allowed me access to A. A. Milne's original manuscript pages, and to records and photographs relating to his time as a student.

Ann Thwaite's *A. A. Milne: The Man Behind Winnie-the-Pooh* (Faber & Faber, 1990) remains the definitive biography and is always a pleasure to read. Her extensive research provides the widest background to the life and work of Alan Milne. Her subsequent book, *The Brilliant Career of Winnie-the-Pooh* (Methuen, 1992) has also much for the reader interested particularly in the Winnie-the-Pooh books. Ernest Shepard's own books of memoirs, *Drawn from Memory* (Methuen, 1957) and *Drawn from Life* (Methuen, 1961), are fascinating in their descriptions of his early life (and unusual in that he drew the illustrations first, and then wrote the stories around them, in a reversal of the usual process).

Curtis Brown has been literary agents to A. A. Milne and E. H. Shepard and their estates for over 100 years, a remarkable partnership which remains harmonious to this day. Stephanie Thwaites continues in a long tradition of providing outstanding help and support to both estates, and she and her colleagues have given me ongoing professional guidance and advice. Michael O'Mara as publisher has similarly given me consistent support and wise counsel, and as editor, Louise Dixon has been supportive, helpful, pragmatic and encouraging. The Pooh Properties Trustees, guardians of the Milne estate, have also been generous in their support.

Farshore, now an imprint of HarperCollins, has generously allowed me to use the coloured-in drawings of Winnie-the-Pooh, recently remastered to an exceptionally high resolution, and John Packard has consistently backed the project. The Garrick Club, a veritable home-from-home for Alan Milne for decades, and the venue for Ernest Shepard's ninetieth birthday celebration lunch, has allowed me to see and reproduce a number of images from their collection of A. A. Milne memorabilia. Mark Burgess, who has been illustrating 'in the style of' E. H. Shepard since 2001 with the support of the Shepard Estate, has kindly given his permission for the reproduction of drawings from more recent times.

My family and close friends have indulged my preoccupation with Milne and Shepard but seem to have enjoyed seeing again the wonderful words and charming decorations for the four Winnie-the-Pooh books, as well as being mostly surprised at the breadth and depth of their other, less well-known, work. As always, my wife Arabee has been stoic in the face of disruption, chaos, muddle, confusion and panic – without her it would not have happened.

Every attempt has been made to identify and credit appropriately copyright owners, but any errors, omissions and failure to acknowledge sources accurately are entirely the responsibility of the author.

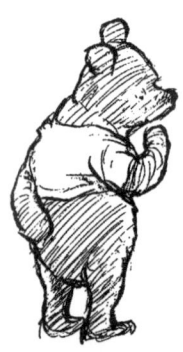

Index

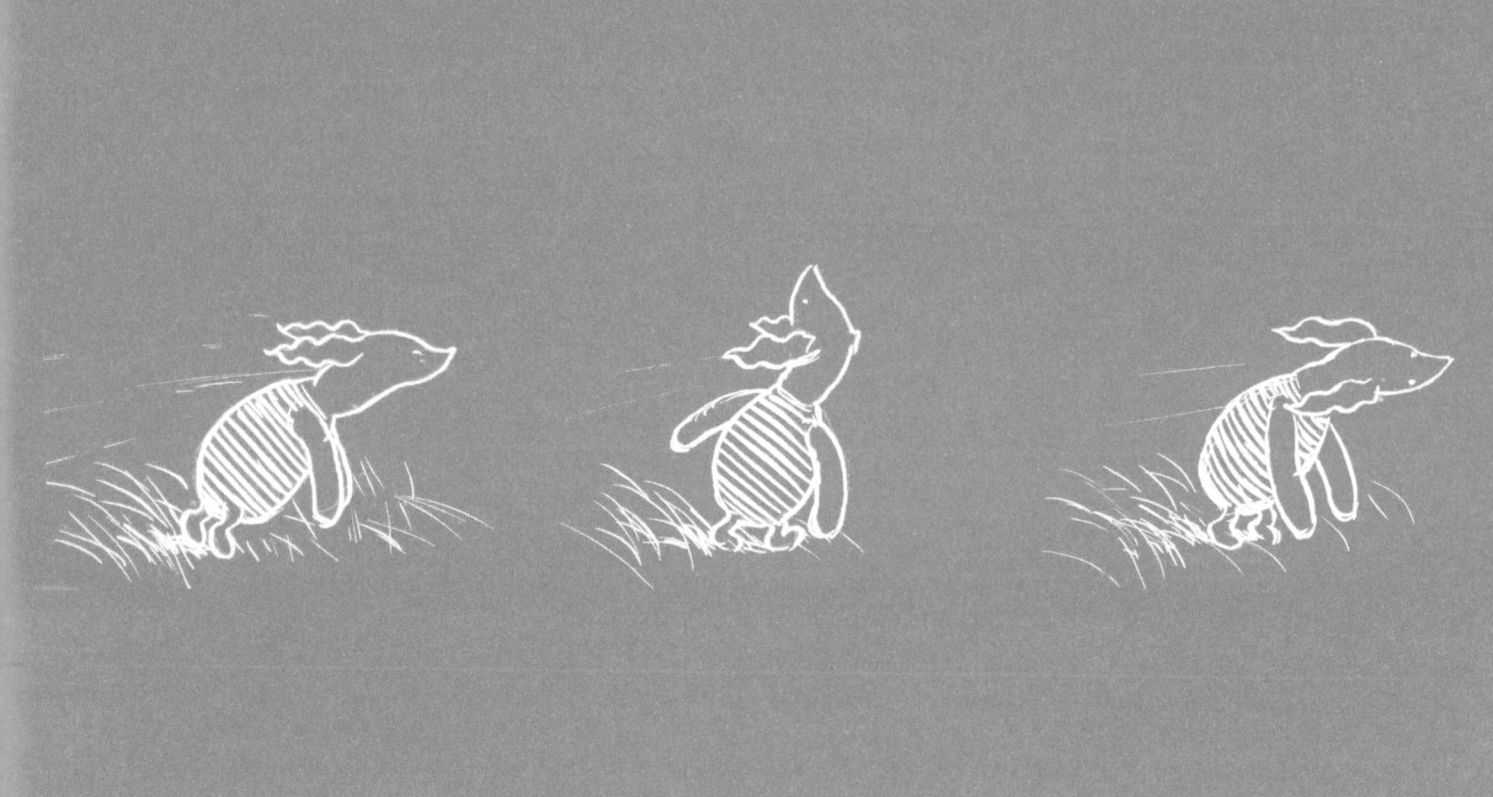